WAR
FOOTING

Your Government has the right to expect of all citizens that they take loyal part in the common work of our common defense . . . from this moment forward.

I have recently set up the machinery for civilian defense. It will rapidly organize, locality by locality. It will depend on the organized effort of men and women everywhere. All will have opportunities and responsibilities to fulfill.

Defense today means more than merely fighting. It means morale, civilian as well as military; it means using every available resource. . . .

As a military force, we were weak when we established our independence, but we successfully stood off tyrants, powerful in their day, tyrants who are now lost in the dust of history.

Odds meant nothing to us then. Shall we now, with all our potential strength, hesitate to take every single measure necessary to maintain our American liberties? Our people and our Government will not hesitate to meet that challenge. . . .

With profound consciousness of my responsibilities to my countrymen and to my country's cause, I have tonight issued a proclamation that an unlimited national emergency exists and requires the strengthening of our defense to the extreme limit of our national power and authority. The nation will expect all individuals and all groups to play their full parts, without stint, and without selfishness, and without doubt that our democracy will triumphantly survive.

I repeat the words of the Signers of the Declaration of Independence—that little band of patriots, fighting long ago against overwhelming odds, but certain, as we are now, of ultimate victory: "With a firm reliance on the protection of Divine Providence, we mutually pledge to each other our lives, our fortunes, and our sacred honor."

Franklin Delano Roosevelt
White House address proclaiming an
Unlimited National Emergency
May 14, 1941

WAR
FOOTING

10 Steps America Must Take to Prevail in the War for the Free World

FRANK J. GAFFNEY and Colleagues

NAVAL INSTITUTE PRESS
ANNAPOLIS, MARYLAND

Naval Institute Press
291 Wood Road
Annapolis, MD 21402

Library of Congress Cataloging-in-Publication Data

War footing : ten steps America must take to prevail in the war for the free world /
    Frank J. Gaffney and colleagues.
                p. cm.
       ISBN 1-59114-301-2 (alk. paper)
       1. United States—Military policy. 2. United States—Defenses. 3. World
politics—21st century. 4. War on Terrorism, 2001– I. Gaffney, Frank J.
UA23.W35358 2006
355´.033573—dc22
                                                                    2005030715

Printed in the United States of America on acid-free paper ∞

12 11 10 09 08 07 06 05   9 8 7 6 5 4 3 2
First printing

Dedicated to

The Ladies in My Life
Marisol, Sarah, and Elizabeth

My Colleagues

and

The Free World

Contents

Foreword

R. James Woolsey

Even among those of us who support both President Bush's overall strategy as set out in September 2001 and the overthrow of Saddam Hussein, there persists a pervasive disquiet. The president's commitment to the cause of democracy and the rule of law is plain. And his courage in moving to bring fundamental change to the Greater Middle East is inspiring. Many of us see the struggle against terrorism and the wars in Afghanistan and Iraq as fundamentally linked to these laudable ends—sharing the view that it is only by offering the people of that part of the world the opportunity to move toward democracy and the rule of law, rocky though the path may be, that we will ultimately defeat Islamist terrorism.

Yet the disquiet persists. Something important is missing in the Bush administration's approach, and it manifests itself in a number of inadequate and sometimes even feckless steps that fail to produce a determined effort, a coherent strategy, or a rallied nation.

I would suggest that the principal missing ingredient is clarity about our enemies' ideas and objectives—their ideology. This lack of clarity proceeds in part from naming our efforts a war against "terrorism," which is after all only a tactic, albeit a terrible one. But we might bypass the nomenclature issue if we would just recognize with whom we are at war.

Failing to do this has led to more than one misstep. We are at war with three movements in the Greater Middle East: Baathism, Shi'ite Theocratic Totalitarianism, and Sunni Theocratic Totalitarianism. The first is essentially 1920s fascism with an Arab nationalist face; it has been badly weakened (may it remain so) by our actions in Iraq. The second—embodied in the rulers of Iran and their proxy, Hezbollah—is very dangerous but fundamentally at odds with the history of Shi'ite Islam and hated by most of the Iranian people. It thus has major vulnerabilites.

But the third movement is growing. It is why the war, whatever we name it, will last for decades. Sunni Theocratic Totalitarianism is fanatically hostile to, among much else, Shi'ite and Sufi Muslims, Jews, Christians, women, music, and democracy. It has two principal faces: the Wahhabis of Saudi Arabia and Salafist Jihadis such as al-Qaeda. Both agree on the above hatreds—they disagree only on whether, in the course of ultimately establishing a worldwide caliphate unifying mosque and state to pursue these hatreds, they should owe allegiance to a single state.

In this regard the two faces of Sunni Theocratic Totalitarianism somewhat resemble the two faces of revolutionary Communism in the 1930s—Trotskyism and Stalinism. Like the Trotskyites and Stalinists, the Salafist Jihadis and the Wahhabis hate each other and kill each other, but their underlying totalitarian dream is the same—they differ only on the key issue of tactics and, thus, leadership.

We may well need, for some years, to work with the state, Saudi Arabia, whom the hate-filled, totalitarian Wahhabis serve. We worked successfully with the Soviet leader, our then-ally, Stalin, during World War II. Years later, when there was a generally reasonable Soviet leader, Gorbachev, we worked with him closely.

In Saudi Arabia, King Abdullah is as good a partner there as we are likely to see for some time. But we should not be confused about whether the Wahhabis who issue fatwas ordering young Saudis to become suicide killers in Iraq, and who fill Pakistani madrassas and American mosques with hate literature, are our enemies. They are so under any Saudi ruler, every bit as much as was the KGB under any Soviet ruler, including Gorbachev.

So as we assess such issues as how to treat Wahhabi–supporting organizations in this country, whether to be tough in barring investments from flowing into terrorist movements, what to ask of our law-enforcement and intelligence officials, and how to construct our public diplomacy, we can either move as suggested by the contributors to this fine volume or we can continue on our current course. Our current posture, showing deference to the Wahhabi-supporting Islamic Society of North America and similar groups, is analogous to what would have been the case if Harry Truman had tried during the early Cold War to reach out to moderates with social-democratic views by embracing (happily he did not) communist front organizations.

Not taking ideology seriously has hindered us from understanding the importance of what should have been—by, at the latest, the afternoon of September 11, 2001—a major government effort: to rally the nation behind moving away from oil dependence. Not only are oil's vulnerabilities to terrorist attack substantial and not only are we at the mercy of regime and policy changes in the turbulent Middle East, but we help fund the Wahhabis' some $4 billion per year of hatred propagation every time we pull up to the gasoline pump.

Other fine contributions to this volume suggest approaches that we should undertake regardless of whether we can bring ourselves to understand the ideology of our enemies: the right way to support our troops abroad; the importance of protecting ourselves against the threat of electromagnetic pulse (EMP) attack, possibly by an al-Qaeda–owned, Scud-carrying tramp steamer; and how to secure our borders.

But the confusion about the nature of our enemies has led us to underestimate their likely persistence, the range of weapons they are willing to use, and the nature of their tentacles into our own society. Bravo for this effort to begin to get it right.

Preface

Think of this book as your owner's manual for the War for the Free World. Whether we like it or not, we "own" this conflict, in which nothing less is at stake than our ability—and that of our children and grandchildren—to live in freedom and prosperity.

We inherited from our parents a Free World, made up of nations that respect and safeguard their citizens' inalienable human and political rights and led by the greatest of all these freedom-loving countries, the United States of America. That community of nations was preserved in the face of brutal totalitarians, at the cost of millions of lives and untold national treasure.

Like this one, the last War for the Free World began long before we started fighting it. With hindsight, we know that the United States—and the world—paid a higher price because we waited until *after* Pearl Harbor to put the nation on a true War Footing. Similarly, the losses we suffered on September 11, 2001, may one day seem trivial when compared with what the future has in store for us if we fail to adopt such a footing—including the steps identified in this book—without further delay.

Make no mistake about it: There are new totalitarians today. In this book we call them Islamofascists, who, together with their friends and allies, are every bit as determined as their predecessors to destroy the Free World.

Whether we are able to bequeath to our heirs a society like the American one we have been privileged to live in and love will be determined in no small measure by whether we use the instruments at our disposal properly and to a far greater degree than we have thus far.

So this book is intended to describe how those instruments—such tools as strategy, statecraft, intelligence, military might, political warfare, diplomacy (both the traditional type and "public diplomacy"), economic and financial measures, law enforcement, and civil preparedness and defense—can be used effectively. If we do that, we can ensure that America, and the Free World that we lead, can survive and prevail.

*   *   *

War Footing sets forth ten "steps" that, although often demanding, are essential to the survival of the United States and the Free World.

We begin in Part I with "Understanding the Problem." America needs, urgently, a clear understanding of the enemy and the hostile ideology we face—an ideology as lethally ambitious as the totalitarian movements of the past century (Step 1). Armed with this understanding, we can further identify the steps we must take to support the critical efforts being made on our behalf by America's matchless armed services (Step 2).

In Part II we examine the nonmilitary weapons that must be marshaled in this war effort. An important priority is the long-overdue necessity of giving discipline and direction to U.S. energy policy, especially in promoting alternative fuels and fuel-saving vehicles (Step 3). The second nonmilitary weapon is the enormous financial leverage of this country—*leverage that can be used to harm our interests if we fail to pay adequate attention* (Step 4).

Part III addresses the urgent priority of "Protecting the Homeland." Our intelligence, law enforcement, and emergency personnel need a much improved level of training, coordination, and support in order to protect our cities and people against terrorist attack (Step 5). A comprehensive defensive approach is also urgently needed if we are to protect our country's technological infrastructure against a catastrophically disabling electromagnetic pulse attack (Step 6). And we need to work diligently to redress the shockingly inadequate policies and practices that currently allow massive undocumented immigration as well as identity fraud (Step 7).

Part IV, finally, gives a tour of the centrally important ideological and political context of this war. We need first of all to understand the political warfare that is directed against us, with deadly effect—and the steps we will need to take to combat it (Step 8). The political dimension of this struggle takes a different form in each region of the globe, and it poses serious threats and calls for positive initiatives in each region (Step 9). Diplomatic engagement is an important aspect of this ideological and political conflict, and we end with an assessment of the problems and potential of three key elements of the diplomatic front: the U.S. Department of State, the United Nations, and American academic institutions (Step 10).

Additional material is provided as appendixes, dealing with energy policy, missile defense, nuclear deterrence, and border and immigration security.

*   *   *

This book is the product of many of the finest national security policy thinkers and practitioners of our time. I am proud to call them not only valued colleagues but cherished friends.

I am grateful to each of them for contributing, on very short notice, their ideas and recommendations for *War Footing*'s ten steps. They have allowed me to fashion those contributions, together with my own, into the chapters you will read here. I take full responsibility for the final form and content of each one; those whose names appear as contributors may or may not agree with everything said even in their section, let alone in the entire book. Yet, we have come together out of a shared conviction that there is much more that our country—and, in particular, its citizens—can, and must, do to secure victory in this War for the Free World.

In addition to my gratitude to each and every one of the named contributors, there are several who provided invaluable inputs but were unable to be formally acknowledged. They include some of the finest public servants I have ever known. I hope to be able in the future to recognize both their contributions to our country while in government and to this book.

It has been a special privilege to work with a dear friend, James T. deGraffenreid, the chief operating officer of the U.S. Naval Institute, and the team he has assembled at the Naval Institute Press—notably, its director, Patricia Pascale, acquisitions editor Eric Mills, and managing editor Linda O'Doughda. Like the storied institution of which they are a part, these men and women are making a real contribution to the nation's security. I will always appreciate their help in enabling me and my friends to try to do the same.

Thanks too are due our literary agent, Don Gastwirth, for his belief in our team from the inception of this project and the importance of our message.

Finally, I am especially grateful to my colleagues at the Center for Security Policy (CSP), led by our vice president for operations, Michael Reilly. This book has largely been drawn from the center's work program. Without the many contributions of the center's staff—drafting, editing, fact-checking, proofreading, and general backstopping, *above and beyond* the work entailed in their day jobs—this book would simply not have been possible. Like the others who have given so much to this collaborative effort, their help is recognized in the Contributors section. Suffice it to say here that they are among the finest professionals with whom I have ever had the pleasure of working. They are a great credit to CSP and indispensable elements of our nation's needed War Footing.

INTRODUCTION

Post-Modern War

Victor Davis Hanson

Since September 11, 2001, there have emerged some general lessons that should guide us in the next difficult round of the struggle against Islamic fascism, the various autocracies that aid and abet it, and the method of terror that so often characterizes it.

1. Political promises must be kept.

Had the United States postponed the scheduled January 2005 elections in Iraq, once the hue and cry of Washington insiders, the insurrection would have overwhelmed Iraq. Only the combination of U.S. arms, the training of indigenous forces, and real Iraqi sovereignty can eliminate the vestiges of hard-core jihadists and Saddamites.

Given our previous record—allowing Saddam to survive in 1991, restoring the Kuwaiti royals after the Gulf War, subsidies for the Mubarak autocracy, and a moral pass given the Saudi royals—we must bank carefully any good will that accrues, if support for democracy is to offer a credible alternative to the old realpolitik. Reformers with no power in Egypt or the Gulf, who oppose such "moderate" autocracies, must, despite all the danger that such a policy entails, be seen in the same positive light as those dissidents in far more peril in Lebanon, Syria, and Iran.

Consistency and principle are the keys, and they will be worth more than a division or an air wing in bringing this war to a close. One of bin Laden's three pretexts—the other two being U.S. troops in the Middle East and the Israeli-Palestinian dispute—is American support for secular autocrats.

It is not just that he is a hypocrite, in being an Islamic totalitarian himself (a fact that explains his current declining popularity). The United States is also clearly taking unusual steps to promote constitutional governments, in a way that cannot be explained away by intellectuals or distorted by even al-Qaeda's propaganda.

2. Any warnings to use needed force should be credible and followed through.

The efforts of the terrorists are aimed at the psychological humiliation and loss of face of American power—not its actual military defeat, which is beyond their capability. Appearance, then, is often as important as reality, especially for those who live in the 8th rather than the 21st century. In a perfect world, in terms of explanations about our use of force, Clintonian lip-biting would be preferable to George Bush's swagger—just as in the execution of policy, Bush's resolve is a much-needed departure from Clinton's equivocation that we witnessed from Haiti to Mogadishu.

After the horrific butchery of Americans in Fallujah in late March 2004, we promised to hunt down the perpetrators—only to pull back in April and May and condemn the city to a subsequent half-year of Islamic terror before retaking it in November. The initial hesitation almost derailed the slated elections; the subsequent siege ensured their success. Nothing has been more deleterious in this war than the promise of hard force to come, followed by temporization, and it is fortunate that by late 2005 the United States went back on the offensive to demonstrate to the terrorists that none of their enclaves were secure. Either silence about our intent or bold military action is required, though a combination of both is preferable.

3. Diplomatic solutions follow, not precede, military reality.

Had we failed in Afghanistan, General Musharaf of Pakistan would be an Islamic nationalist today, for the sake of his own survival, while Dr. A.Q. Khan's nuclear dispensary would be still operating. Withdrawing from Iraq in defeat would have meant no progress in Lebanon, nor pressure on the Mubarak autocracy, nor any change of behavior in Libya.

Some hope has followed in the Middle East only because the Intifada was crushed and Arafat is in paradise. In no small way, the end of the threat of Saddam's Scuds, of his suicide bomber bounties, and of his constant bloody rhetoric has given the region greater chance of dialogue. There will be no more powerful image for the region's dictators than Saddam in chains, the worst of the region's lot now demurring to a constitutionally appointed judge in a televised trial.

The Muslim scholars of Iraq talk somewhat differently now than a year ago because thousands of their sympathetic terrorists have been killed in the Sunni Triangle. Even the would-be Great Mahdi Moqtada Sadr has become more a buffoon than a Khomeini reborn since his militia was crushed last year. His resurrection will depend on how well his militias are able to intimidate the innocent and weak, and how much latitude the U.S. and British militaries mistakenly decide to grant him.

A quarter-century of terror, from the Iranian hostage-taking to September 11, should have taught us the wages of thinking that an Arafat, bin Laden, assorted hostage-takers, an Iranian mullah, Saddam, or Mullah Omar might listen to a reasoned diplomat in striped pants. Our mistake has been not so much that appeasement and empty threats made no impression on such cutthroats; most sober thinking people know that temporization can only do harm.

The real tragedy, instead, was that onlookers who wished to ally with us shuddered that the United States either would talk to, or keep its hands off, almost any monster or mass murderer in the Middle East, as long as such accommodation meant a continuation of the not-so-bothersome status quo. In contrast, the fact that bin Laden and Mullah Omar are in hiding, Saddam in chains, Dr. Khan exposed, the young Assad panicking, and Colonel Gadhafi on better behavior will slowly teach others the wages of their killing and terrorism—and that the United States is as unpredictable in using force as it is constant in supporting democratic reformers.

4. The worst attitude toward the Europeans and the UN is publicly to deprecate their impotent machinations while enlisting their aid *in extremis*.

After being slurred by both the Europeans and the UN, we then asked for their military help, peacekeepers, and political intervention—so far winning no aid of consequence except their contempt in addition to inaction. Chancellor Schroeder of Germany did nothing but harm to the U.S. effort in Iraq; the fact that we once sought his participation proved a monotonous refrain in all his subsequent campaigning, as he reminded Germans how he stood up to American pressures. Yet had he assented, we would have had very little real help anyway in Iraq from his forces.

Pressuring the Europeans and the UN to do what they really don't want to only leads to their gratuitous embarrassment and the need to get even for it in the most petty and superficial ways.

The UN's efforts to retard the American removal of Saddam interrupted the timetable of invasion. Its immediate flight after the bombing of its head-quarters emboldened the terrorists. And a viable U.S. coalition was carica-tured by its obsequious (and unsuccessful) efforts to lure in France and Germany. Due to their hostility and caricature, most think that our so-called coalition of the willing is a Potemkin alliance, when in fact more countries are participating in the effort, both in numbers and troops sent, than was true of the UN-mandated campaign in Korea, when the United States' troops rep-resented a larger percentage of total allied forces than they do now in Iraq.

We should look to the UN and Old Europe only in times of post-bellum calm, when it is in the national interest of the United States to give credit for the favorable results of our own daring to opportunistic others—occasions that are not as rare as we might think. Afghanistan is a good example. The Europeans did almost nothing to remove the Taliban. Their promises of mus-cular peacekeeping in real force have likewise proved mostly disappointing. Yet, Afghanistan to them is the "good war," because their contingents face lit-tle risk and they can claim to be doing humanitarian rather than martial work. Thus it made sense to welcome their presence, as it will again in Iraq when the constitutional government is secure, more lucrative contracts are bid out, and the world wishes to claim credit for the democratic calm after the storm of Saddam and the insurrectionists has passed.

5. Do not look for logic and consistency in the Middle East, where they are not to be found.

It makes no sense to be frustrated that Arab intellectuals and reformers damn us for removing Saddam while they simultaneously now praise the democratic rumblings that followed his fall. We should accept that the only palatable sce-nario for the Arab Street was one equally fanciful: Brave demonstrators took to the barricades, forced Saddam's departure, created a constitution, held elec-tions, and then invited other Arab reformers into Baghdad to spread such indigenous reform—all resulting in a society as sophisticated, wealthy, free, and modern as the West, but felt to be morally superior because of its alle-giance to Islam.

That is the dream that they find preferable to these realities: The Amer-icans alone took out the monster of the Middle East; any peaceful protest against Saddam would have ended in another genocide; and adherence to Islamic fundamentalism is a prescription for economic stagnation.

Ever since the departure of the European colonials, the United States, due to its power and principled support for democratic Israel, has served a Middle Eastern psychological need to account for its own self-created impotence and misery. This is a pathology abetted by our own past realpolitik and nurtured by the very autocrats that we sought to accommodate and who now, in their 11th hour, have turned on us for following principles rather than their own promises to maintain order and the status quo.

After all these years, do not expect praise or gratitude for billions poured into Iraq, Egypt, Jordan, or Palestine—or thanks for the liberation of Kuwait, protection of Saudi Arabia in 1990, or the removal of Saddam, much less for American concern for Muslims in Bosnia, Kosovo, Chechnya, Somalia, the Sudan, or Afghanistan. Our past sins always must be magnified as much as our more recent benefactions are slighted.

In response, American policy should be predicated not simply on friendship or the desire for appreciation but on what is in our national interest and what is right, a symbiosis that is possible only through the current policy of consistently promoting democracy. Constitutional government—the rule of law, human rights, and fair and free voting—is not utopia. It is, however, the only proper antidote for the sickness in the Middle East, the one medicine that hateful jihadists, dictators, kings, terrorists, and theocrats all agree that they alike hate. It is, after all, ironic now for the United States to be as damned as much in the Arab press for our naïveté and idealism about democracy as in the past for our cynical support for Arab autocrats.

The events that followed September 11 are the most complex in our history since the end of World War II, as we try to distance ourselves from dictators who in the short term offer help in putting down terrorism, even as we know in the long term their repression only encourages and abets it.

The great chain of events that began on September 11 continues to unfold, as the war against the terrorists who planned that mass murder has expanded to include the regimes that aid and abet Islamic fascists and that create the conditions that ensure their sanctuary and appeal. The president has declared in the aftermath of the wreckage of September 11 that the world must choose sides, either with the terrorists or against them.

What that bold declaration really means is that those in the Middle East have a great decision before them. They can either join the free nations of the world in their embrace of consensual government, freedom of the individual, open markets, and the rule of law. Or they can continue with the old pathology of autocratic government, blaming others for its own self-induced misery—and using parasitical terrorists, who promise a return to some mythical caliphate, to deflect the anger of the masses onto the West and in particular to attack the United States. We can appeal to the wisdom and good sense of those in the Middle East, but the choice for their free future is, and should be, theirs alone—and equally, after September 11, the consequences will be ours to address as we must.

PART I
Understanding the Problem

I
t seems obvious by now that we are *not* fighting a "War on Terror." Terror is, after all, an instrument of war, not an enemy.

That said, we certainly have a war going on. Usually when people talk about it, however, they mean the "War in Iraq."

The truth is very different. And if we don't understand the enemy we are fighting and the actual nature of this conflict, we have little likelihood of surviving this war, let alone prevailing in it. We are in the midst of the War for the Free World.

The first section of this book, therefore, clarifies both points:

♦ Step 1 explains that we are at war primarily with adherents to a dangerous, totalitarian ideology—Islamofascism—and with the states and organizations that enable its global ambitions. Terror is the trademark and tool of choice of the Islamofascists. To the extent that Islamofascists are willing to kill themselves in the process of killing others, every foot soldier in this ideological vanguard is a potentially lethal precision-guided weapon.

We describe in Step 1 how this ideology (*not* a religion) came to be the worldwide menace it is today, both to America and to other freedom-loving people, and we explain the critical role this ideology plays in the Islamofascists' efforts to take over the Muslim faith and, in due course, the world. And, as will be developed more fully in subsequent chapters, we offer ways in which—having understood what we are up against—the United States and its true friends can counter and defeat this metastasizing disease.

♦ Step 2 shows how the military fits into this war. It lays out the considerable successes our armed forces have achieved since the September 11,

2001, attacks. It also describes decisions made and policies adopted that have complicated the military's task in this global conflict.

We make clear in this chapter that, although there are many nonmilitary aspects to our War Footing, we must field, maintain, train, and use effectively America's armed forces in the aspects of this global war where these forces are appropriate. To do so will require a substantially greater and sustained investment of resources. It will also entail supporting our troops in another critically important way: by giving them, and those that lead them—civilian and uniformed alike—the best intelligence this nation can provide.

STEP 1

Know the Enemy

With Contributions from Alex Alexiev

I n the four years since September 11, 2001, the United States can claim some important successes in the so-called War on Terror. America and our allies successfully eliminated al-Qaeda's base of operations in Afghanistan in fall 2001. Since then, many of the organization's senior operatives have been neutralized and its operations disrupted.

The U.S.-led "coalition of the willing" removed the brutal dictatorship of Saddam Hussein through Operation Iraqi Freedom. By so doing, we precluded that rogue regime from further developing and using weapons of mass destruction or supplying them to fellow terrorists.[1]

On the domestic front, significant strides have also been made in shoring up homeland security. As of this writing, the United States has avoided a single significant terrorist attack since September 11, 2001—an unbroken four-year record that seemed extremely unlikely in the chaotic aftermath of the September 11 attacks.

In fact, a number of threats have been preempted by U.S. authorities. Most recently, as many as thirteen alleged terrorists serving time at the New Folsom State Prison in California reportedly plotted attacks against National Guard sites as well as the Israeli consulate and synagogues in the Los Angeles area.

---

1 In a stunning lapse of logic, the failure of investigators to "find" any stocks of biological or chemical weapons has been generally taken as evidence that they did not exist. Yet, the U.S.-led inspection team's reports described unmistakable evidence of a coordinated cover-up by Saddamite forces, including smashed computer drives, scrubbed surfaces, and piles of still-warm ashes (presumably of incriminating documents). Inspectors were well aware, too, that the sources they relied on for information had everything to lose and nothing to gain from cooperating. (See the Congressional testimony of two then-directors of the Iraq Survey Group: David Kay, statement to Congress, October 2, 2003, available at http://www.nti.org/eoresearch/officialodocs/cia/cia100203.pdf; Charles Duelfer, statement to Congress, March 30, 2004, available at http://www.cia.gov/cia/publicaffairs/speeches/2004/tenetotestimonyo03302004.html.)

Despite these very positive developments, it would be highly premature to claim that we are close to winning the War for the Free World. The July 2005 terrorist attacks in London are a vivid reminder that terrorist networks and groups retain considerable ability to wreak havoc.

The likelihood that we will be able to survive, let alone prevail, against such enemies over the longer term depends critically on our understanding the nature of the enemy we confront in this war, his purposes and methods of operations, and his strengths and vulnerabilities.

The True Threat

The problem facing the United States and the Free World is neither al-Qaeda nor, for that matter, terrorism itself. Murderous and disruptive as Osama bin Laden and his ilk are, they are just symptoms of a larger problem: a totalitarian ideology that has come to be known as Islamofascism (or Islamism), which seeks to dominate the Muslim faith and, in due course, the non-Muslim world.

Islamofascism inspires and characterizes most of the terrorist groups of our time. Although it uses a perverted interpretation of the Muslim faith as its banner, this ideology has, in its essence, more in common with Nazism and Communism than with traditional Islam.

Like its fellow totalitarian ideologies, Islamofascism rejects reason and glorifies violence. In order to justify its extremely violent tactics, Islamists seek to dehumanize their designated enemies. What Jews, Gypsies, and Slavs were for the Nazis, and what the "class enemy" was for the Communists, infidels, and Muslim "apostates" are for the Islamists just another category of subhumans deserving extermination.

Islamofascism on the March

Forty years ago, there was but one state—Saudi Arabia—ruled by the Islamists' brutally repressive version of the Islamic religious code, known as Shari'a. Today, there are a half-dozen countries that are either fully or partially subjected to Shari'a, and several others appear to be heading that way. (Six regions in which Islamofascism and other totalitarian threats to freedom are emerging are discussed in Step 9.)

◆   Since 2001, radical Islamist rule has been consolidated in twelve states in **Northern Nigeria.** The result has been systematic abuse of constitutionally guaranteed human rights. The country has been brought to the brink of civil war.

♦ **Bangladesh** has been critically undermined as a secular democracy by an Islamist reign of terror in the countryside, with the complicity of its current government, which includes a radical Islamist party as a key coalition partner.

♦ **Pakistan** moved squarely into the Islamist camp starting with the seizure of the presidency by Gen. Zia ul-Haq in 1978. With massive Saudi funding, Islamicization continued under a succession of Pakistani military dictators and corrupt politicians who have aided and abetted Islamic extremism at the expense of civil society. In the process, Pakistan has been transformed into an international haven of extremism and terrorism, with thousands of jihadist madrassas, dozens of terrorist training camps, and assorted centers of Islamist indoctrination, to say nothing of its role as a proliferator of nuclear weapons technology to other rogue states.

♦ Perhaps most disturbing is the case of **Turkey**, a Muslim country with eighty years of unbroken secular rule, where the Islamist government of Prime Minister Recep Tayyip Erdogan is methodically destroying Kemal Ataturk's legacy.

In addition, Islamist insurgencies flourish from Chechnya to the Philippines and from Iraq to the brand-new jihad theater in Thailand. At the same time, Sudanese government-sponsored Islamist thugs in Darfur commit genocide against fellow Muslims, to the shocked dismay of a seemingly paralyzed international community.

Islamofascism in the West

Islamic extremism has made huge strides in the burgeoning Muslim expatriate communities in many large European cities, as a newly dominant creed. Under Islamist control, these enclaves are being transformed into separatist, crime-ridden antisocieties that wholly reject Western civilization and its norms. The fall 2005 Parisian riots are cases in point.

Such communities are openly supported by outside Islamofascist sources. For example, the large group of Turkish Islamists in Europe, known as Milli Görüsh—widely regarded as an extremist organization with terrorist sympathies—has nevertheless been embraced and sponsored by Prime Minister Erdogan's government in Turkey. The effect of such support is unmistakable. Many European Muslims are increasingly willing to engage in violence against their democratic host societies. Thirteen percent of British Muslims, according to a 2004 Home Office survey, approve of terrorism, and 1 percent—a staggering sixteen thousand—said they had "engaged in terrorist activity at home or abroad, or supported such activity."[2] The danger is no less acute on the Continent. For example, German studies have indicated that 25 percent of German Muslim school students are ready to use violence on behalf of Islam.[3]

The longer-term prospects are just as unpalatable. The native European population is now contracting at 2.2 million per year because of low birth rates. At the same time, the Muslim community in Europe is growing at 50 percent per decade. If current trends prevail, in twenty-five years we will see the Islamist-radicalized youth become a majority of the youth cohort in large European urban centers. We can only speculate as to what kind of European society will emerge should the rising tide of Islamofascism continue among Muslims there.

Islamofascism in America

In the United States, the purveyors of fanatical Islamic agendas exercise considerable influence within the Muslim community. Well funded, well disciplined, and well organized, they profess to speak for all Muslims while supporting extremist and terrorist causes.

Since September 11, the Islamists have conducted a massive propaganda campaign, aimed at convincing Muslims that American antiterror efforts are nothing more than a veiled war on Islam. The purpose is to alienate American Muslims from the government and make them more receptive to Islamic extremism. Under the guise of concern for the rights of suspected terrorists (and often in conjunction with far-left organizations), Islamists are also doing their best to emasculate the Patriot Act and otherwise impede the campaign against terrorism (see Step 5).

Despite such hostile activities, Islamist operatives have been afforded frequent access to high-level administration officials, including meetings and receptions at the White House and periodic "outreach" sessions. Among those hosting such sessions have been the leadership of America's top counterterror organization, the FBI.

Incredibly, one of the most notorious of these Islamofascists, Abdurahman Alamoudi, was not only allowed to participate in such sessions, he was even permitted to run Islamist recruitment operations inside America's

---

2   A link to the document is available at http://www.timesonline.co.uk/article/0,,2087-1688261,00.html.
3   Wilhelm Heitmeyer, Joachim Müller, and Helmut Schröder, *Verlockender Fundamentalismus: Türkische Jugendliche in Deutschland,* Frankfurt, 1997.

prisons and military at the same time as he was associated with many of the Wahhabi-financed front organizations in this country. Alamoudi is currently serving a twenty-three-year sentence in federal prison for terrorism-related crimes.[4]

Where Did Islamofascism Come From?

It is impossible to defeat a violent movement such as radical Islam without understanding the ideology motivating it. This has been made more difficult because of efforts undertaken—particularly of late—by some of the Islamists' sympathizers and apologists to obscure the true nature and purposes of the extremists.

Prime examples of such efforts have been the various statements and "fatwas" issued recently that purportedly reject terrorism but fail to denounce by name any who are engaged in it. Still, by examining the roots of this hateful ideology, we can better penetrate its subterfuges and counteract its jihadist agenda in our own time.

The rise of Islamic extremism is not a new development. The first movement resembling today's phenomenon, that of the Kharijites, appeared shortly after the birth of Islam in the 7th century and was further developed by Islamic scholars in the 13th century.

In the mid-18th century, Islamofascism became institutionalized. The theories advanced by a radical cleric of the Arabian Peninsula, Muhammad ibn Abd al-Wahhab, became the state religion of a kingdom established there by Abdul Aziz Ibn Saud, the founder of Saudi Arabia.

Wahhabism, as this creed came to be known, claimed that the practice of Islam had become corrupted by Muslims who failed to follow the ostensibly pure Islam of the time of the Prophet and his companions. In fact, however, Wahhab's extreme doctrines contradicted and attacked major tenets of traditional Islam. On a wide array of religious and social topics, Wahhab's version of Islam represents *an outright falsification* of the Muslim faith.

To name just one egregious example, Wahhab claimed that Muslims who did not accept his doctrines are not actually Muslims at all, but nonbelievers

---

4   See Frank Gaffney Jr., "A Troubling Influence," *FrontPage Magazine*, December 9, 2003, available at http://www.frontpagemag.com/articles/readarticle.asp?ID=11210; Michael Waller, "FBI Polarized by 'Wahhabi Lobby,'" *Insight Magazine*, July 11, 2003, available at http://www.insightmag.com/main.cfm?include=detail&storyid=446224); "Know Thine Enemy," Center for Security Policy, Decision Brief: May 16, 2005; "Whose Partner is Abu Mazen?" Center for Security Policy, Decision Brief: May 26, 2005.

and apostates. He taught that violence and jihad against such people was not only allowed, it was obligatory.

This claim violates two fundamental tenets of the Muslim holy book, the Koran:

1. Invoking jihad against fellow Muslims is not permitted.
2. A Muslim's profession of faith must be taken at face value; only God may judge his or her sincerity on Judgment Day.

Wahhabism was useful to the House of Saud, however. Wahhab's teachings provided a religious pretext and legitimization for violence against and conquest of other Muslims. By 1746, just two years after Ibn Saud embraced Wahhabism, the new Saudi-Wahhabi state proclaimed jihad against all neighboring Muslim tribes that refused to subscribe to the new religion.

From that day to this, the history of Saudi Arabia is replete with violent campaigns to force other Muslims to submit politically and theologically. Such behavior violates yet another fundamental principle of the Koran, which prohibits the use of compulsion in religion.

Islamism Is About Political Power, Not Religion

Today's Wahhabism is not about religion. Like other ideological scourges of the 20th century, it is essentially an instrument for obtaining and holding onto power. It is a vehicle for political sedition, subversion, incitement to violence and terror, and, ultimately, conquest.

Though known for the selective use of Koranic principles to justify its practice, Islamism—like Nazism and Communism—is really about global domination. It strives for the restoration of a mythical caliphate and the worldwide rule of Islam, a utopian goal similar to the Nazi "Thousand Year Reich," or the world Communism hailed by the Bolsheviks as the final stage of societal progress.

Once upon a time, it was fashionable—though extremely foolish—to dismiss the declared ambitions of megalomaniacs like Hitler, Lenin, and Stalin. Today, it is no less dangerous to discount the Islamofascists' determination to realize their goals.

Islamofascism resembles its totalitarian antecedents in another way: violence is seen as a *first resort* against enemies who are blamed for a litany of injuries, real or perceived. In particular, Islamism sees itself, and all Islam, as victimized by the West. It views fundamental Western norms—such as democracy, secularism, human rights, and separation of church and state—as grievous threats to its quest for power and world domination. According to the Islamofascists, there can be no compromise and *no peaceful coexistence* with those who do not subscribe to their worldview.

It follows that, according to the Islamofascists, there must be a no-holds-barred struggle between their faith and the "world of unbelief." It can only end apocalyptically, when all the "infidels" have been either converted or killed.

One of the founding fathers of Islamism, Hassan al-Banna, spelled this out explicitly. Blaming Western secularism for having delayed "the advancement of the Muslim world for centuries," he urged his followers to "pursue this evil force to its own lands, invade its Western heartland, and struggle to overcome it until all the world shouts by the name of the Prophet."[5]

Undoubtedly, this sounds like the fantastical ravings of a madman. But the fantasy is a deadly one, and, unfortunately, it is much less of a fantasy today than when these words were written a half-century ago.

The Islamists' Other Enemy

Another key to the character of Islamofascism—and potentially the secret to its undoing—is to be found in those described as the "enemy." To be sure, Jews, Christians, Hindus, and other "idolaters" are the main enemy in the long term.

But a special enmity is reserved for those Muslims who stand in the way of the Islamists' takeover of the faith. They are labeled *takfir* (apostates) and *munafiqin* (hypocrites). Their numbers include hundreds of millions of Muslims whose practice of the faith draws on the tolerant and peaceable traditions that the Wahhabi Islamofascists reject. Such Muslims belong to sects like the mainstream Shi'as, Sufis, Ismailis, Ahmadis, and many others.

Although these moderate Muslims collectively represent the vast majority of the faith's practitioners, the Islamists treat them with scorn and contempt. In the United States, thanks to Saudi domination of the Islamic establishment, the bona fide moderate Muslims are usually excluded from Muslim-American and Arab-American organizations that nevertheless purport to be "mainstream" groups. Their exclusion contributes to the widespread perception in the non-Muslim world that there are no real alternatives to the pro-Islamist factions.

The Islamists' methods of inducing conformity include threats of economic retaliation, physical violence, and ostracism—the standard totalitarian methods of enforcing submission. These threats have instilled real fear

---

5   Fathi Yakun, *To Be a Muslim*, Riyadh, Saudi Arabia: International Islamic Publishing House, 1996. Cited in "Saudi Publications on Hate Ideology Invade American Mosques," Center for Religious Freedom, Freedom House, Washington DC, 2005, p. 59.

among moderate Muslims. For example, the dramatic increase over the past decade in compliance with severe Islamic dress codes in Muslim communities in modern, tolerant Europe is a product of relentless intimidation and physical coercion.

Islamic fanatics—from the Wahhabis to members of the Muslim Brotherhood, from bin Laden to the Jordanian terrorist Musab al-Zarqawi—are as skillful as al-Wahhab himself at distorting and even misrepresenting the teachings of the Koran. Like him, they call other Muslims unbelievers and threaten them with the ultimate punishment.

Being declared an apostate is tantamount to a death sentence in Islam. No Muslim can safely ignore this sort of threat. In fact, the mass murder of other Muslims has become the hallmark of Islamism: over the past quarter-century, at *least 90 percent of its estimated 350,000 victims were innocent Muslims.*

As appalling as these sorts of statistics may be, they should come as no surprise given the ambitions of Islamofascism. Islamists see the majority of peaceable, tolerant, and law-abiding Muslims as the immediate obstacle in their quest for control of the Muslim community. Dominating the moderates of the faith is an essential first step toward taking their jihad to the infidels.

The extremists have been making steady progress in the past several decades, principally due to the largesse of the Saudi regime and, to a lesser extent, its Shi'a counterpart in Iran. Nowhere is this progress more evident than in the rapidly growing Muslim communities in Western Europe. As the recent London bombings have shown, their insular ghettos are rapidly becoming prime breeding grounds of Islamic fanaticism.

Many find it surprising that people fleeing oppressive and poverty-ridden Muslim societies would come to the wealthy, tolerant, and generous West, only to fall prey to a hate-filled creed. Many Americans and Western Europeans turn to familiar notions about poverty, racism, unemployment, and discrimination to explain the "root causes" of Islamofascism. Such an analysis involves a fundamental misunderstanding of the ideology's roots and sponsors. Indulging in it is a formula for the further metastasizing of the Islamist cancer, to the grave peril of moderate Muslims and the rest of us.

Radicalization and "Root Causes"

Westerners find it particularly difficult to comprehend the rabid intolerance of the contemporary Wahhabi ideology. Wahhabism adheres dogmatically to a set of beliefs and prescribed behavior that is fundamentally at odds with those accepted by the vast majority of the world's Muslims. Wahhabi beliefs include:

♦ Violence and jihad as pillars of Islamic virtue.

♦ Enforced conformity to the approved practice of the faith.

♦ Institutionalized oppression of women.

♦ The modern world, secular government, and democratic institutions are contrary to Islam.

♦ Non-Wahhabi Muslims are considered illegitimate, at best.

♦ The Shi'a creed is denounced as a "Jewish conspiracy" against Islam.

Given the extremism of these views, how is it that Wahhabism has become the dominant strain of Islamism, as well as the prototype ideology of all extremist and terrorist groups—including groups that despise its patrons, the House of Saud? The short answer is *money*, abetted by the acute crisis of legitimacy suffered by the Muslim world, in the last quarter of the 20th century.

Funds controlled directly and indirectly by the Saudi royal family have provided much of the impetus behind Islamofascism's ascendancy. Without a pervasive sense of grievance, however, money alone would not have produced the current dangerous situation.

The centuries-long decline of Islam as a dominant civilization reached bottom in 1924, when Mustafa Kemal Ataturk, as the first President of Turkey,

♦ Abolished the last remnants of the caliphate and the Ottoman Empire;

♦ Instituted a secular, pro-Western Turkish republic.

For the conservative adherents of the old sultanate, Ataturk's overthrow of the caliphate—the very symbol of Muslim community—was traumatic indeed. Worse was to come, with the establishment of European colonial rule over much of the Muslim world. In short order, there began to emerge (particularly in the Arab world) movements and ideologies determined to restore the lost power and glory of the faith.

The first of these, founded in 1928, was the Muslim Brotherhood; it was followed by similar movements founded by Islamist ideologues. These initiatives began to establish a strong presence in the Muslim world during the second half of the 20th century and ramped up dramatically as streams of Saudi financing came on line, beginning in the 1970s.

Deobandism, a prime example. Named after a Muslim seminary in the town of Deoband in Uttar Pradesh, India, the Deobandis preach a particularly virulent Islamist creed. Its hatred of infidels and Shi'a Muslims is pathologic. Jihadist fervor is cultivated from a very young age, through Koranic schools (madrassas). Women are relegated to second-class status at best.

The Deobandis represent a small minority of the Muslim population in Pakistan. Thanks to Saudi funding, however, coupled with strong government support beginning with General Zia, the Deobandis have played a pivotal role in the Islamicization of Pakistan. They have established an estimated eighteen hundred madrassas, producing every year tens of thousands of graduates prepared solely for jihad. The Deobandis were responsible, in fact, for installing the Taliban in Afghanistan.

Currently, the Deobandis are a decisive influence in the Islamist government of Pakistan's Northwest Frontier Province, which is diligently Talibanizing this strategic region. For example, it recently passed a law mandating the formation of a religious police force.

Some contend that these developments are the result of "blowback"—an unintended and undesirable consequence of the U.S.-led liberation of Afghanistan and Iraq. In fact, Deobandi Jihadi groups, of whom there are at least a half-dozen in Pakistan, were practicing terrorism and suicide bombings against Christians, Hindus, Shi'as, and the Barelvi Muslim sect long before September 11.

Wahhabi terror. In the 1970s and 1980s, Islamic terrorist groups began appearing in the Middle East and South Asia (including Al Jihad and Gamaa Islamiya in Egypt, and the Front for National Salvation [FIS] in Algeria). These groups shared many of the Wahhabi tenets and practices. Their numbers grew after the Soviet invasion of Afghanistan.

As the Islamist terror groups were violently suppressed in places like Egypt and Algeria, the Saudis quickly moved to co-opt them, providing sanctuary and financial assistance both in Saudi Arabia and elsewhere. The economic and logistical dependence of many of these extremists on the Saudis fed into the ongoing radicalization of Wahhabism itself, in a synergistic relationship, despite the deep resentment of the Saudi regime felt by many practicing jihadists (like Osama bin Laden).

More than anything else, then, as today, it was the vast outlay of Saudi funds that made Wahhabism the dominant influence within the Islamofascist phenomenon. If we are seeking "root causes" of terrorism, we will need to pay close attention to the flow of money.

The Infrastructure of Islamism

The Wahhabis have always been sympathetic to Sunni Muslim extremists. There is evidence that they supported such people financially as early as a century ago. The Saudi offensive to spread Wahhabism did not begin in earnest, however, until the mid-1970s.

The impetus was the kingdom's financial windfall, as oil prices rocketed after the Saudi-led oil embargo of the United States in 1973. "It was only when oil revenues began to generate real wealth," says a Saudi government publication, that "the Kingdom could fulfill its ambitions of spreading the word of Islam to every corner of the world."[6]

How Much Are the Saudis Investing in Islamofascism?

Significantly, there are even today no published Western estimates of the actual expenditures made by the Saudis to construct the worldwide Wahhabi edifice—striking evidence of our inattention to this campaign waged by a nation that is both our principal oil supplier *and* a major state-sponsor of terror. But even the occasional tidbits provided by official Saudi sources suggest a campaign of unprecedented magnitude.

Between 1975 and 1987, the Saudis' reported expenditure on "official development assistance" was merely $48 billion ($4 billion per year). By the end of 2002, that figure had grown to more than $70 billion.[7] It is clear from Saudi statements (in the government-controlled media as well as official documents) that the vast majority of these funds support "Islamic activities" rather than real development projects. (By way of comparison, the Soviet Union is believed to have spent only $1 billion per year on external propaganda at the peak of Moscow's power in the 1970s.) Such staggering amounts make a mockery of the $5 million in terrorist accounts the Saudis claim to have frozen since September 11.

Where the Saudis' Money Goes

Saudi financing appears to be allocated according to a carefully crafted plan designed to enhance Wahhabi influence and to control foreign mosques—to the detriment of mainstream Muslims. Much of the aid (as much as $350 million annually for Pakistan alone)[8] goes to fund religious schools that teach little more than hatred of the infidels while producing barely literate Jihadi

---

6 "Billions Spent By Saudi Royal Family to Spread Islam to Every Corner of the Earth," *Ain-Al-Yaqeen*, (Saudi government-controlled newspaper), March 1, 2002.

7 See "Saudi Aid to the Developing World," November 2002, in www.sauclinf.com/main/1102.htm and statement by Dr. Ibrahim Al-Assaf, Saudi Minister of Finance and National Economy, as reported by Saudi Online, January 2, 2003 (www.saudionline.com/news2003/newsjan03/news2.shtml). Ninety-six percent of these aid amounts are said to be grants.

8 For details on Saudi funding of the madrassas, see Alex Alexiev, "The Pakistani Time Bomb," *Commentary*, March 2003.

cadres. There are now tens of thousands of these madrassas run by the Wahhabis and their Deobandi allies in South Asia and Southeast Asia.

The Saudi funding has also been linked directly to organizations associated with terrorist activities in places like Afghanistan, the Philippines, Indonesia, Chechnya, and Bosnia. The mechanisms used for this purpose include most of the large Saudi foundations.[9]

But these are merely the sums reported as Saudi state aid. Additional so-called private donations are made by members of the royal family, favored businesses, the Wahhabi apparatus, and, especially, by state-controlled charities.

The Saudis claim that the charities that have been associated with Islamist financing, terrorist financing, or both are independent and nongovernmental—charities such as Al Haramain, the World Muslim League (WML), the World Assembly of Muslim Youth (WAMY), and the International Islamic Relief Organization (IIRO). There is, nevertheless, conclusive evidence from Saudi sources that these organizations are in fact tightly controlled by the government and, more often than not, literally run by government officials.[10] For example:

- ♦ The WML and the IIRO are under the direct supervision of the Grand Mufti of Saudi Arabia, the highest religious authority in the kingdom.
- ♦ WAMY and Al Haramain are chaired by the Saudi Minister of Islamic Affairs.
- ♦ As early as 1993, the kingdom passed a law stipulating that all donations to Muslim charities must be funneled through a fund controlled by a Saudi prince.

Consider a report on the yearly activities of the Wahhabi Al Haramain Foundation—a charity described as "keen on spreading the proper Islamic culture":

> It printed 13 million [Islamic] books, launched six Internet sites, employed more than 3,000 callers [proselytizers], founded 1,100 mosques, schools and cultural Islamic centers and posted more than 350,000 letters of call [invitations to convert to Islam].[11]

---

9   For a detailed account of the involvement of Saudi organizations and charities in sponsoring terrorist groups and activities, see U.S. Government Evidentiary Proffer Supporting the Admissibility of Co-Conspirator Statements, United States v. Enaam Arnaout, No. 02-CR-892 (Northern District of Illinois.) filed January 6, 2003.

10   See http://www.saudhouse.com/salmanobinoabduloaziz.htm.

11   *Ain-Al-Yaqeen* (Saudi government-controlled newspaper), December 8, 2000.

Another key Saudi "charity," IIRO, claims to have completed thirty-eight hundred mosques, spent $45 million for Islamic education, and employed six thousand proselytizers.[12] Both IIRO and Al Haramain currently operate directly out of Saudi embassies in countries in which they do not have their own offices. And both have been implicated in terrorist activities by U.S. authorities.

The Wahhabis' Totalitarian Strategy

Early on in the Wahhabi ideological campaign, the penetration of the Muslim communities in non-Muslim Western societies was made a key priority, designed to ensure Wahhabi dominance in the local Muslim establishments. This involved taking over existing mosques (or building Saudi-style new ones), establishing Islamic centers and educational institutions, and endowing Islamic chairs at various universities.

Taking over a mosque, of course, means more than building and maintaining the structures. It also means:

♦ assigning Saudi-trained imams.
♦ ensuring that only Saudi-published Wahhabi literature is used on the premises.
♦ selecting those who will be allowed to make the obligatory pilgrimage to Mecca.
♦ granting all-expenses-paid scholarships in Saudi Arabia.

In short, it allows the Saudis to proselytize freely and to exercise control over every aspect of the operations of the mosque and the community it serves.

Moreover, the leadership of the mosque is responsible for the collection of *zakat*—the yearly donation, equal to 2.5 percent of annual income, that observant Muslims must give to charity through the mosque. Wahhabi clerics naturally direct these funds to favored extremist organizations. For example, most Pakistani mosques in the United Kingdom have reportedly been taken over by the Wahhabi/Deobandi group, even though their members belong primarily to the moderate Barelvi creed. As a result, millions of pounds sterling in donations are now supporting terrorist groups in Pakistan.

Wahhabism in the West.

No one knows for sure how much the Saudis have spent to secure a foothold in non-Muslim regions, especially in Western Europe and North America.

---

12 Ibid.

The sums, however, are undoubtedly staggering. Some indication can be discerned from the Saudis' own data: they acknowledge having built more than 1,500 mosques, 210 Islamic centers, 202 Islamic colleges, and 2,000 schools for educating Muslims in non-Muslim countries.[13] Most of these institutions continue to receive annual donations from Saudi sources, ensuring that Wahhabi control is not likely to weaken in the near future.

What have the Saudis managed to buy in North America with such unprecedented Islamic largesse? In the United States and Canada, an estimated *80 percent* of all Islamic religious institutions are said to be supported financially by the Saudis.[14] The Saudi-funded Muslim Student Association chapters on U.S. college campuses are largely dominated by Islamist and anti-American agendas, as are most of the many Islamic Studies centers and schools financed by the Saudis. In addition, there are a growing number of Deobandi schools in the United States, usually subsidized by the Saudis, teaching intolerance and rejection of American and democratic ideals.

The Saudis have also focused on spreading radical Islam in the American black community. As noted above, their front groups operate programs aimed specifically at converting inmates in America's prisons, many of whom are black or Hispanic. The alleged terrorist plot recently uncovered at New Folsom State Prison in California would appear to be a product of this ominous recruitment operation.

The Role of Other Islamofascist States

Saudi Arabia may be the most important state sponsor of extremism, but it is far from being the only one. A number of countries—notably Iran, Sudan, and Syria—are unabashed supporters of radical Islamism and terrorism and make no secret of their hostility toward the United States.

Even more worrisome, however, are those Islamist regimes that, like Saudi Arabia, are key state sponsors of Islamofascism while pretending to be our "strategic allies" in the War on Terror.

Pakistan is a case in point. It is impossible to comprehend fully the extent of the cancerous spread of jihadist Islam in South Asia and, for that matter, in Britain, without an appreciation of the Islamofascists' continuing control over Pakistan's governing institutions and territory.[15]

---

13 *Ain al-Yaqeen*, March 1, 2002.
14 See note 6.
15 Most British radical Islamist organizations and affiliated madrassas are direct offshoots of Pakistani Deobandi, Ahle Hadith, and Jamiat-e-Islami Islamist organizations. See International Crisis Group (ICG) Report, "Pakistan: Madrassas, Extremism and the Military," Asia Report #36, July 29, 2002, p. 16.

Four years have passed since September 11, when General Musharaf caused his government overnight to switch sides from being a patron of the Taliban and al-Qaeda to an avowed ally of the United States. Tens of billions of dollars in U.S. aid have been provided to ensure that his government stays on our team.

But there is scant evidence that Musharaf's dictatorship is doing much to stem the incitement of hateful Islamist propaganda, churned out every day by Pakistan's thousands of Jihadi madrassas or to curb its still-operating terrorist training camps.

Even the nominally "secular" Pakistani curriculum continues to indoctrinate children to strive for jihad and martyrdom.[16] By allowing the continued indoctrination and training of thousands of foreign jihadists, Islamabad is directly complicit in the sponsorship of extremism and terrorism, from Western Europe to East Asia.[17]

In the wake of the August 2005 London bombings, General Musharaf finally publicly acknowledged that, until then, he had done little to curtail his country's pervasive Jihadi networks and madrassa hate factories. Indeed, Pakistan's actual contribution to the War for the Free World has largely been limited to helping to arrest several hundred foreign jihadists that had been operating freely on Pakistani soil.

The general's excuse is that he was constrained by a lack of power at the time (a curious admission on the part of an absolute military dictator). Now, he says, he finally has enough power and will get serious about using it against the Islamofascists. Although there is some truth to Musharaf's claim that he is constrained in acting against his country's Islamists, this fact suggests that he will continue to do nothing. The devastating October 2005 earthquake will doubtless provide fresh excuses for inaction.

The reality is that Pakistan is not a state with a military establishment—it is a military establishment that owns a state (including a large chunk of its industrial and real estate assets). For nearly thirty years, this military establishment has had a close, synergistic relationship with Islamic zealots, using them as proxies in Kashmir and Afghanistan as well as against its own civil society. To expect that the military and Musharaf will break this relationship to please us is a foolish delusion.

---

16 See, for instance, A.H. Nayyar and Ahmed Salim, *The Subtle Subversion*, available at www.sdpi.org/archive/nayyaroreport.htm.

17 Karachi madrassas have become a center for indoctrination of Thai Islamic militants and have contributed immeasurably to the violent Islamist insurgency now spreading in Southern Thailand. See B. Raman, "Pakistani Madrassas: Questions and Answers," South Asia Analysis Group (SAAG), August 5, 2005. Available at http://www.saag.org/papers15/pare1487.html.

Knowing the Enemy

It is important to bear in mind that the Wahhabi creed is practiced by roughly 20 million people around the world. That is *less than 2 percent* of the planet's Muslim population.

As we have seen, however, thanks to the cumulative investment by Saudi sources over the past three decades, Wahhabism (together with its allied ideologies) has become a dominant factor in the international Islamic establishment.

A particularly noteworthy example of this influence can be seen in what has become of the venerable Al-Azhar mosque and university in Cairo. These institutions have long been regarded as examples of Islamic moderation, yet they have now been taken over by the Wahhabis and regularly spew extremist propaganda.[18] Two of their recent fatwas make it a religious duty for Muslims to acquire nuclear weapons to fight the infidels and justify suicide attacks against American troops in Iraq.

The Wahhabi project has contributed immeasurably to Islamic radicalization and destabilization in a number of countries. Notwithstanding September 11 and all that has happened since, Riyadh continues to finance extremist networks around the world, providing terrorist groups and individuals with safe havens, financial underwriting, and other forms of support.

Amazingly, even Islamofascist terrorist attacks in Saudi Arabia itself do not seem likely to bring about meaningful change. Riyadh's unremitting hostility toward America shows no signs of abating. If anything, it is intensifying, as the House of Saud appreciates that American success—in the so-called War on Terror, and in the effort to promote a new democratic order in the Middle East—would spell the regime's doom.

What Needs to Be Done

Little lasting progress in the War for the Free World can be expected if we fail to grasp two important realities.

1. Islamism, though parading as a religion, is in fact a totalitarian ideology that promotes political and religious sedition and incitement to violence. Like other such ideologies before it, unless defeated, this one will stop at nothing short of the destruction of our tolerant society and constitutional government.

---

18 For details on the Wahhabi takeover of Al-Azhar, see the testimony of Islamic scholar Khaled Abou al-Fadl cited in Frank Foer, "Moral Hazard," *The New Republic*, November 18, 2002.

2. In virtually all cases, Islamism and its terrorist manifestations have been—
    and continue to be—state sponsored.

The chapters that follow address a variety of challenges; each recommends
War Footing steps that will enable us to meet and surmount them. None of
these is more important, however, than the first step: Know the enemy.

STEP 2

Really Support the Troops

With Contributions from Lt. Gen. Tom McInerney, USAF (Ret.), Maj. Gen. Paul E. Vallely, USA (Ret.), Dr. Daniel Goure, and Dr. Michael Rubin

---

M any millions of Americans all over the country are committed to supporting our troops serving in Afghanistan and Iraq. The message can be seen everywhere, pasted on car bumpers and posted on Web sites. But how exactly can we best "support the troops"?

Every page of this book is about how we can—and must—support the war effort and the troops that carry much of the burden of it, principally by promoting coherent and informed policies. But for the sake of troops on the front lines, it is also important that we focus clearly on what their role in this war is and what they will need to perform it. This chapter will explain their mission in Iraq (and elsewhere) and the factors that have complicated it.

Understanding the Challenge

The "War in Afghanistan" and the "War in Iraq" are the obvious arenas of the current conflict, and these operations are certainly the most difficult and dangerous tasks we've entrusted to our soldiers so far. But these arenas are really just two fronts of a far larger, and extremely complex, conflict: the War for the Free World.

Waging Three Kinds of War

This larger conflict consists of three elements: a conventional war, a counterinsurgency war, and a war of ideas.

◆ **The conventional war.** In identifiable geographic "theaters of operations," our troops confront known enemies using traditional military means.

◆ **The counterinsurgency war.** A battle that must be fought almost everywhere, not only with conventional troops but also using secret (covert) means, against a largely unknown enemy (or enemies) who target civilian populations.

◆ **The war of ideas.** An array of nonmilitary weapons of political warfare and strategic communication—laptop computers, Web sites and blogs, and radio broadcasts—can help secure victory and may save soldiers' lives.

Although this multifaceted war may be different from those that preceded it, victory will come as has been the case in other great conflicts: step by step, in a string of engagements, battles, and campaigns. We know that progress may be difficult to track, whereas setbacks, such as deadly suicide bombings, will be highly visible and widely reported.

Moreover, victory in this war is unlikely to be signaled by a formal surrender or treaty. In some of the places in which we are fighting—or will fight—the victory can only come from *within the local society*, when popular opposition to Islamofascist regimes and their allies decisively rejects the totalitarian ideology that fuels this conflict.

A Long-Delayed Offense

Tragically, in spite of two decades of provocation, it took the attacks of September 11, 2001, to bring the United States to the point of employing military means against the terrorists' safe havens. We can pinpoint the beginning of the overt conflict as the attacks by Islamofascist agents on the U.S. embassy in Iran in 1979 and the American embassy and Marine barracks in Lebanon in the early 1980s.

Prior to September 11, the United States was playing a generally defensive game in response to those attacks and others that followed. Washington (like the rest of the Western world) generally adopted a law-enforcement approach (in other words, a defense-only strategy) to deal with international terrorism perpetrated by al-Qaeda, Hezbollah, and other Islamist groups (see Step 5).

◆ The Clinton administration's response to al-Qaeda's 1998 bombings of two U.S. embassies in Africa in 1998 was a single cruise-missile strike on a training camp in Afghanistan.

◆ Michael Scheuer, who formerly ran the CIA's al-Qaeda task force, documents at least *ten instances* when the United States failed to take advantage of an opportunity to go after Osama bin Laden. As a direct result, bin Laden's embryonic terrorist organization was able to create a secure base of operations in Afghanistan.

We lost a lot of ground in those two decades—literally. The U.S. military today has been tasked to recapture territory that was lost in those years to our terrorism-wielding enemies.

By now, however, America's armed forces are applying a hard-learned lesson: *no nation can win a war by defense alone.*

- By playing defense, we allow the adversary the advantage of choosing the time, place, and level of his attacks. This strategy also permitted the enemy to create and maintain safe havens in which to organize and orchestrate his next offensive.
- Winning wars is about defeating hostile forces, whether disciplined conventional armies or loosely organized terrorist cells—denying their capacity to wage war and their will to continue the fight. To accomplish these goals, *the war must be taken to the enemy.*

The Dangers of One-Way "Dialogue"

But even after the September 11 attacks compelled the United States to go on the offensive, the war effort was hampered from the outset by a dangerous misconception. Much of America's political leadership was persuaded that, before military force could be employed, every opportunity for "dialogue" and negotiation had to be exhausted.

In the case of Afghanistan, fortunately the delay was brief. The Taliban mistakenly believed that the United States would not or could not destroy their regime. They foolishly refused to surrender bin Laden, and the United States was free to move swiftly to prove them wrong.

Launching the Iraq front of this war was a very different story. Much is written daily about the problems of planning and intelligence gathering that hampered that operation. But it is clear that America's military effort was undermined, most of all, by the many months of planning that was afforded the regime of Saddam Hussein while the United States deferred a military attack in the name of "giving peace a chance" at the United Nations.

A Compromised United Nations

The critics' clear purpose was to block U.S. action against the regime of Saddam Hussein—a state sponsor of terror that had

◆ repeatedly used weapons of mass destruction on its own people and its neighbors
◆ refused to comply with UN-imposed weapons inspections
◆ pledged to exact revenge for its humiliation in Operation Desert Storm
◆ celebrated the terrorist attacks of September 11, 2001 (the only country to do so openly).

In the post-September 11 world, President Bush was right to regard such a regime as an intolerable threat.

Yet, various United Nations bureaucrats, ostensible U.S. allies (notably, France and Germany), and Russia and China were determined to prevent President Bush from eliminating that threat. Without the UN Security Council's blessing, they reasoned, the White House would be politically unable to take action against Iraq. UN Secretary General Kofi Annan went so far as to declare that, unless the UN authorized the use of force (a nearly unprecedented circumstance), military action would be "illegal" (see Step 10).

We now know that a number of those who opposed the liberation of Iraq were in Saddam's pocket, if not actually on his payroll. There was much to be gained, on many sides, from the continuation of the UN's porous "Oil for Food" program in Iraq.

It is often alleged that the Bush administration's policy to liberate Iraq was motivated by a U.S. desire for Iraq's oil. It should be clear by now, however, that oil was more of a consideration for at least some of the governments who cooperated with Saddam Hussein's regime.

Six months of diplomacy ended, predictably, in failure. In the end, the American-led "coalition of the willing" was able to overthrow the Iraqi paymaster and his brutal regime without UN approval. Regrettably, however, we were not able to do so before material harm was done to the cause, both in Iraq and beyond.

The Lessons of Iraq

The diplomatic delay was costlier than is generally understood. A regime that had constructed elaborate underground facilities was granted ample time to organize a strategic retreat, so as to continue a semblance of a terrorist regime as a well-equipped, well-funded insurgent mob. The delay, moreover, allowed our adversaries beyond Iraq to develop a coordinated response to any assault on that country.

The consequences of delay were grave indeed. Saddam Hussein's government used the delay to damaging effect. He had learned a hard lesson from his 1991 defeat in Operation Desert Storm: he had counted on a UN process to forestall a U.S.-led invasion of Kuwait—a grave miscalculation.

In 2003, therefore, he hedged his bets. In the event that his friends at the UN failed to deliver on their promises to prevent another invasion—this time, of the Iraqi homeland—*Saddam began planning the insurgency* that continues to claim lives of coalition and Iraqi forces, and of countless civilians, to this day.

Iran, Syria, and Saudi Islamists also took advantage of the breathing space to gain a foothold in Iraq:

- By the time the United States finally went to war, the chief source of international news for Iraqis was the vitriolic *al-Alam*, an Iran-based Arabic-language television network.
- Iran's Islamic Revolutionary Guard Corps and the Iranian intelligence services collaborated with the Syrian government to plan their own campaign of insurgency and destabilization; U.S. forces later captured Iranian infiltrators, along with documents outlining Iran's plans for destabilizing liberated Iraq.
- Iran's Syrian allies established a kind of covert passage to transport terrorists—many of whom came from Saudi Arabia—into Iraq.
- North Korea, like Iran, exploited the window afforded by America's dithering with the UN, as well as the distractions associated with the subsequent invasion, by ramping up their respective long-standing covert nuclear weapons programs.[1]

A Squandered Opportunity

But if the diplomatic delay was a valuable opportunity for enemy tacticians, it was also a lost opportunity as far as U.S. preparations were concerned. Keenly aware that any war preparations would be viewed as undermining the negotiations over weapons inspections, Secretary of State Colin Powell and

---

1   Both North Korea and Iran also became more openly defiant of international obligations and watchdogs in response to the administration's ill-advised participation in feckless negotiations led (respectively) by China and the EU-3 (Britain, France, and Germany).

National Security Advisor Condoleezza Rice decided to defer any action on two critically important initiatives:

♦ **A full-up postwar planning office for Iraq.** This would have been the "command center" for serious work on alternative post-invasion scenarios and possible responses.

♦ **A Free Iraqi Force consisting of trained Iraqi exiles.** The U.S. military had begun to train just a handful of Iraqis when the invasion was launched. Instead of helping to liberate their country, these volunteers sat out the first weeks of the conflict in Hungary, huddled around radios listening for news.

This is why, in the post-invasion period, the insurgents seemed to have a free hand for so long. We were woefully ill prepared to contend with the insurgency prepared by Saddam, the Syrians, Iranians, and Saudis for post-invasion Iraq.

There were further ramifications to this lack of preparedness.

In Iraqi eyes, a Free Iraqi Forces component could have spelled the difference between occupation and liberation. On April 9, 2003, in a pivotal symbolic event, to be shown again and again in news clips, it was an American Marine corporal—and not an Iraqi—who draped a flag over the statue of Saddam Hussein; and it was (famously) an American flag rather than the flag of Iraq.

On the ground, U.S. troops lacking Iraqi interpreters lost critical early opportunities and made inevitable errors of judgment. The U.S. mission in Iraq has suffered ever since from the lack of a trusted, proficient Iraqi military partner. It has proved difficult indeed to train a new Iraqi army in the field, under fire from a determined and well-supplied insurgency.

Diplomacy is not always a neutral tactic. We need to be especially wary of accommodating the demands of parties whose standard mode of operations is to use diplomacy to block U.S. interests, especially when we have reason to believe that, as with Iraq, such negotiations will make it more difficult to support our troops and protect our vital interests.

Just as military preparations may undercut negotiations, the reverse is also true: negotiations can forestall military preparedness, without necessarily resolving the underlying conflict. In this case, it can be argued, diplomacy was a diversion that proved damaging to our vital interests and especially harmful to our fighting forces.

"Engaging" with the Enemy

The "reconciliation" negotiations conducted in Iraq post-invasion have proved, similarly, to be a non-neutral tactic. The theory has been that efforts to bring enemy forces into the political process will promote security. Unfortunately, among Islamist radicals (and in Middle East societies generally) such a process is likely to have the opposite effect. Premature reconciliation is seen as a signal of weakness and thus invites further violence.

We tend to forget that President Bush's decision to oust Saddam Hussein was initially popular with the vast majority of Iraqis. Iraqis celebrated their liberation. Many greeted American troops warmly. For a time, Iraqi men, women, and children cooperated with U.S. troops, alerting them to improvised explosive devices (IEDs) and fingering insurgents.

The honeymoon collapsed, however, amid confusion about U.S. intentions. Initiatives that American civilian and military personnel intended as constructive acts of reconciliation were seen by ordinary Iraqis as incipient betrayals—as collaboration with the feared Baathist thugs.

Americans can scarcely imagine what it is like to have lived for thirty-five years under the sort of capricious and utterly ruthless repression imposed by Saddam Hussein's Baathist dictatorship. In such an environment, it becomes second nature for everyone, citizens and officials alike, to keep their heads down. No one will risk doing *anything* that could get them or their families in serious trouble. One develops a keen instinct for survival, highly attuned to the slightest signals emanating from the power structure.

Iraqis were confused, therefore, when, shortly after the fall of Baghdad, Gen. Jay Garner (the first American director of postwar reconstruction in Iraq) had dinner with an Iraqi businessman named Saad al-Janabi. Al-Janabi was widely known as a key member of Saddam's Baath Party, a man who had been closely identified with one of the dictator's most feared subordinates and relatives, his late son-in-law, Hussein Kemal. For Iraqis, Garner's outreach to one of Saddam Hussein's key allies was an ominous sign that the United States was considering some kind of deal with the Baathists.

This perception played into profound Iraqi fears. Would the Americans once again abandon the people of Iraq to their jailers? This had been the story once before, when, after the Gulf War in 1991, President George H.W. Bush had encouraged Iraqis to rise up in rebellion against Saddam Hussein. When many of them did so, the United States failed to come to their aid, and thousands were slaughtered. Americans may have forgotten the episode, but Iraqis most assuredly remember.

For their part, the Baathists took a similar message from the American attempt at outreach and reconciliation. For Garner to dine with al-Janabi signaled that the United States had no intention of rounding up regime officials and bringing them to justice. Power was within their reach, if they would only go for it. Meanwhile, the Iranian government could point to such evidence of American outreach as a way of convincing Iraq's Shi'ites that Tehran, and not Washington, would be their reliable protector.

The Costs of "Re-Baathification"

The policy of "engaging" the enemy has very serious implications that go beyond the matter of how our intentions may be perceived. U.S. officials, critical of the Iraqis' de-Baathification program, largely refused to support it. Indeed, the American leaders in Iraq have actually engaged in *re*-Baathification, a process that can be directly associated with increased violence and insurgency.

The U.S. "big tent" approach, for example, merely served to transform Mosul from a relatively peaceful city into a "no-go" area:

- Rather than confront Baathists and Islamists, it was decided to empower them. This was a catastrophic failure. After one of Saddam's former generals, Muhammed al-Maris, was put in charge of the Iraqi Border Police at the Syrian border, Mosul became a transit point for insurgents.
- Another former Baathist general, Muhammad Kha'iri Barhawi, was selected as Mosul's police chief. By day, Barhawi served the new Iraq, but by night he plotted the return of the "old guard." In November 2004, with U.S. forces preoccupied with Fallujah, Barhawi handed control of Iraq's second-largest city to insurgents.
- The outreach extended to Islamofascist elements, too: in Mosul, Islamists were placed on the city council and in key security positions.

To be sure, Mosul became relatively calm. But that quiet was purchased at a high price. "Reconciliation" led not to genuine peace but to the Islamicization of the city and the creation of a new safe haven for the export of terror. Americans, as well as Iraqis, are dying as a result.

Never Reward Violence

Terrorists—like a malignancy—must be *eliminated* rather than soothed with a diplomatic Band-Aid. It is an extremely grave mistake to try to co-opt them with concessions. Just as ransoming hostages engenders further kidnappings, rewarding violence sparks a cascading increase in violence.

Consider Fallujah. On March 31, 2004, terrorists in Fallujah ambushed, killed, and mutilated four nonmilitary U.S. security contractors. The following day, President Bush declared, "America will never be intimidated by thugs and assassins."

But in the eyes of our opponents, America was indeed intimidated: the payoff for terrorism came swiftly. For twenty-four days, Coalition forces had encircled Fallujah. But now, instead of taking the city and ridding it of its "thugs and assassins," the United States decided to empower them. It turned the city over to a newly created "Fallujah Brigade"—*made up of former insurgents.*

Upon learning of the deal, the Fallujah insurgents drove through the streets shouting, "We redeem Islam with our blood." Minaret-mounted loudspeakers declared, "Victory over the Americans!" In the twenty-four days that followed the creation of the Fallujah Brigade, car bombings increased by *600 percent.* Ultimately, Fallujah had to be taken by force, but this delay cost us dearly in Iraqi and American lives and in Iraq's confidence in the U.S. commitment.

The War for Public Opinion

Our opponents in this war, whether in Iraq or elsewhere, respect strength, not compromise. They are merely emboldened by signs that their strategy of murder and mayhem is succeeding in the critical battle they believe they *can* win: the contest to influence American public opinion (see Step 8).

For all the loose talk comparing this conflict to the Vietnam War, there are more differences than similarities between them. Today's enemy, however, clearly has learned the central lesson of Vietnam: a strategic victory over America becomes possible at the point when the American public becomes so demoralized and alienated that it insists the war be abandoned.

The insurgents' car bombs and suicide attacks are not really a military tactic. Instead, these are weapons in the war for public opinion—Iraqi and American. The aim is not to win converts to their cause but simply to convince the liberators, and the liberated, that their efforts are futile.

This is why the terrorists in Iraq seek to slaughter as many Americans, Iraqis, and Coalition personnel—military and civilian—as possible. Their key aims are to obscure any evidence of progress, to escalate the costs of securing the new Iraq, and to thus lend support to those Americans who imagine that we can safely pull out our troops and walk away.[2]

---

2   See intercepted letter from Ayman Zawahiri to Abu Musab Zarqawi, July 2005, Office of Director National Intelligence, News Release No. 2-05, available at http:www.ndi.gov.

Surrender Is Not an Option

Anyone who thinks we can just walk away from the "war" in Iraq—as we ultimately did in Vietnam—lacks a clear understanding of either of these conflicts.

The American defeat in Southeast Asia had a profoundly adverse effect on our security, prestige, and influence. It not only signaled to our foes that large-enough casualties would cause us to retreat; it also put American allies throughout the world on notice that we would abandon them if we thought doing so would serve our interests. Simply put, the surrender of 1975 was the nadir of American power in the late-20th century.

But the effects of abandoning Iraq would be far worse. It would hand the Islamofascists and their allies a far more significant victory than did the boldly executed attacks of September 11. It would validate the Islamists' most powerful recruiting tool: their claim that weak Americans and other infidels will inevitably be defeated by the jihadist warriors—that the future belongs to a new despotism, which seeks to impose the pitiless tyranny of radicalized Islam.

The effect on friendly nations would be no less devastating. Especially in states that are themselves under threat from the Islamists, many will conclude that their best hope lies in appeasing these enemies rather than expecting us to help defeat them.

Finally, our defeat in Iraq would validate the means by which radical Islamists have fought in Iraq: mass murder and assassination. There can be no doubt that terrorism would intensify all over the Free World—including within the United States—as dogmatic Islamists recommit ruthlessly to pursue their stated goal of a worldwide caliphate.

What Needs to Be Done

If failure is not an option, what needs to be done to support our troops in Iraq, Afghanistan, and elsewhere?

1. Win in Iraq

For the time being, we cannot responsibly consider—and we should stop debating—any major reduction of U.S. forces on the ground in Iraq, let alone their complete withdrawal. Instead, we need to make a redoubled effort to accomplish the following tasks:

The Military Imperative

Use our troops to deny the enemy safe havens and isolate them from the populations they rely on for cover, support, and recruits. This task will require the number of U.S. troops in the country to remain at its current level for the foreseeable future. (Indeed, there may need to be temporary *increases* in our deployments, to help assure security at the time of critical referenda and elections.)

Be a Reliable Ally

Work to restore the confidence of the Iraqi people in our commitment to their future security and freedom, by making no further outreach or concessions to Baathists, Islamofascists, and others associated with the insurgency.

Develop the Iraqi Security Forces

Continue to build and support strong, well-disciplined, and well-trained Iraqi security forces. There are now roughly 170,000 Iraqi personnel in various stages of training, including army, national guard, police, and other security forces. By the end of summer 2006, these forces will number 250,000 courageous men and women, who daily take the fight to the enemy in the face of threats and violence directed against them and their families.

Iraq's growing forces need our training to develop not only military skills but also a strong sense of ethics, honor, and respect for civil-military relations at all ranks and grades. Without an ethos of selfless service to the public, the trainees are unlikely to earn the respect and confidence of the Iraqi people.

We also need to provide Iraq's security forces the equipment they need to execute their duties, including "up-armored" Humvees and heavier armored fighting vehicles; more powerful weapons, such as artillery and mortars; and aircraft, especially helicopters. They also will need adequate communications, logistics, and maintenance capabilities.

U.S. forces will, of course, leave Iraq at some point in the future; but we must reject any notion that an arbitrary date should be set for their withdrawal. Such a deadline would certainly encourage the terrorists to bide their time, preparing a new offensive in which they will no longer be facing U.S. troops. Top U.S. and Iraqi commanders must instead develop a plan that ties U.S. force withdrawals to the achievement of specific goals, related among other things to benchmarks of size, sophistication, and battlefield effectiveness of the Iraqi security forces.

2. Stay on the Offensive

In Step 9, we will consider nonmilitary strategies for dealing with various actual and potential adversaries. Whether or not those strategies are successful, we need to be mindful that, if we fail to keep our enemies off balance and on the run, we risk having to fight them some day within our national borders. If nonmilitary strategies are insufficient, military options are called for.

3. Transform the Military

With the end of the Cold War, the U.S. government—executive and legislative branches alike—allowed U.S. military capabilities to erode dramatically. Although officials continued to claim that America's military was adequate to fight two major regional conflicts nearly simultaneously, our enemies readily understood that this was merely "talking the talk."

We must do everything necessary to maintain the military forces we need today and to prepare for the likely needs of tomorrow. Given the stakes, we simply cannot afford to undergo the sort of hollowing-out that will result from trying to wage war on the cheap.

Current preparedness requires that we:

♦ meet the costs associated with the war effort
♦ ensure that we sustain the technological edge of our armed forces
♦ continue to field the most professional and best-trained forces in the world
♦ maintain the ability to project power rapidly and globally.

Even though we are currently facing determined, aggressive foes in Afghanistan and Iraq, these campaigns cannot distract us from the need to prepare our military—every element of it—for tomorrow's major battles. There are two essential elements to this effort.

Assure That Our Troops Have the Resources They Need

We need make a realistic commitment to supply the resources needed to accomplish our military aims. This can best be accomplished by increasing the defense budget in relation to the gross domestic product (GDP). Currently, defense spending consumes roughly 3.2 percent of our GDP—a small fraction of what we committed when, during past wars, our national survival was at stake as it is today. Congress should *increase defense spending to the equivalent of 4 percent of GDP in fiscal year 2006, 4.5 percent in fiscal year 2007, and 5 percent in fiscal year 2008.*

Budgeting at this level (and backed by rigorous oversight and budgetary review) will permit our military to meet the pressing demands of its day-to-day combat operations, and make possible necessary, and in some cases long overdue, modernization programs.

Target the Leaders of Terrorist Organizations

We must Enhance the U.S. capability to target terrorist leaders, even on the territory of neutral or friendly countries, if necessary. This may require creating dedicated combined-arms units that can pack more punch than our Special Operations forces. Such units could include elite conventional ground combat elements as well as dedicated intelligence assets, unmanned aerial vehicles (such as Predator, Global Hawk, or Scan Eagle), and mobility capabilities (notably, the formidable V-22 tiltrotor). These units should be located in theaters of interest and ready to move at a moment's notice.

4. Fashion New Alliances

The current War for the Free World will be a long one. It will have to be fought in, and primarily by, those nations where the threat has arisen. That is why the United States must aggressively pursue the creation of new alliances designed to support the long-term global war on terrorism. These alliances will entail:

- ◆ arrangements less formal than the NATO model, yet more durable than the ad hoc coalitions created to support operations in Afghanistan and Iraq;
- ◆ long-term relationships that will support sensible intelligence sharing, training, interoperability, and multinational operations. Such relationships can make partner countries less vulnerable to becoming sanctuaries for terrorist organizations.

5. Recognize the Real Limits of Diplomacy[3]

Our experience in Iraq, both before and after the conflict, underscores the importance of being realistic about the potential drawbacks of diplomatic negotiations involving implacable and duplicitous, yet patient, adversaries.

It is a firm tenet of democratic foreign policy that it is invariably better to discuss differences than to fight over them, and this is surely true, as far as it goes. However, if the real choice is between fighting a weak enemy today or a stronger one tomorrow, the diplomatic process may be merely a dangerous illusion. To the extent that discussions buy precious time for our foes to become more dangerous, they merely postpone the conflict to a time and circumstance of the enemy's choosing.

---

3   See Step 10 for more detail.

6. Provide Quality Intelligence

In recent years, the U.S. intelligence community has been repeatedly criticized for a variety of shortcomings, including serious problems with the quality and conduct of intelligence gathering and analysis. CIA Director Porter Goss has begun to make personnel and management changes, in the face of stiff resistance from below and above; he deserves our strong support.

The following critical changes must be made (including undoing some recent, ill-considered reforms that have only made matters worse):

Encourage More Risk-Taking and Competitive Analysis

Intelligence analysis today is a bland, cautious, stultified business. Analysts are generally gun-shy—afraid to stick their necks out or to offer well-supported yet imaginative conclusions about the workings and intentions of secretive and hostile states.

The analyst who is inclined to be more creative is likely to be required to "tone it down," to toe the accepted "party line." To question the agencies' preferred conclusions—which, by the way, bear a startling resemblance to the conventional wisdom of the foreign policy establishment and the *New York Times* editorial board—is to jeopardize one's career.

Do Some Serious Housecleaning—in Both the CIA and Defense Intelligence Agency (DIA) Analysis "Shops"

Careerists, many of whom were chosen by and promoted during a Clinton administration hostile to effective intelligence operations, should be replaced with professionals capable of thinking outside the box—the kind of thinking our adversaries often engage in. CIA Director Goss has made some modest personnel and other changes aimed at reforming CIA analysis but not enough to serve our urgent needs in time of war.

Bring Intelligence Professionalism into the State Department

The most political "intelligence" agency is the U.S. State Department's Bureau for Intelligence and Research (INR). INR's highly partisan officers are closely allied with very liberal State Department careerists (see Step 10). Although INR is a small organization and nominally writes analysis only for the secretary of state, it is obtrusively active in interagency assessments, especially National Intelligence Community papers.

The mainstream media and some Democratic members of Congress have lionized INR for "getting it right" on Iraq's weapons of mass destruction (WMDs) programs. This claim is only partly true. INR did object to some aspects of the pre-war intelligence assessments of Iraq's WMDs program (mostly concerning an alleged Iraqi nuclear weapons program). The bureau did not object, though, to the intelligence community's analysis that Iraq had covert chemical and biological weapons programs. And INR was dead wrong when, in 1991, it objected to analysis that Iraq had a covert nuclear program before the Gulf War.

INR's problems stem from unavoidable conflicts of interests arising from its peculiar composition and mandate: INR is ostensibly an intelligence agency, yet it is located within a policy agency and staffed by State Department officers. To correct this conflict, at least half of INR's personnel should be managers and analysts on loan from other intelligence agencies. And to minimize the overt politicization of INR intelligence support, the bureau's career officers should be required to attend intelligence analyst training courses at the CIA and the DIA and to serve on assignments in these agencies for significant portions of their careers.

Liberate U.S. Intelligence Collection

American efforts to gather intelligence through human and technical means has long suffered from bureaucratic problems that inhibit our ability to gather crucial information and to transmit it quickly to policy makers and commanders in the field. The human-source intelligence divisions (HUMINT) at CIA and DIA are especially bureaucratized, oriented to meeting internal agency goals that have little to do with needs of policy makers. Innovation and risk taking are, accordingly, discouraged.

Although most details regarding the CIA human intelligence operation are classified, the House Select Committee on Intelligence published this summary in the unclassified version of a June 2004 report:

> After years of trying to convince, suggest, urge, entice, cajole, and pressure CIA to make wide-reaching changes to the way it conducts its HUMINT mission, . . . CIA, in the Committee's view, continues down a road leading over a proverbial cliff. The damage to the HUMINT mission through its misallocation and redirection of resources, poor prioritization of objectives, micromanagement of field operations, and a continued political aversion to operational risk is, in the Committee's judgment, significant and could likely be long-lasting.

Undo Recent, Harmful Intelligence "Reforms"

Putting U.S. intelligence on a true War Footing will mean more than reforming the intelligence community. It will also require dealing with and undoing ill-advised changes implemented over the past year, at the recommendation of the National Commission on Terrorist Attacks upon the United States ("The 9/11 Commission"). These changes—including, notably, the creation of a new layer of bureaucracy, in the form of a Director of National Intelligence (DNI) and his staff—were previously considered, and rejected, by the Congress. They were quite sensibly resisted by the Bush administration, until a combination of political circumstances induced the president to acquiesce and appoint Ambassador John Negroponte to serve as the first DNI.

A number of serious problems have flowed from this "reform." For instance, the DNI's office has sapped so many resources from CIA and DIA offices to create its new bureaucracy that intelligence support of senior policy makers has actually been *reduced*. And Ambassador Negroponte has put two Foreign Service colleagues in key positions for which they are poorly suited: Thomas Fingar as Deputy Director for Analysis and former ambassador Kenneth Brill as Director of the National Counter-Proliferation Center.

Thomas Fingar, now Deputy Director for Analysis, was previously part of the problematic and politicized management of the INR. The questionable accuracy of his testimony against John Bolton's nomination to be UN ambassador raised doubts that he can assure the integrity and competence of the intelligence community's analytical personnel.

Ambassador Kenneth Brill, newly named Director of the National Counter-Proliferation Center, was a perennial apologist for proliferators in his prior post as U.S. ambassador to the International Atomic Energy Agency. Shortly after he took up his current duties, the intelligence community leaked its conclusion regarding Iran's weapons program: They decreed that Iran was, incredibly, at least 10 years away from having nuclear weapons. (This bizarre analysis is discussed in Step 9.)

This catalogue of intelligence deficiencies is not news. Factors such as these, however, contributed to the inability to collect and disseminate intelligence that might have either forewarned of the September terrorist attacks or produced accurate information on the true state of Iraq's WMDs programs. That being so, it is deeply troubling that they remain largely uncorrected.

Our military forces, government policy makers, and law-enforcement officials all rely heavily on the work of the intelligence community. As long as it remains seriously dysfunctional in many areas, neither our military nor our civilian leaders will receive the quality of intelligence they require to prevail in this war.

We can win this War for the Free World being waged against Islamo-fascism and its sponsors only if we clearly understand how to support our troops—the men and women who are putting their lives on the line every day for our country.

If these various lessons can be learned and corrective actions taken as part of putting America on a real War Footing, the U.S. military and intelligence communities will be able to perform their vital roles in this global conflict. By so doing, they will give us the time and opportunity to implement the other, nonmilitary steps described in the chapters that follow.

PART II
Wielding America's Economic and Financial "Weapons"

merica is fighting this war, as the saying goes, with one arm tied behind its back. To date, we have failed to make use of some of our most important strengths—our nonmilitary "weapons"—to enhance our security and to hurt our enemies. This section illustrates how, by harnessing two of these powerful instruments, we can bring to bear what the military calls "force-multipliers"; capabilities that will greatly improve our chances of surviving and prevailing over our Islamofascist foes and their totalitarian ideology.

- ◆ Step 3 offers insights into the national security risks associated with our dependence on foreign oil, most of which is used to power our cars, planes, and other vehicles. It describes how a combination of forces—ranging from unstable and hostile suppliers to terrorists attacking the oil infrastructure to skyrocketing demand from Communist China—are making the nation's reliance on such imported energy an increasingly unsustainable vulnerability.

Most importantly, we provide tangible suggestions for ways in which Americans and their elected representatives could stop sending tens of billions of dollars every year to state sponsors of terror and their friends who are trying to kill us. In other words, energy security is a "two-fer." It allows us to reduce a dangerous strategic vulnerability, and it permits us to deny our enemies the resources they use to endanger us.

- ◆ Step 4 shows how Americans can similarly use the financial power of our institutional and private investments to strengthen our country and hurt its foes. We provide shocking information about the immense amounts of money being made available to state sponsors of terror through their dealings with businesses listed on the U.S. stock exchanges. More alarming still, most U.S. investors have no idea that they are investing in companies partnering with terrorist regimes, let alone the potential financial risks associated with doing so.

If we are serious about winning this war, we need to adopt a War Footing stance that includes measures that use our money to punish our enemies and their business partners while rewarding the responsible—and profitable—companies that are on our side.

STEP 3

Provide for U.S. Energy Security

With Contributions from Dr. Gal Luft and Anne Korin

T hree years ago, one of America's most thoughtful strategists and security-policy practitioners, former CIA director R. James Woolsey, described the central challenge in our death struggle with Islamofascism and its sponsors:

> We are at war. We should start by asking what we can do, as soon as possible, to undercut our enemies' power. Other considerations should now follow, not lead . . . . If we do not act now, we will leave major levers over our fate in the hands of regimes that have attacked us or have fallen under the sway of fanatics who spread hatred of the US, and indeed of freedom itself. For all of them, their power derives from their oil. It is time to break their sword.[1]

Mr. Woolsey is calling to mind a lesson no victor in the history of military conflict has ever ignored: It is a grave mistake to enrich one's enemy in a time of war.

The flip side of that coin is that any winning strategy involves denying the other side the economic means necessary to keep up the fight. In World War II, as our soldiers clashed on the beaches of Normandy and Guadalcanal, the Allies made a concerted effort to cut the economic lifeline of the Axis.

In fact, it was only when the German and Japanese war industries ran out of cash and raw materials—when their urban centers of economic activity

---

1 R. James Woolsey, "Spiking the Oil Weapon," *Wall Street Journal*, September 19, 2002.

were reduced to rubble and their supply lines severed—that the Thousand Year Reich and the Greater East Asia Co-Prosperity Sphere were finally destroyed.

The Cold War might still be with us had it not been for President Ronald Reagan. He reversed his predecessors' and allied efforts to prop up the Soviet Union with political détente and grain sales, trade, loans, and other forms of assistance. Instead, he set out to destroy the "Evil Empire" by integrating *economic warfare* measures with other instruments, to empty the Kremlin's coffers and compound the failed system's many deficiencies.[2]

Energy Lessons Unlearned

Today, in our War for the Free World, we are standing this historical experience on its head. We are enriching our enemies instead of curtailing their economic power. And we are so dependent on their principal resource, oil, that we have left our economic jugular exposed and invitingly vulnerable to attack.

Under the sands that spawned radical Islam sit most of the world's oil reserves. Seventy percent of proven oil reserves are concentrated in the Middle East, primarily in Saudi Arabia, Iran, Iraq, Kuwait, United Arab Emirates, and Libya.

This is a significant problem because oil lubricates, literally and figuratively, the wheels of America's economy. The statistics are mind-boggling:

♦ The United States consumes a quarter of the world's oil supply, yet it is the locus of a mere 3 percent of global oil reserves. Consequently, the United States is heavily—and *increasingly*—dependent on foreign oil.

♦ In fact, America's dependence on foreign oil has grown from 30 percent in 1973—when the cartel known as the Organization of Petroleum Exporting Countries (OPEC) imposed its oil embargo—to 60 percent today.

♦ According to the U.S. Department of Energy, this dependence is projected to reach almost 70 percent by 2025.[3] And a growing share of the oil we import comes from the Persian Gulf.

---

2 See Peter Schweizer, *Victory: The Reagan Administration's Secret Strategy That Hastened the Collapse of the Soviet Union*, Atlantic Monthly Press, 1994.

3 U.S. Department of Energy, *Annual Energy Outlook 2005 with Projections to 2025*, Report no. DOE/EIA-0383, 2005.

- Oil imports constitute a quarter of the U.S. trade deficit and are a major contributor to the loss of jobs and investment opportunities in this country.
- More importantly, while the U.S. economy is bleeding, oil-producing nations sympathetic to—if not directly supportive of—our Islamist foes are experiencing staggering windfalls, to the detriment of our national security. Collectively, these exporters are garnering *billions of dollars a day*.
- In turn, an undetermined portion of these revenues finds its way—through official government handouts, intelligence slush-funds, so-called charities, and well-connected businesses—to the jihadists committed to America's destruction. Underwriting Islamofascist terror can take the form of subsidies for radicalized madrassas and mosques, as well as outright support of terrorist groups.

Our Enemies and the Oil Weapon

Saudi Arabia. Fifteen of the nineteen perpetrators of the September 11, 2001, terror attacks were Saudi nationals. This revelation exposed the true face of the country that many Americans had comfortably regarded as "our gas station" in the Middle East. After September 11, we could no longer ignore the fact that, while Saudi Arabia is home to a quarter of the world's reserves, it has also played by far the greatest role in advancing global Islamist militancy.

As noted in Step 1, the kingdom's oil wealth has directly enabled the spread of the virulent strain of Islamofascism known as Wahhabism around the world, from Nigeria to Canada, from Gaza to Pakistan, from Chechnya to the United States, from the Balkans to Latin America's lawless Tri-Border area.

Such aggressive proselytizing has been accomplished through the Saudis' use of oil funds to control 95 percent of Arabic language media, as well as large numbers of mosques around the world, including some 80 percent of those in the United States. In particular, petrodollars garnered from this country and elsewhere are being used by Saudi Arabia systematically to provide social services, build Wahhabi "Islamic centers" and schools, pay preachers' salaries, and, in many cases, fund terror organizations.

An October 2002 report by the Council on Foreign Relations Independent Task Force on Terrorist Financing concluded:

> It is worth stating clearly and unambiguously what official
> U.S. government spokesmen have not: For years, individuals

and charities based in Saudi Arabia have been the most important source of funds for al-Qaeda, and for years, Saudi officials have turned a blind eye to the problem.[4]

In July 2005, Under Secretary of the Treasury Stuart Levey, testifying in the Senate, noted:

> Wealthy Saudi financiers and charities have funded terrorist organizations and causes that support terrorism and the ideology that fuels the terrorists' agenda. *Even today*, we believe that Saudi donors may still be a significant source of terrorist financing, including for the insurgency in Iraq.[5] [Emphasis added.]

Iran. If Saudi Arabia is the financial engine of radical Sunni Islam, its Persian Gulf neighbor, Iran, is the powerhouse behind the proliferation of a no less intolerant and violent version of Shi'ite Islam. Iran is OPEC's second-largest oil producer, holding 10 percent of the world's proven oil reserves, and it has the world's second-largest natural gas reserve. With oil and gas revenues constituting more than 80 percent of its total export earnings and 50 percent of its gross domestic product, Iran is heavily dependent on petrodollars.

Iran's oil revenues serve also, of course, to support its version of Islamofascism and to underwrite the support Tehran gives to some of the world's most dangerous Islamist movements. Notable among these is the Lebanon-based terrorist group Hezbollah.

Iran's mullahs are fully aware of the power of their oil. Their supreme leader, Ayatollah Ali Khamenei, warned in 2002: "If the West did not receive oil, their factories would grind to a halt. This will shake the world!"[6] Unfortunately, as the world's demand for oil increases, Iran grows richer. Its oil revenues have jumped 25 percent in 2005 alone. Such wealth makes the mullahs ever more confident of their ability to defy American and allied efforts to bring international pressure to bear in preventing Tehran from developing nuclear weapons.

Terrorist groups. Al-Qaeda and its affiliates believe that the way to bring down a superpower is to weaken its economy through protracted guerrilla

---

4   "Terrorist Financing," Report of an Independent Task Force Sponsored by the Council on Foreign Relations, November 25, 2005. Available at http://www.cfr.org/content/publications/attachments/TerroristoFinancingoTF.pdf.
5   Testimony of Stuart Levey, Under Secretary, Office of Terrorism and Financial Intelligence, U.S. Department of the Treasury, before the Senate Committee on Banking, Housing, and Urban Affairs, July 13, 2005. Available at http://www.treas.gov/press/releases/js2629.htm.
6   "Iran Wields Oil Embargo Threat," *BBC News*, April 5, 2002.

warfare. In various public statements, Osama bin Laden has mentioned economic warfare as a pillar of his strategy.

For example, bin Laden claims that economic pressure brought the jihadists victory over the Soviets in Afghanistan during the 1980s—and subsequently caused the fall of the Soviet Union. He boasted in an October 2004 videotaped message, "[We] bled Russia for ten years until it went bankrupt and was forced to withdraw in defeat."[7]

This strategy is now being applied against the United States. "We are continuing in the same policy to make America bleed profusely to the point of bankruptcy," said bin Laden.[8] His logic—flawed as it may be—is simple: To cause America to suffer a fate similar to that of the Soviet Union, the terrorists need to drain U.S. resources to the point that we can no longer afford to preserve our military and economic dominance.

Bin Laden believes that, as the United States loses standing in the Middle East, the jihadists can gain ground. He is confident that, without our support, regimes that are corrupt and illegitimate—such as Saudi Arabia's royal family—can be toppled by al-Qaeda.

Al-Qaeda believes these ends can be accomplished by mortally weakening America's economic power through attacks against financial hubs, like the World Trade Center. And with cause: The September 11 attack alone cost the U.S. economy close to a trillion dollars.

To the extent that our efforts to secure our homeland (discussed in Step 5) are successful in making attacks on America's assets at home more difficult to execute, the vulnerable overseas sources of U.S. energy supplies will become the terrorists' targets of choice.[9]

Soft Underbelly of the World's Economy

In fact, terrorist organizations like al-Qaeda have identified the world's energy system as a "two-fer": The jihadists call it "the provision line and the feeding [tube] to the artery of the life of the crusader's nation."[10] It is also a way of increasing the revenues garnered by their oil-exporting sponsors.

The strategy is simple. At a time when the oil market suffers from an acute shortage of spare production capacity, infrastructure attacks immediately translate into higher prices. This means a historic transfer of wealth from

---

7   Gal Luft, "Osama's War on America's Wealth," *FrontPage Magazine*, December 15, 2004.
8   Ibid.
9   See *Financial Times*, October 5, 2005.
10 Gal Luft and Anne Korin, "Terror's Next Target," *The Journal of International Security Affairs*, December 2003.

oil-consuming countries—primarily the United States—to the Muslim part of the world, where three-quarters of global oil reserves are concentrated.

So far, this strategy has worked extremely well. Pipelines, oil rigs, and pumping stations are easy to sabotage. For the most part, they are located in areas where terrorists enjoy local support. "We call our brothers in the battlefields to direct some of their great efforts toward the oil wells and pipelines," reads a jihadist Web site. "The killing of 10 American soldiers is nothing compared to the impact of the rise in oil prices on America and the disruption that it causes in the international economy."[11]

Regrettably, it seems that the calls for jihadists to attack oil infrastructure are being increasingly heeded. To cite but a few examples:

- Oil facilities, oil workers, or both have been struck in Saudi Arabia, India, Nigeria, Pakistan, Russia, and the Philippines.
- In summer 2002, a group of Saudis was arrested for involvement in a plot to sabotage Ras Tanura, the world's largest oil terminal through which a tenth of the world's oil supply flows daily.
- In September 2005, Saudi security forces thwarted a group of jihadists intent on attacking Saudi oil facilities.

Should a major attack on a Saudi oil installation succeed, it is likely to have devastating implications for the global economy. Former CIA Middle East field officer Robert Baer estimated that a sufficiently large attack would "be more economically damaging than a dirty nuclear bomb set off in midtown Manhattan or across from the White House in Lafayette Square." This "would be enough to bring the world's oil-addicted economies to their knees, America's along with them," he wrote.[12]

If there were any doubt about the danger posed by bin Laden's economic warfare strategy, consider the results of an ongoing and sustained, if low-grade, terrorism campaign against Iraq's oil sector:

- Since April 2003, oil pipelines, refineries, and pumping stations have been attacked more than three hundred times, causing a loss of tens of billions of dollars in oil revenues.[13]
- The sabotage campaign has also forced the Iraqi oil industry into playing one long game of catch-up. It is focusing at the moment on fixing the damage, rather than developing Iraq's potential. The inhospitable investment

---

11 SITE Institute.
12 Robert Baer, "The Fall of the House of Saud," *Atlantic Monthly*, May 2003.
13 Iraq Pipeline Watch, Institute for the Analysis of Global Security, available at http://www.iags.org/iraqpipelinewatch.htm.

climate for multinational oil companies caused by the sabotage deters them from sending personnel and expensive equipment to Iraq.

♦ Oil terrorism also has a corrosive influence on the *morale* of the Iraqi people and their attitude toward the Coalition. It slows reconstruction progress and disrupts civilian life with a lack of reliable supply of electricity—which, in Iraq, is generated from oil. It also forces interruptions in supplies of refined products.

Enter the Dragon

Islamist terrorists and their sponsors are able to translate supply disruptions into such immense wealth, to the detriment of our security, largely because of burgeoning demand from two new quarters: Communist China and India.

With 1.3 billion people, the People's Republic of China (PRC) is the world's most populous country. It has also emerged as second only to the United States in its consumption of oil. India, with a billion people, is not far behind. The two Asian neighbors and longtime rivals have been rapidly industrializing, and they now enjoy what are among the fastest-growing economies in the world—developments directly tied to access to petroleum products.

As both nations seek secure sources of oil to meet, in particular, the demands of their transportation sectors, they are becoming increasingly dependent on the Middle East. Today, almost 60 percent of China's oil imports and 70 percent of India's come from the region, largely from Saudi Arabia and Iran.

Quite apart from the impact that these new energy-importing states are having on the price of oil, there is an ominous strategic aspect to their budding relationships with the two leading Islamist regimes, Saudi Arabi and Iran. China and India are cementing multibillion dollar energy deals with these suppliers, affording them in return political protection, non-Western revenue streams, and arms.

To take one example, U.S. and European Union (EU) efforts to secure international opposition to Iran's nuclear weapons program have not met with favor in Beijing and New Delhi. China has gone so far as to signal its willingness to veto any effort to secure UN sanctions against Iran, a further sign that Tehran has successfully parlayed its oil into a Chinese checkmate of American power. The Sino-Iranian relationship promises to bring America and other freedom-loving people more grief in the future.

Unfortunately, Chinese deals go beyond these Islamofascist Persian Gulf states. The PRC is also buying up reserves in places like Siberia, Venezuela,

Indonesia, Sudan, Canada, Kazakhstan, Azerbaijan, and Cuba (see Step 9). These transactions appear designed not only to secure oil to meet Chinese needs, they also have the effect of taking these reserves off a global market upon which the United States is increasingly dependent.

That being the case, it would appear that we will inevitably find ourselves on a collision course with Communist China over oil. Things might be different if the world were still awash with cheap oil, but this is no longer the case.

To the contrary, the rest of the world is—like the Chinese—waking up to the idea that oil is a commodity in increasingly limited supply. Even the major U.S. oil companies have begun to acknowledge that the growth in world demand is expected easily to exceed available world supplies for the foreseeable future. For instance, David O'Reilly, the chairman and CEO of Chevron Corporation, stunned the energy industry recently when he admitted in an open letter

> The era of easy oil is over . . . . Many of the world's oil and gas fields are maturing. And new energy discoveries are mainly occurring in places where resources are difficult to extract—physically, technically, economically, and politically. When growing demand meets tighter supplies, the result is more competition for the same resources.[14]

Some oil analysts believe that, to make matters worse, Saudi Arabia—the world's largest oil producer—is facing an imminent *and irreversible* decline in its production capacity.[15] If true, this would only exacerbate the problem.

Situation Intolerable

Four years after September 11, with the price of oil high and likely to go higher, it is essential that Americans recognize the huge strategic as well as financial costs associated with our oil dependence. Such a recognition must then reinforce the message delivered by James Woolsey in 2002: It will be extremely difficult to win the war against Islamofascism as long as we continue to send huge amounts of petrodollars to those who wish us harm.

The following statistics tell the story:

---

14 Chevron advertising campaign, Summer 2005, available at http://www.willyoujoinus.com/ downloads/manifesto.pdf.

15 Matthew Simmons, *Twilight in the Desert: The Coming Saudi Oil Shock and the World Economy,* John Wiley & Sons, 2005.

- In November 2001, a barrel of oil was selling for $18. In less than four years, the price has jumped to $70.
- The United States is, therefore, forced to pay an extra $50 over the 2001 price for every barrel it imports. Because the United States imports 11 million barrels per day (mbd), this represents a loss of more than *$550 million per day*—or $200 billion per year—as a result of the recent rise in oil prices.
- Looking at it another way, Saudi Arabia—which currently exports about 10 mbd—receives *an extra half billion dollars every day* from oil-consuming nations.
- For its part, Iran—which exports 2.5 mbd—garners an *extra* $125 million each day.

This data confirms Mr. Woolsey's thesis: The United States is in the untenable situation of simultaneously funding both sides in the war on terrorism. It funds the defense of the Free World against its sworn enemies through our tax dollars. At the same time, it supports hostile regimes through the transfer of petrodollars.

If we continue on this crazy course, we will bleed more dollars each year as our enemies gather strength. Steady increases in world demand for oil mean further enrichment of the "oiligarchs" in the Persian Gulf and continued access by terrorist groups to a viable financial network, allowing them to remain a lethal threat to the United States and its allies.

Quite simply, America can no longer afford to postpone urgent action on energy security. For decades, the goal of reducing the nation's dependence on foreign oil has been a matter on which virtually all Americans could agree. Unfortunately, progress has been invariably stymied by differences regarding how best to accomplish that goal—with what means, how rapidly, and at what cost to taxpayers, industry, and consumers. Now, national security imperatives dictate that this intolerable situation must change.

Time for Realism

To change course, we must first dispense with certain misconceptions.

Diversification of Oil Supply Will Not Suffice

One of the most common misconceptions is the belief that the United States can insulate itself from price spikes and supply disruptions by simply shifting its sources of oil imports from the Middle East to other parts of the world. Because oil is a fungible commodity, it does not matter what proportion of the oil the United States imports comes from the Middle East. What matters is the share of Middle East producers in overall supply.

Think of it this way: The oil market is like a huge pool; producers pour in oil while consumers draw it out. Prices and supply levels are determined in the international markets.

If all we do is rearrange our sources of oil supply—while *demand* for oil does not drop—the flow of petrodollars to proliferators and apologists for radical Islam would remain the same, as would the vulnerability of the United States to international oil terrorism. That would be the case even if America no longer imported *a single drop of oil* from the Middle East.

One of the much-touted ways to diversify supplies has been through enhanced exploitation of oil resources from places in the developing world outside the Middle East. Suggested locations include West Africa and the former Soviet Union.

The Islamists are *there*, too. Unfortunately, the emerging non–Middle Eastern oil producers are not likely to become the reliable sources of supply we might like. They tend to be scarred by corruption, ethnic violence, and economic stagnation. Many of them have, not coincidentally, been the target of the Islamofascists (see Step 9)[16].

Take the case of Nigeria. It has the biggest known oil reserves in Africa. It is also the fifth-largest oil supplier to the United States. And half of Nigeria is now under a repressive form of Shari'a law.

What's more, Osama bin Laden is known to have sent emissaries to Nigeria, as well as to other African countries, in an effort to expand the Islamists' influence and to unite Islamic groups under the umbrella of al-Qaeda. In February 2003, al Jazeera television aired a message allegedly from bin Laden listing Nigeria as one of six countries that needed to be "liberated" from America's "enslavement."[17] In a recent report, the U.S. National Intelligence Council concluded ominously that Nigeria faces "outright collapse" within the next fifteen years and that this collapse may "drag down a large part of the West African region."[18]

The picture is not much more promising in places like the energy-rich republics of the Caspian region. They, too, face increasing threats of Islamist

---

16 See "Oil groups face rise in threats to security," *Financial Times*, October 5, 2005. Available at http://news.ft.com/cms/s/4efc9980-353e-11da-9e12-00000e2511c8.html.

17 "Special Report: al-Qaeda," *The Guardian*, February 12, 2003. Available at http://www.guardian.co.uk/alqaida/story/0,12469,893984,00.html.

18 *Mapping Sub-Saharan Africa's Future*, National Intelligence Council, March 2005. Available at http://www.cia.gov/nic/confreportsoafricaofuture.html.

terror from groups operating in Central Asia and in the Caucasus. Such groups include the Islamic Party of Eastern Turkistan, the Islamic Movement of Uzbekistan (IMU), and Chechen and Uighur separatists.

Perhaps the most dangerous Islamofascist organization operating in this area (among others), however, is Hizb ut-Tahrir al-Islami—the Islamic Party of Liberation. It is estimated to have five thousand to ten thousand adherents in Uzbekistan, Kyrgyzstan, Tajikistan, and in oil-rich Kazakhstan. Hizb seeks to seize power and supplant existing governments with a Shari'a-based caliphate that will carry on jihad against the West.

In our own hemisphere as well, the influence of Islamists and others unfriendly to the United States is growing (see the treatment of Latin America in Step 9). Of particular concern is the increasingly authoritarian, and virulently anti-American, president of Venezuela, Hugo Chavez, who has been making common cause with terrorist-sponsoring states like Iran and Libya. He is using his oil revenues to destabilize Latin and Central America, particularly energy-rich nations like Bolivia, Ecuador, and Peru. He has even threatened to end Venezuela's role as the United States' third largest supplier of oil.

In other words, the regions often hailed as the new oil el Dorados are already rife with the same ills prevalent in the Middle East. Or they likely soon will be.

All roads lead to the Middle East. Even if the developing world's alternative sources of oil were more promising, there is another problem with an energy strategy that continues to rely exclusively on oil, albeit from diversified sources. It is a mistake to buy increasing quantities of oil from producers outside of the Middle East for any purpose other than as a stop-gap solution, to play for time while we seriously develop alternative, non-oil-based energy sources. Doing so will only create, in the long run, a stronger direct U.S. dependency on the Middle East.

After all, reserves in non-OPEC countries are relatively small. OPEC producers more or less stick to a quota, whereas non-OPEC producers typically do not. As a result, the latter will deplete their oil reserves faster than will OPEC. In fact, at current rates of production of known holdings, non-OPEC countries will use up their reserves in about fifteen years, compared with roughly eighty years for OPEC countries.

Exxon Mobil Corporation has estimated that non-OPEC production will peak within a decade.[19] This includes Russia and West Africa. *At that point, there will be little easily recoverable oil left outside of the Middle East.*

---

19 "Exxon president predicts non-OPEC peak in 10 years," *Oil and Gas Journal*, December 13, 2004.

Domestic Resources Will Not Suffice, Either

Some people believe that another alternative exists to the present, unwise U.S. reliance on imported oil from the Mideast; namely, expanded recovery of America's own oil and gas resources. Historically, the problem with this option has been the successful opposition of environmentalists to drilling in places like Alaska's Arctic National Wildlife Refuge (ANWR), as well as in and off the coasts of the Lower 48.

Regardless of where one stands on the environmental concerns, it is naive to think that America can drill itself out of its energy dependence. At most, tapping ANWR will bring the U.S. share of world oil up from 2.9 percent of global reserves to 3.3 percent. With the economy projected to grow at an average annual rate of 3 percent in the next two decades, and with the attendant increasing needs for oil, the United States simply is no longer capable of meeting its demand for petroleum from domestic resources.

Unconventional Sources of Oil Will Not Solve the Problem

Modern technology makes it possible to recover petroleum from nontraditional sources like oil shale and tar sands that exist in abundance in parts of the Western United States and Canada. Unfortunately, the theoretically vast quantities of energy to be found in these deposits are not a panacea either.

For one thing, the energy required to extract the oil is so huge as to offset the amount of energy that oil will produce. In addition, production requires strip-mining or other measures that are expensive and cause severe environmental damage. Though unconventional oil supplies are a welcomed addition to our energy basket, it will be extremely difficult for them to compete with the cheaply extracted and easily refined Arabian crude.

Natural Gas Entails Similar Problems

Today, natural gas accounts for one-fifth of all energy used in the United States. It can be, and is, used for electricity generation as well as for transportation. As such, natural gas will continue to play an important role in meeting our energy needs. But it cannot be a successor to oil.

After all, natural gas is, like oil, a finite resource that is mainly concentrated in the Middle East. And, as with oil, America's share of global reserves is only 3 percent. From a national security point of view, replacing our oil-based economy with a natural gas-based one would be like swapping cancer for heart disease.

In addition, the United States is already facing a severe natural gas shortage. The price of this commodity had tripled in the past four years, even before the effects of Hurricanes Katrina and Rita on the Gulf States' energy complex were felt. Federal Reserve Chairman Alan Greenspan recently warned that tight natural gas supplies present "a very serious problem" and are having an adverse impact on the U.S. economy.[20] Given these tight supply conditions, it would be foolish to rely more heavily on the natural gas market to assure America's future energy needs.

What Needs to Be Done

Let us be clear: We will always need oil. What we must do is reduce the strategic importance of oil to the global economy. We must shift oil from being a strategic commodity—one whose disruption can hold our economy hostage—to a commodity that is *interchangeable with other energy resources*.

Because two-thirds of the oil we use is consumed in the transportation sector (mostly in cars and trucks), long-term security and economic prosperity require diversifying our energy sources in that sector. This can be done via a technological shift to an economy based on nonpetroleum, next-generation fuels and vehicles designed to use them.

It is worth noting that diversification away from imported oil to domestic energy sources has already been accomplished in another sector of the economy—the generation of electricity. In the 1970s, nearly a third of U.S. electricity was produced by burning oil. Today, this figure is down to just 2 percent.

A number of public policy institutes, trade unions, and other organizations have joined forces under the banner of the Set America Free Coalition to advance a blueprint for effecting a similar change in the U.S. transportation sector. (The Coalition's blueprint can be viewed in full at Appendix III.) This plan offers ways in which the nation's oil imports can be cut in half within two decades through the widespread use in our cars and other vehicles of a variety of currently available technologies.

A Program for Energy Security

The main ingredients of the Set America Free blueprint are as follows.

1. Fuel Choice

One of the highest virtues of the American way of life is freedom of choice. Think of any consumer good—from a cup of coffee to a carpet—and consider

---

20 "Greenspan Warns of Serious Natgas Problems," *Reuters*, May 21, 2003.

the range of choices we have. But when it comes to transportation fuel, Americans have essentially no choice. Driving into a gas station, oil-based products like gasoline and diesel are the only substances with which we can fill our tanks.

The fact that a single liquid fuels virtually our entire society is a formula for disaster. If for whatever reason petroleum supplies are disrupted, we currently do not have a fallback option.

The first step to enabling fuel choice is to ensure that all new cars are flexible fuel vehicles (FFVs). FFVs look and perform just like "regular" vehicles, with one difference: instead of running solely on gasoline, they are designed to burn alcohol-based fuels (ethanol and methanol), gasoline, or any mixture of the two.

This is not a new technology. Henry Ford's 1908 Model T was an FFV. And some 4 million FFVs have been manufactured in the United States since 1996, including such popular models as Ford Taurus, Chevy Silverado, and Dodge Caravan. Because FFVs can also run on gasoline, drivers can refuel even in places where pumps have not yet been modified to dispense alcohol-based fuels.

The only difference between a gasoline-only car and an FFV is that the FFV engine is equipped with a modified control chip and some different fittings in the fuel line to accommodate the characteristics of alcohol. The marginal additional cost associated with the production of a flexible fuel vehicle is currently under $150—less than the cost of a typical CD player.

That cost would be reduced further as the volume of production of such cars increases. That would be particularly true if flexible fuel designs were to become the industry standard—as they should, *effective immediately*.

Ethanol. Also known as grain alcohol, ethanol is a liquid that can be produced domestically from fermented agricultural products, including (but *not exclusively*) from corn. The U.S. industry currently has a capacity of 3.4 billion gallons a year and has increased production by an average of 25 percent per year over the past three years.

The main barrier preventing ethanol from becoming a massively used transportation fuel in the United States is its cost and the limited supply of corn. Ethanol benefits from federal subsidies amounting to 51 cents per gallon.

Fortunately, there are feedstocks other than corn that can be converted to ethanol without the need for such massive government assistance. For example, a great deal of effort is being expended to develop processes for the economic conversion of cellulosic biomass into ethanol. Such processes will allow production of fuel from switch grass and other dedicated energy crops.

Until such technology becomes economical, however, there is another source of ethanol that makes economic sense and that does not require a government subsidy: sugar cane. In Brazil, at least 25 percent of the fuel sold in gas stations is sugar-based ethanol. In addition to Brazil, Latin American and Caribbean countries like Guatemala, Panama, Trinidad and Tobago, Costa Rica, El Salvador, and Jamaica are all low-cost sugar cane producers. These nations could become key to U.S. energy security if large numbers of American vehicles were FFVs—and if imported ethanol could be freed from the current, heavy U.S. tariffs on sugar.

Expanding U.S. fuel choice to include biofuels imported from our neighbors in the Western Hemisphere would not only help increase our energy independence from Islamofascist Middle Eastern suppliers. It would also have clear geopolitical benefits. By encouraging these countries to increase their output and become major fuel suppliers, we could greatly enhance the U.S. posture in the Western Hemisphere. As we shall see in Step 9, such a change is increasingly urgent in light of the oil-bankrolled subversion practiced by Venezuela's Chavez and his mentor, Cuban dictator Fidel Castro, as well as China's growing activity in the region.

To put it bluntly, we cannot hope to enjoy energy security through renewable fuels unless we are also willing to open the U.S. ethanol market to imports. It defies common sense to tax ethanol coming in from our neighbors when we do not tax oil imported from Saudi Arabia.

Methanol. Another alcohol that can be used in flexible fuel vehicles is well-known to Indianapolis 500 fans: wood alcohol, or methanol. Today, this liquid fuel is produced mostly from natural gas. Greatly expanded domestic production can be achieved, however, by producing methanol from coal, a resource the United States has in abundance. The commercial feasibility of coal-to-methanol technology has been demonstrated as part of the Department of Energy's "clean coal" technology effort. Currently, methanol is being cleanly produced from coal on a commercial scale for around 50 cents a gallon. Methanol can also be produced from agricultural waste.

2. Electrify Transportation

As the price of gasoline has mounted, there has been growing consumer demand for so-called hybrid vehicles. Hybrids combine a traditional internal combustion engine with an electric motor to improve gas mileage. The motor is powered by a battery, continuously recharged by capturing braking energy that would otherwise be wasted.

Hybrids get anywhere from 20 percent to more than twice the mileage of conventional gasoline engines, without compromising performance. However, their only external fuel source is gasoline. Increasing fuel choice calls for taking hybrids one step further.

Plug-in hybrids. For many years, electricity has been the source of power for all our home appliances. Why not use electricity to power our cars as well? Because less than 2 percent of U.S. electricity is generated from oil, using electricity as a transportation fuel would greatly reduce our dependence on imported petroleum. Vehicles that meet consumer needs could tap America's electrical grid to supply energy for transportation, allowing more efficient use of such domestic sources of electricity as coal, solar, wind, geothermal, hydroelectric, and nuclear power.

During the 1980s, some auto companies put battery-operated electric vehicles on the road. While these cars were generally clean, quiet, and highly efficient, they failed to achieve large-scale penetration of the market. Among the stumbling blocks were the limited range (driving distance) and the reduced performance of electric-only vehicles.

Plug-in hybrid electric vehicles (PHEVs) offer the benefits of electric vehicles without the range and performance penalties. PHEVs are souped-up hybrids that can optionally be plugged in. Like first-generation hybrids, plug-ins have a liquid fuel tank and internal combustion engine, so they have the same driving range as a standard car. Although they look and perform much like regular hybrid cars, they can in addition be plugged into a 120-volt outlet at home (or in a parking garage) and recharged.

Plug-ins can run on their batteries' stored energy for much of a typical day's driving. Depending on the size of the battery, that might be up to 60 miles per charge—far beyond the daily commute of an average American. And, when the charge is used up, the PHEV automatically switches over to run on the engine powered by its fuel tank. Someone who drives a distance shorter every day than the car's electric range could do so exclusively by recharging the battery and never having to dip into the fuel tank.

PHEVs can reach fuel economy levels of a hundred miles per gallon of gasoline consumed. Because 50 percent of cars on the road in the United States are driven twenty miles a day or less, a plug-in with a twenty-mile-range battery would reduce gasoline consumption by, on average, 85 percent.

Five hundred miles per gallon of gasoline performance. If, moreover, a plug-in vehicle were designed as an FFV, fueled with 80 percent alcohol and 20 percent gasoline, fuel economy could reach *five hundred miles per gallon of gasoline.*

Notice we say "per gallon of gasoline" and not "per gallon." The object of expanding fuel choice is not to reduce the energy consumption of a vehicle. Rather, it is to shift the balance in the transportation sector away from oil to more secure energy resources, by stretching each gallon of gasoline further by substituting alcohol fuels and electricity.

Ideally, plug-in hybrid vehicles would be charged in home or apartment garages at night, when electric utilities have significant excess capacity. The Electric Power Research Institute estimates that up to *30 percent* of the U.S. vehicle market could shift to PHEVs with a twenty-mile electric range, without any additional electricity-generating capacity.

At present, the estimated retail price of a plug-in hybrid would be higher than that of corresponding conventional vehicles, because of the cost of extra batteries to extend the range in electric mode. The exact difference in price depends on the size of the battery, but, roughly speaking, every additional 10 miles of vehicle range adds about $1,000 to the cost.

This price difference is partly offset, however, by the lower operating costs of plug-ins. At current gas prices, it costs well over 10 cents per mile to refuel a conventional car with gasoline, whereas refueling a plug-in with electricity is only 3 cents per mile. That means that the lifetime overall cost of mass-produced plug-in hybrid vehicles would be equivalent to that of gasoline-only vehicles.

In light of the national and energy security benefits of achieving such a dramatic reduction in demand for gasoline, the president and other officials should be doing everything possible to encourage the widest and fastest possible penetration of plug-in hybrid vehicles into the market. One way of doing that would be for the difference in the up-front price of PHEVs to be covered by federal and state tax credits and by rebates designed to reward consumers for reducing consumption of petroleum-based fuels and emissions. This strategy is proving very effective in getting hybrid electric vehicles past the early-adopter hump and into the mainstream.

3. Stretch a Gallon Still Further

The Bush administration describes conservation as one of the important elements of a sound energy policy. It notes that in the past three decades, the American economy has grown nearly five times faster than energy use—proof positive that conservation can go hand-in-hand with increases in productivity.

Indeed, the last time the United States made a concerted effort to improve energy efficiency—between 1979 and 1985, in response to OPEC's oil embargo—its oil consumption decreased by *15 percent.* Conservation does not necessarily entail compromising our lifestyles, or settling for smaller, slower, or less comfortable cars. And, given the benefits for our energy security, encouraging conservation must be a central ingredient in our War Footing strategy.

Individual initiatives. The most immediate measures to improve the efficiency of America's automobile fleet are in the hands of individual motorists:

- properly inflating tires
- tuning the engine
- maintaining air filters
- removing excess weight from the trunk
- driving at a steady pace
- consolidating trips
- choosing to take the "broadband highway" to work, using the Internet to telecommute from a home office.

Better materials. At least two-thirds of fuel use by a typical consumer vehicle is caused by its weight. Reducing the weight and drag of a vehicle need not require reducing its size or safety, but it can greatly increase gas mileage. Today, we can achieve this objective thanks to advances in both metals and plastics. Cars made from advanced composites and next-generation steels can be affordably manufactured with current technologies. They can roughly halve fuel consumption without compromising size, safety, performance, or cost-effectiveness.

In fact, crash tests and race-car experience have shown that these vehicles are actually safer. As a report commissioned by the Pentagon notes, "Ultra-strong carbon fiber composite auto bodies can save oil and lives at the same time, and by greatly simplifying manufacturing, can give automakers a decisive competitive advantage."[21]

Modern diesels. Significant progress toward better efficiency can also be reached in the realm of diesel engines. Modern diesel vehicles are becoming increasingly popular in Europe, which is one major reason why average fleet mileage there is so much higher than in the United States. Hybrid diesel engines can combine the benefits of both technologies to reach even higher efficiency gains.

Diesel fuels currently account for almost 20 percent of U.S. oil consumption. New technologies are available to use nonfossil sources for its production. For example, diesel fuel can be made from waste, such as garbage, tires,

---

21 Amory B. Lovins, *Winning the Oil Endgame*, Rocky Mountain Institute, 2004, p. 57.

and animal by-products. In fact, it is currently being commercially produced from turkey carcasses and other offal.

An innovative biodiesel fuel can be commercially produced from soybeans and other vegetable oils. Such fuels are compatible with the current distribution infrastructure, and blends of up to 20 percent can be used in existing vehicles.

Needed: A New National Initiative

There is no shortage of other longer-term technological solutions to our energy problem. Although many of them hold great promise, it is not clear that they will be available by the time we need them.

After all, the average lifetime of a vehicle in the United States is more than sixteen years. Thus, the technological transformation of the transportation sector will take roughly fifteen to twenty years, as new vehicles replace old ones.

That is why it is imperative to begin the process *without delay*. Every day we wait is one more day that America will struggle under the yoke of a dangerous and ruinously expensive oil dependence, with all its national security implications.

We have no time to wait for commercialization of promising but immature technologies, such as hydrogen fuel cells, which still face significant technological barriers. Nor do we have time to wait for expensive and time-consuming infrastructure change. The focus should be on using alternative approaches—like fuel choice and plug-in hybrids—that can be implemented relatively quickly and that permit the maximum possible use of existing refueling facilities and automotive assembly lines.

In 1942, President Roosevelt mobilized the nation's scientific and financial resources to launch the Manhattan Project—a top-priority effort to build an atomic weapon in response to threats to America's survival. The outcome was an end to the war with Japan, followed by the development of a wide new array of nuclear-based technologies in energy, medical treatment, and other fields.

In 1962, President Kennedy launched the Apollo Man to the Moon Project, driven in part by mounting threats to U.S. and international security posed by Soviet space dominance. The outcome was an extraordinary strategic and technological success for the United States. It engendered a wide array of spin-offs that improved virtually every aspect of modern life.

In 1983, President Reagan responded to the danger of Soviet ballistic missiles by unveiling the Strategic Defense Initiative (SDI), a major program to develop the means to destroy such missiles in-flight. We now know that SDI played an important part in the success of Mr. Reagan's strategy for destroying the Soviet Union. It compounded the Kremlin's already acute economic problems and contributed to the breakup of the USSR, creating unprecedented potential for a more peaceful and prosperous world.

In all three of these historic cases, a U.S. president called upon America's ingenuity and the power of technology to address a global threat. In each case, that threat came from an enemy determined to change the existing world order and to extinguish the Western values and way of life we cherish. Today, the security of the United States and, indeed, that of the world, is no less threatened. This time, the threat comes from another totalitarian ideology, Islamofascism, fueled by petrodollars. Fortunately, we do not need an expensive new Manhattan Project to conduct groundbreaking research into new and exotic technologies and fuels that will, over many years, enhance energy efficiency and cut our dependence on foreign oil from the Islamists and their friends.

The truth is that the technologies that will allow us to make the leap into the post-oil era are *already with us*. All that is needed now is leadership and the support of the American people for a national commitment to energy security. Putting the nation on a War Footing is the opportunity to bring these assets to bear and to begin weaning our country from its oil dependency and the associated vulnerabilities.

Today, the United States imports 11 million barrels per day (mbd), and it is projected to import almost 20 mbd by 2025. According to the Set America Free blueprint, if all cars on the road by 2025 are hybrids and half are plug-in hybrid vehicles, U.S. oil imports would drop by 8 mbd. If all of these cars were also flexible fuel vehicles, U.S. oil imports would drop by as much as 12 mbd.

Such a leap toward energy security is a big idea—but the American people have never shied away from big ideas. During World War II, Winston Churchill observed that "Americans' national psychology is such that the bigger the idea, the more wholeheartedly and obstinately do they throw themselves into making it a success. It is an admirable characteristic, provided the idea is good."[22]

Breaking the hold of Middle East autocracies over the global economy is a good idea whose time has come. For more than two centuries, the United States has been the harbinger of freedom and democracy in the world, to the benefit of millions of people. Now it is time for America to lead the Free World in an effort to liberate us all from our current dependence on those that would do us harm.

---

22 Winston S. Churchill, The *Second World War: Closing the Ring (Volume V)*, Houghton Mifflin, 1951, p. 561.

STEP 4

Stop Investing in Terror

With Contributions from
Christopher Holton

O ne of the most important fronts in this War for the Free World—
yet one of the least recognized—is the financial one. This is also
the most readily "accessible" front, one on which millions of ordinary Americans could engage, with potentially devastating effect on our
enemies.

Terrorism costs money. To be sure, the operations immediately involved in
individual attacks may not be expensive to plan and execute: the costs to al-
Qaeda of the September 11, 2001, attacks are estimated to have been only
about $500,000.

This figure does not take into account, however, the part played—or the
costs incurred—by state sponsors who enable these and other terrorist
attacks. Their outlays are far greater, providing our enemies with safe haven,
intelligence support, material assistance, training, and arms (including possibly weapons of mass destruction). We must find ways to cut off this sort of
funding, starting with the U.S. State Department's list of officially designated
state sponsors of terror: Iran, Libya, Syria, Sudan, North Korea, and Cuba.

Unfortunately, not only are we largely failing to reduce that funding, but
also: citizens of this country are actually unwittingly and indirectly helping it
to continue and even to *expand*. If we are serious about surviving, let alone
prevailing, in this War for the Free World, we need to understand and use our
financial leverage.

What Is the Financial Front?

The necessity for cutting off revenue streams to terrorist organizations has long been recognized. Since the September 11 attacks, the newly created Office of Terrorism and Financial Intelligence (TFI) of the U.S. Treasury has been devoted primarily to the task of depriving terrorists of their means of support.

In addition to its own efforts in this area, the U.S. government has developed working relationships with a number of international organizations and groups. For example, an international interagency working group called the Financial Action Task Force has targeted foreign and domestic "charities"—informal banking operations (known as *hawalas*) and phony businesses that serve as fronts for the terrorists' money-laundering and weapons-acquisition operations.

The good news is that, as President Bush has observed, these efforts have resulted in the denial of some $144 million in funds from 396 entities or individuals, funds that might otherwise have flowed to those bent on killing us.[1] The bad news is that this sum, though impressive, is but a small fraction of the American money terrorist organizations have access to, thanks to their state sponsors' business dealings with publicly traded companies.

How Corporations Indirectly Support Terrorism

There are roughly 450 companies listed on international equity exchanges—the vast majority of which are foreign-owned and foreign operated—that are known to be doing business in Iran, North Korea, Libya, Syria, Sudan, or a combination of these countries. Once such countries are designated as state sponsors of terror, they are subjected to official sanctions barring U.S. companies from working there.[2]

Just how important are measures like the 1996 Iran-Libya Sanctions Act to the war effort? According to Richard Newcomb, the former director of the Treasury Department's Office of Foreign Assets Control, they play an important role. He testified before Congress that U.S. terrorism-related sanctions are "intended to deprive the target of the use of its assets and deny the target

---

1 U.S. Department of the Treasury, Press Release, JS-2164, December 21, 2004. Available at http://www.treasury.gov/press/releases/js2164.htm.
2 Only a few American-owned companies have used a loophole in the law to use offshore subsidiaries to circumvent the sanctions.

access to the U.S. financial system and the benefits of trade, transactions and services involving U.S. markets."[3]

Incredibly, at the same time as the Bush administration properly seeks to curtail funding for governments that sponsor terrorism, publicly traded companies doing business with such governments are able to undermine the objectives of U.S. sanctions policy. Typically, they do so in three ways:

1. **Publicly traded companies develop and exploit terrorist sponsors' natural resources,** particularly oil and natural gas. For example, the Italian energy giant ENI Spa has one of the largest footprints of any Western company in terrorist-sponsoring states. ENI projects in Iran and Libya are estimated to be valued at nearly *$10 billion.*

   In Sudan, Chinese companies play a similar role. China National Petroleum Corporation (CNPC), along with its subsidiary, PetroChina, and Sinopec Group support the odious regime in Khartoum with large investments in the Sudanese oil sector. In 2004, Chinese oil imports from Sudan topped 12 percent of the PRC's daily consumption. According to some estimates, China has also stationed some four thousand troops in Sudan to safeguard its interests there.

   In October 2004, one of the largest energy deals in recent history was signed between China's Sinopec Group and Iran. The deal guarantees Beijing more than 270 million tons of natural gas over thirty years, valued at roughly $70 billion. The deal offers China rights to explore and tap additional Iranian oil fields worth an estimated $100 billion.

   As we have seen in Step 3, this sort of transaction involves more than the transfer of huge sums to the world's most consistent and unabashed state sponsor of terror. It also represents a strategically ominous political liaison. Commenting on the contract, Iran's deputy minister of petroleum Hadi Nejad Hosseinian said, "What we have right now is trade with China. But when we invest in each other for 30 years, this is a marriage."[4] Given Iran's ambitions to export its version of Islamofascist revolution and its nuclear ambitions, the prospect that such a "marriage" will underwrite, legitimate, or protect the government in Tehran must be considered an extremely unfriendly act.

2. **Publicly traded companies transfer high technology and advanced equipment to terrorist-sponsoring regimes.** Often, such technology is

---

3   Testimony of R. Richard Newcomb, Director, Office of Foreign Assets Control, U.S. Department of the Treasury, before the Committee on Banking, Housing, and Urban Affairs, United States Senate, JS-1670, May 20, 2004. Available at http://www.treas.gov/press/releases/js1670.htm.
4   Vivienne Walt, "Iran Looks East," *Fortune Magazine,* February 8, 2005.

"dual use"—that is, of a kind that can be used for military as well as civilian applications.

For instance, the French-headquartered telecommunications giant, Alcatel, has had operations in terrorist-sponsoring states over the past five years worth more than $300 million. Until recently, one of these states was Saddam Hussein's Iraq, whose fiber-optic infrastructure Alcatel reportedly substantially upgraded prior to Operation Iraqi Freedom. It did so despite the U.S. government's announced concerns that the project could advance Iraqi military capabilities—and potentially cost American lives.

3. **Publicly traded banks and financial service companies facilitate financial transactions.** These services include assisting with bond offerings of rogue-state governments. In some cases, such transactions involve the direct underwriting of new projects in state sponsors of terror.

For example, banks like France's BNP Paribas and Switzerland's UBS have aided rogue-state regimes by making loans or otherwise underwriting their business activities. UBS was recently fined $100 million by the U.S. Federal Reserve for illegally transferring American banknotes to terrorist-sponsoring states, including Iran and Libya. (As discussed below, within twenty-four hours of the Fed's action the share value of UBS reportedly dropped some 3½ percent.)

Money is, of course, fungible: What is given for a benign purpose can be used for a malevolent one. At the very least, loans can free up funding for terror that might otherwise have been used for humanitarian or other legitimate purposes. Because the regimes in question are notoriously non-transparent, there is no way to be sure whether funds transferred to them actually wind up getting applied in non-threatening ways.

Bad business in Korea. A particularly egregious example of corporate support for terror-sponsoring regimes involves the South Korean–based Hyundai Merchant Marine (HMM). Published reports indicate that the company engaged in secret, illegal fund transfers to Pyongyang totaling as much as $186 million in the immediate run-up to an important 2000 summit between the North and South Korean governments.

The South Korean government was allegedly aware and supportive of what amounted to a bribe to North Korean dictator Kim Jong-Il to participate in the meeting with his South Korean counterpart, then-president Kim Dae Jong. The goal was to help salvage the latter's dubious pursuit of detente with the North, dubbed the "Sunshine Policy." In late 2004, after an investigation by the South Korean Financial Supervisory Service, HMM and at least two Hyundai directors were fined more than $2 million for accounting irregularities related to the 2000 summit cash transfer.

Hyundai showed remarkable indifference to the potentially dangerous consequences of its actions in North Korea. A senior Hyundai official, Kim Yoon Kyu, has been quoted as saying, "We made clear and told them [the North Koreans] half-jokingly not to use the money in making missiles." He then revealed the contempt rogue states must feel toward those willing, as Lenin reportedly remarked, to provide the rope with which they can hang their enemies—namely, us: "I asked them where they used the money from us. They said they can't tell us the details, but they sure didn't use the money to make missiles." Wink, wink.

Terror and the U.S. Capital Markets

As it happens, the bulk of the terrorist sponsors' publicly traded business partners raise funds for their investment activities and other operations in the U.S. capital markets. Their stocks may be held in the portfolios of institutional investors, as well as those of many individuals. The former are investment funds with more than $500 million under management. They include public pension funds, 401(k) plans, mutual funds, college and university endowments, and life insurance companies.

An indication of the magnitude of Americans' investments in companies partnering with state sponsors of terror was revealed in August 2004 by the Center for Security Policy (CSP). In a 120-page report entitled "The Terrorism Investments of the 50 States," CSP performed the first national-security-oriented statistical analysis of the investment patterns of 100 of America's leading public pension funds.

Data supplied by 87 of these funds about their equity holdings confirmed troubling connections between publicly traded corporations and the unholy nexus of designated terrorist-sponsoring states, proliferation of WMDs, and the spread of ballistic missile delivery systems.

CSP's analysis arrived at a stunning conclusion: These funds alone have approximately *$188 billion* invested in companies that do business with our enemies' sponsors.

To get a sense of the extent to which the economic life blood of terrorist-sponsoring rogue regimes is being provided by the pension systems and other investment portfolios of Americans, consider the following findings:

- On average, America's top 100 pension systems invest between 15 percent and 23 percent of their portfolios in companies that do business in terrorist-sponsoring states.
- On average, the top 100 pension systems invest in 101 companies that have business activities in terrorist-sponsoring states.
- On average, the top 100 public pension funds included the following unsavory holdings: 73 companies doing business in Iran; 24 companies doing business in Libya; 26 companies doing business in Sudan; 31 companies doing business in Syria; and 9 companies doing business in North Korea.

We cannot extrapolate with confidence from these pension fund data to calculate the total worth of Americans' holdings of the stock of such companies. It seems reasonable to believe, however, that the aggregate amount likely equals hundreds of billions of dollars.

To be sure, not all of this money is finding its way into the hands of terrorists, nor is all of it funneled to their state sponsors. It seems clear, nevertheless, that a significant portion of the investments made by publicly traded companies is translating into "found money" for rogue-state regimes. A conservative accounting of the leading public pension funds' $188 billion holdings (as presented in the CSP report) suggests that these funds alone are associated with approximately *$73 billion* worth of projects in Iran, North Korea, and the other state sponsors of terror.

American investments in terror's friends do matter. Some naively contend that, just because a company or subsidiary has a business tie to a country on the State Department's terrorism list, this does not mean that our enemies are being aided or abetted. Yet, as former Clinton administration Under Secretary of State Peter Tarnoff once observed: "A straight line links Iran's oil income and its ability to sponsor terrorism, build weapons of mass destruction, and acquire sophisticated armaments. Any government or private company that helps Iran to expand its oil must accept that it is contributing to this menace."[5]

In short, projects underwritten by American and other investors create revenue streams (including, in at least some cases, bribes) for terrorist-sponsoring governments' agencies and officials—and their cronies, relatives, and favored business associates. There is no way to estimate with confidence exactly how much of these cash flows make their way into support for terror.

---

5   Testimony of former Under Secretary of State for Policy, Peter Tarnoff, before the Senate Banking Committee, October 11, 1995.

But, if Saddam Hussein's success in diverting the UN's notorious Oil-for-Food funds to his own purposes is any guide, it surely is worth *billions of dollars* to our terrorist foes.

Doing Our Part

Whatever the precise amount flowing from U.S. investors to terrorists, it is surely too much to suit the average American investor in a pension or mutual fund. Such investors, after all, include millions of law-enforcement officials, firefighters, teachers, and other public employees, together with countless other patriotic citizens. It is inconceivable that such Americans would want the companies that manage their life savings to be providing vital hard currency flows, political cover, and dual-use technology to support and strengthen the states that threaten their security and that of their children and grandchildren.

We all need to determine what is actually being done with our money—and to keep it from being used, even indirectly, to try to kill Americans. Once investors become aware of this problem, it seems certain that there would be a considerable market for what might be called "security responsible" mutual funds that are "terror-free."

A New Type of Risk for Investors: "Global Security Risk"

A further consideration adds to the need for such transparency and corrective action. The Securities and Exchange Commission (SEC) has warned investors about what it calls "global security risk." That is the material risk associated with investing in companies whose reputation and share value could be dramatically, rapidly, and adversely affected should something go wrong in their business dealings with terrorist-sponsoring states. In November 2003, the then-chairman of the Securities and Exchange Commission, William Donaldson, informed Congress that global security risk is "a crucial issue for investors." Last year, Congress insisted that the SEC establish an Office of Global Security Risk to address this dramatic financial risk.

To illustrate how this risk might affect investors' equities, consider the following scenario, recently described in *American Legion* magazine[6]:

---

6   Frank J. Gaffney Jr., "How NOT To Make A Killing," *American Legion Magazine*, April 2005, pp. 34–36.

A plot to detonate a nuclear weapon in a US city is discovered in the nick of time. The perpetrators, Islamic terrorists, are arrested and the bomb safely dismantled. When government physicists examine the device, however, they are shocked to find that its electronic triggers are jury-rigged switches known as lithotripters, sold to Iran by a prominent and profitable French multinational company—let's call it Acme Francais.

As word spreads that Acme Francais' products were very nearly used by terrorists to kill tens of thousands of Americans, the reaction is swift and dramatic: the company's reputation is severely damaged with the public, and its stock-market value drops like a stone.

Those who count on their investments in public-pension systems, mutual funds, 401(k) plans, and personal portfolios are angered and frustrated to discover that Acme Francais' loss is their loss, too. Since Acme is a blue-chip international company, with worldwide and highly diversified businesses that consistently offer strong return on investment, many stock indexes and fund managers viewed it as a good bet. But that was before anyone was aware of the company's business dealings with a U.S.-government-designated state sponsor of terror.

There is a growing awareness among influential public officials of the strategic and financial implications of publicly traded companies doing business with terrorist-sponsoring regimes. These critics include U.S. Sen. Frank Lautenberg (Democrat of New Jersey) and U.S. Sen. Jon Kyl (Republican of Arizona), who together sought in 2005 to close the loophole that allows American corporations' offshore subsidiaries to ignore U.S. sanctions laws.

Similarly, in the House of Representatives, U.S. Rep. Frank Wolf (Republican of Virginia) has played a decisive role in his capacity as chairman of the Appropriations subcommittee charged with oversight of the SEC. Congressman Wolf was the prime mover behind legislation that created the SEC's Office of Global Security Risk. The accompanying report language included the following statement:

[Congress] is concerned that American investors may be unwittingly investing in companies with ties to countries that sponsor terrorism and countries linked to human rights violations. . . . [It] believes that a company's association with sponsors of terrorism and human rights abuses, no matter how large or small, can have a material adverse effect on a public company's operations, financial condition, earnings, and stock prices, all of which can negatively affect the value of an investment.[7]

U.S. Rep. Barbara Lee (Democrat of California), supported by other members of the Congressional Black Caucus, has taken a special interest in the support the terrorist-sponsoring and genocidal regime of Sudan is getting from Chinese and other corporations. Writing in the *Los Angeles Times* in January 2005, Congresswoman Lee argued: "Now is the time for California and the California Public Employees Retirement System (CalPERS) to put our money where our values are. It should conduct a real investigation to identify those companies doing business in Sudan and voluntarily divest from them."[8]

Irresponsible Resistance from the Investment Community

Unfortunately, CalPERS and most other public pension funds have, to date, been unwilling to do their part for the war effort. In fact, with the notable exception of a few—including those representing New York State's teachers and New York City's police and firefighters—institutional investor fund managers and boards have been, to put it charitably, AWOL.

Typically, these institutional investors have ignored appeals to foster security-minded corporate governance with respect to firms willing to partner with terrorist-sponsoring states. Needless to say, they have been even more resistant to calls for divestment of such companies' stocks or other uses of their financial leverage in support of the war effort.

Indeed, most public pension systems and university endowments have systematically resisted even calling for the *identification of such companies* held in porfolio. Why? They fear, presumably, that if the American people discover the truth about such investments, they will demand divestment.

An untenable position. These institutional investors' objections to transparency, good governance, and corporate accountability in this context are strikingly out of character. Public pension funds and other institutional investors have religiously promoted these accepted good-business standards for many years; companies that appear unduly resistant to such concerns are likely to find their stocks promptly dumped from the portfolios of these funds.

Organizations like CalPERS, moreover, have shown little hesitation to divest or otherwise punish companies for engaging in lines of work they find

---

7 Excerpted from House Rpt. 108-221, Departments of Commerce, Justice, and State, the Judiciary, and Related Agencies Appropriations Bill, Fiscal Year 2004, Monday, January 26, 2004.
8 "Erase the Darfur Blood Stain From California's Pensions," *Los Angeles Times*, January 30, 2005.

objectionable. The model is a familiar one. It was used twenty years ago with considerable effect against the apartheid government of South Africa. In the 1980s, when American colleges and universities, public pension funds, and other investors decided to divest stocks of companies whose businesses helped prop up that racist regime's business partners, the effect was dramatic: first, the South African government was forced to abandon apartheid, and that step ultimately resulted in its fall from power.

More recently, the divestment model has been employed by a host of "socially responsible" investors. They have targeted businesses involved in activities deemed unacceptable on moral, political, or other grounds. These have included involvement with environmental degradation, tobacco, gaming, gun manufacturing, alcohol, sweatshops, and the repressive military regime in Burma.

Today, an intense divestment campaign is being mounted by various Protestant denominations and on some college campuses. The object of this initiative? To remove from church portfolios the stocks of companies doing business with a democratic friend and ally of the United States, Israel.

The question occurs: If divestment is good enough for a regime that was beastly to its own people like South Africa; if it is good enough for companies that engage in what are considered to be socially irresponsible activities; if it could conceivably be acceptable for use against corporations involved with Israel, one of our country's most strategically important allies; then on what possible grounds could we foreclose using this instrument in our life-and-death struggle against Islamofascists and other terrorists bent on our destruction?

The bottom line is this: If pension funds can exclude some stocks without undermining their profitability, why not exclude those companies that provide revenues, technology, equipment, and moral cover to governments that sponsor terrorists and threaten our vital security interests?

Volunteers in the Financial War on Terror

Fortunately, increasing numbers of Americans believe we must wage this war on the financial front as well. They have recognized an empowering fact: Divestment is a practical way of ensuring that their investments are not used to underwrite the economies of the world's most grave security threats.

Another approach has been pioneered by New York City comptroller William Thompson, who oversees some $88 billion invested on behalf of

New York City's five pension funds. Last year, Comptroller Thompson filed shareholder resolutions on behalf of those five funds against five U.S. companies: Conoco-Phillips, Halliburton, General Electric, Cooper Cameron, and Aon. As a result, the companies decided to change course:

♦ Halliburton agreed not to pursue additional contracts with Tehran. Conoco stated that it would no longer permit subsidiaries to do business in U.S.-sanctioned countries. Aon agreed to establish a committee to assess such ties.

♦ Comptroller Thompson leveraged the retirement funds' $1 billion worth of stock in General Electric to persuade the company to reconsider its contracts in Iran. In early 2005, GE did just that. It announced to investors that it would not renew or extend any contracts in Iran starting February 1. GE, which had invested roughly $270 million through subsidiaries in Iran in 2004, stated that the country's "uncertain conditions" contributed to its decision.

♦ The New York pension funds held about $52 million worth of stock issued by Cooper Cameron Corporation, a publicly traded manufacturer of oil and gas technology. Under pressure from those funds, the company agreed to divest its business venture in Iran. At the time, Comptroller Thompson declared, "I hope Cooper Cameron's decision will encourage other companies to thoroughly examine their relationships with rogue nations. We believe that American companies should nonetheless adhere to the spirit, as well as the letter, of the law."

In the end, with his shareholder activism strategy vindicated, Mr. Thompson voluntarily withdrew all his resolutions.

These success stories prove beyond any doubt that the effort to cut off indirect funding of terror sponsors, by focusing on corporations that do business with such rogue states, can—and will—work.

Another promising step with respect to public pension systems came in the State of Louisiana in May 2005, when the legislature moved to increase transparency with respect to investments by the state's public pension systems in companies that do business in and with terrorist-sponsoring nations. The Louisiana law has three important aspects:

1. It requires portfolio managers doing business with Louisiana's thirteen pension systems to screen for companies that do business with terrorist-sponsoring nations, as defined by the U.S. State Department in "Patterns of Global Terrorism: Iran, Syria, Libya, Sudan and North Korea."

2. It requires state public pension funds to report semiannually to the legislature on those companies in portfolio that have business ties in Iran, Syria, Libya, Sudan, and North Korea.
3. The law also authorizes the state's thirteen pension funds to divest from companies doing business in and with the terrorist-sponsoring nations.

Meanwhile, in two other states—Arizona (with the leadership of State Treasurer David Petersen) and Tennessee—legislation has been introduced mandating biannual disclosure of state monies invested in all companies doing business with state sponsors of terror. According to Treasurer Petersen, "If we don't say anything and something were to happen, to me we didn't do our fiduciary responsibility."

Despite such impressive gains, however, there are many in the pension system who continue to assert that "divesting terror" would disrupt their management of their public fund and substantially affect returns on investment. Although the success of environmentally friendly, tobacco-free, and similar socially driven funds disprove this argument, the Missouri Investment Trust (MIT) is poised to provide the first public pension fund case study for investing "terror-free." The MIT has sent out a request for proposal asking that asset managers bid on a $5 million international equity portfolio that screens out companies that partner with terrorist-supporting governments.

A Case Study: Sudan

Particularly noteworthy progress has been made around the country in bringing the financial war on terror to one of the most egregious Islamofascist enemies of freedom: the government of Sudan. (Although these initiatives primarily reflect public concern over ongoing, massive human rights violations in that country, they helpfully penalize as well a regime that sponsors terror.) State legislators in Maryland, Massachusetts, New Jersey, California, Illinois, and Texas have introduced legislation prohibiting the investment of state monies in companies active in Sudan. Illinois and New Jersey have already enacted this divestment initiative.

For their part, student activists have urged college administrators and state officials to stop investing in companies doing business in Sudan. At Harvard University, students launched HarvardDivest.com, a Web site petition that challenged Harvard's endowment investment arm, the Harvard Management Company, to divest its $3.5 million holdings in PetroChina. Harvard has proceeded with this divestment after more than fifteen hundred Harvard alumni, students, and professors signed the petition supporting it.

Other students are working, with the help of the Boston-based American Anti-Slavery Group, to establish a national student network to build on Harvard's success. Its purpose is to pressure officials in states across America to introduce legislation prohibiting the use of public money for investments in companies active in Sudan.

One of the first achievements of this network was the result of efforts by students at Williams College, who prevailed on Massachusetts state legislators to take action. Legislation was introduced in June 2005 calling for the Massachusetts Investment Board to divest its holdings in companies operating in Sudan. According to the bill's sponsor, Sen. Andrea Nuciforo: "One way in which the Commonwealth can have an impact is to ensure that state pension funds are not contributing, in any way, to this tragedy. . . . Many overseas corporations are still engaged, either knowingly or not, in perpetuating these heinous crimes."

Learn How to Fight the Financial War on Terror

The Center for Security Policy has created a Web resource to help empower concerned Americans to use financial leverage against our enemies. This site, DivestTerror.org, provides suggestions for public pension fund beneficiaries, taxpayers, and other investors to take steps to ensure that their money is not being put, even indirectly, in the service of terrorists.

The center specifically recommends for this purpose a tried-and-true model: divesting stocks issued by companies that do business with state sponsors of terror. Were such companies to sever their ties with terror-sponsoring regimes, the effect on these governments would be crippling.

Widespread divestment would force public companies to choose between their operations in terrorist-supporting countries and their corporate reputation and stock value in America. When the South Africa divestment campaign forced corporations to make a similar choice, they withdrew from that country—and apartheid became a relic of history.

Employed effectively, a divestment campaign today might once again accomplish changes in the policies, and perhaps the governments, of the targeted nations. At the very least, it can compel the companies that do business with them to terminate operations in countries that persist in sponsoring terror. Either way, the effect would be highly salutary to the War on Terror.

During the South Africa divestment campaign, pension systems were reluctant to divest—until pressure from activists and students prompted lawmakers to compel them to do so. That is why a central element of the DivestTerror.org campaign is to encourage and enable Americans to petition their state lawmakers, as well as public pension system and university endow-ment administrators.

What Needs to Be Done

There are a number of specific steps and initiatives that individuals can undertake to advance this divestment campaign:

1. *Organize to reach state officials*: Write state officials asking the legislature to require state and local public pension funds to divest the stock of any company that does business in terrorist-sponsoring nations. Have members of the community sign and send this letter to the governor, state treasurer, leading state senators, and representatives or assembly-men. Naturally, the Internet is a great force multiplier for such efforts (sample letters can be downloaded from DivestTerror.org).

2. *Create a buzz*: It is easier to ignore the view of one person than those of scores, hundreds, or perhaps thousands. Send an e-mail to family, friends, neighbors, congregation leaders and members, and business associates to educate them about this issue, with the goal of generating more awareness of the need to divest terror.

3. *Engage the media*: Make this an issue of central importance for local, community, and state media: newspapers, talk radio, and television.

4. *Don't take "No" for an answer:* If past experience is any guide, pension fund managers and state and local officials will probably hope that they can ignore any pressure for divestment of companies that partner with terror-sponsoring regimes. They will stall in the hope that such cam-paigns will peter out over time. Accordingly, lay down markers and timetables for action. Ensure that the media are well aware of any com-mitments that are made—and whether they are in fact met.

The war against Islamofascist terror is unlike any other we have ever faced. Even so, the financial weapons that have been successfully wielded for other causes can and must be applied as part of the War Footing strategy. More than any other element of our strategy, this is one critically important area in which concerned Americans can play a direct and decisive part in winning the War for the Free World.

PART III
Protecting the Homeland

For the nation to be considered truly on a War Footing, and for it to become as safe as we can make it, a far more comprehensive effort is going to have to be undertaken to protect the territory, people, economy, and infrastructure of the United States.

We have recently witnessed the devastation wrought in one region of the country by a natural disaster, Hurricane Katrina—devastation that was compounded by a succession of human errors prior to, during, and after the storm. This was a vivid reminder of how woefully ill-prepared we are for the sorts of mass destruction that determined, state-sponsored Islamofascist terrorists could inflict.

This section addresses three steps we must take to provide better protection for our homeland in the face of such a threat:

- ◆ Step 5 addresses ways in which we can better equip our law-enforcement authorities and other leaders with the legal instruments, intelligence, training, and public support required to keep America safe—and free.

- ◆ Step 6 describes how the United States could become "unplugged"—suffering the loss on a *national* basis of the sorts of interruptions of power, energy resources, telecommunications, transportation, food supplies, and critical infrastructure that the Gulf States experienced during and after Katrina. It lays out measures needed to deter, defeat, and, if necessary, mitigate the consequences of the mega-terrorist threat: a "catastrophic" electromagnetic pulse (EMP) attack.

- Step 7 deals with the need to address the national security imperatives arising from three interrelated problems:

  - America's porous and regularly penetrated borders.
  - Our dysfunctional policy and programmatic approaches to legal and illegal immigration.
  - The fraud-plagued identity documentation systems upon which we rely to secure everything from airplanes, to government and private facilities, to bank accounts.

STEP 5

Equip the Home Front

With Contributions from Andrew C. McCarthy, Timothy Connors, and Mark Chussil

T wo grim realities emerge from the global war against Islamofascists and their state sponsors:

1. It is impossible to protect everything we care about all the time. We face people who are determined to hurt us—some of whom are willing to kill themselves in the process. Each and every such terrorist becomes the equivalent of a precision-guided weapon. As long as ours remains an open and free society, these sorts of weapons will be able to do at least *some* harm. This is in fact why the United States must pursue an offensively oriented strategy in this war (see Step 2).

2. We must nevertheless do what we can to protect our citizens, society, infrastructure, and way of life. Security is, after all, the first responsibility of government.

What steps must be taken by the American people, and their elected officials, that can make a real difference in our safety and security at home? This chapter will discuss three such initiatives.

- ◆ Provide our law-enforcement authorities with the *intelligence and legal tools* they need.
- ◆ Ensure that our police are *properly trained* to contend with the threat posed by the Islamofascists and other terrorists.
- ◆ *Prepare officials, community leaders, and the public to deal with crises,* whether man-made or natural. Officials at all levels of government need to be taught to work together, as well as with other community leaders, as a team. The public must be included in preparing and implementing evacuation and other crisis-mitigation plans.

Waging the Counterterror War at Home

The terrorist attacks on September 11, 2001, put a spotlight on the limits of America's law-enforcement approach to the Islamofascist threat. The response was (1) to adopt a far more comprehensive and offensively oriented strategy, and (2) to introduce some long-overdue improvements in the tools and methods available to the criminal justice system.

It is tragic that thousands of Americans had to die to prompt a reconsideration of counterterrorism strategy. The practice had been to rely almost exclusively on criminal indictments and prosecutions to combat terrorists, including suicide bombers. The failure of this approach should have been clear long before: even though the membership of anti-U.S. terror organizations was growing into the thousands, the government had managed to neutralize just twenty-nine terrorists, most of them low-ranking operatives.

But there is much more to the story than the paltry results. Prosecution is an ineffective counterterror strategy because *it is not designed for that purpose.* Prosecution is part of domestic policing, an aspect of executive power very different from national security.

Former Attorney General William Barr highlighted this distinction in his testimony before the House Intelligence Committee in October 2003.[1] He noted that because the government has, essentially, a monopoly on the legitimate use of force vis-à-vis a defendant in the justice system, our court procedures are designed to provide a kind of counterweight to government powers of prosecution.

- ◆ Under the Constitution, our criminal process is structured to protect the rights of defendants, by embracing the right of privacy and the presumption of innocence on the part of the accused.
- ◆ In addition, the defendant is assured a lawyer who is responsible for challenging the government's case and whose job is essentially to make it difficult for the client to be found guilty (whether he is or not).

Our system of justice, in effect, deems it preferable for government to fail in the prosecution of an offender rather than for an innocent person to be wrongly convicted or otherwise deprived of his rights.

---

1 Testimony of former U.S. Attorney General William P. Barr before the House Select Committee on Intelligence, October 30, 2003. Available at http://www.globalsecurity.org/intell/library/congress/2003ohr/031030-barr.pdf.

We Are at War

This stance differs dramatically, of course, from the national security response to external threats; in particular, from hostile nations and terrorist organizations that claim the right to use force against us.

Here the executive branch has a very different responsibility: to use the government's national defense powers against hostile agents, at home or abroad, who are determined to inflict harm on us. As it happens, most of these enemy agents have been foreign nationals who are not entitled to our constitutional protections.

In such cases, the overriding concern must be to defeat the enemy and, as former Attorney General Barr put it, to "preserve the very foundation of all our civil liberties." In this case, the government must not be permitted to fail if we are to continue to enjoy the right, as our Founders put it, to life, liberty, and the pursuit of happiness.

Viewed in this light, a prosecution-based approach to combating terrorism actually *endangers* the public. According to our system of justice, the same military enemy who would be presumed a deadly threat on the battlefield is presumed innocent (by definition) in the courtroom.

Under the law-enforcement approach, any terrorist accused of planning the mass murder of Americans gets the same procedural advantages as someone charged with tax evasion. Most importantly, because the prosecution must satisfy our system's demanding requirements for a fair trial, the government is obliged to disclose to the defendant detailed information about its investigation. This can include highly sensitive intelligence about:

- suspected co-conspirators in a plot to harm the American people
- related activities and organizational structure
- the methods and sources used to collect such information (whose disclosure often destroys their further usefulness).

Even if al-Qaeda had managed to construct its own CIA, it could not have amassed anything like the information it gleaned from being prosecuted in American courtrooms.

A New Approach, At Last

After September 11, as the government brought to bear a comprehensive mobilization of military, intelligence, financial, and diplomatic resources to combat the Islamofascists, prosecution moved from the forefront of the counterterrorism effort to a secondary (but crucial) supporting role.

Within law enforcement itself, moreover, a mini-revolution took place.

1. There was a new recognition of the true peril posed by terrorism; namely, the possibility of an attack, using weapons of mass destruction, that could dwarf even the losses we sustained on September 11.
2. It was explicitly recognized that intelligence and prevention had to be given precedence over investigation and prosecution—that thwarting active conspiracies, and gutting their support networks, must become the priorities rather than merely bringing terrorists to justice *after* the mass murder has occurred.

All this sounds sensible enough. Implementing the new priorities, however, has sparked a war within the war.

Libertarian extremists—drawn from both the far left and far right—have vigorously opposed virtually every measure, no matter how modest, aimed at improving the government's ability to detect and interrupt terrorism. The battlelines have been most sharply drawn over the Patriot Act, racial and ethnic "profiling," and laws prohibiting material support to terrorist organizations. These tools are the subject of the next section.

Tools for War on the Home Front

1. The Patriot Act

Despite the impassioned claims of critics, the Patriot Act is *not* an assault on the basic freedoms enshrined in the Bill of Rights. Rather, it is an eminently sensible overhaul of the government's antiquated counterterror arsenal, an overhaul that reflects the realization that we cannot hope to fight a 21st-century war using 20th-century legal instruments.

The Patriot Act's single most important improvement has been to dismantle the barrier often referred to as "the Wall": the set of legal and regulatory practices, constructed over the past three decades, designed specifically to impede the flow of information between law enforcement and the intelligence community.

The Wall reflected a fundamental misunderstanding of the 1978 Foreign Intelligence Surveillance Act (FISA). That law authorized the FBI to conduct electronic surveillance and physical searches in foreign counterintelligence investigations, applying standards that are different from those that apply in conventional criminal cases.[2] The concern arose that the government might

---

2   In criminal cases, the government generally must establish probable cause that a crime has been or is being committed in order to obtain a court warrant to eavesdrop or search. Intelligence cases, on the other hand, require probable cause that the target of the investigation is an agent of a foreign power; essentially, a spy or a terrorist.

misuse this national security authority. Specifically, some feared that criminal investigations might now be conducted without affording defendants their right to fair trials with the traditional constitutional protections.

As a result, a series of missteps by the U.S. Justice Department and the courts caused astonishing procedural barriers to be created to curb information sharing between criminal and intelligence investigators. These missteps culminated in regulations issued by the department in 1995 that dramatically *increased* the original restrictions—just at the time that terrorist attacks on American targets overseas were beginning to increase.

The effect of the Wall on law enforcement was extraordinary. To give just one notable example: only a few weeks before the September 11 attacks, FBI headquarters refused to allow its criminal division to assist its own intelligence division in the attempt to locate two suspected terrorists. The two men were believed—correctly, as it turned out—to be already in the United States. These two known suspects, Khalid al-Midhar and Nawaf al-Hazmi, were thus accorded the freedom of movement that allowed them to fly the hijacked Flight 77 into the Pentagon.

With respect to the Wall, as in so many other areas, the Patriot Act has applied common sense to reforming the existing rules and procedures governing counterterrorism law enforcement. The act established that intelligence agents, criminal investigators, and prosecutors are not only allowed but actually *encouraged* to pool their information.

Tearing down the Wall paid almost immediate dividends.[3] At last permitted to connect all the dots, the Justice Department has been able to

- Shut down terrorist conspiracies in upstate New York, Virginia, southern California, and Portland, Oregon.
- Disable terrorist financiers in Chicago, Texas, and New York.
- File major indictments against operatives of al-Qaeda, Hamas, and Palestinian Islamic Jihad.

The Patriot Act has been invaluable in other ways, as well. It extended to national security investigations the same investigative methods long available to law-enforcement agents probing the vast majority of federal crimes.

- The Patriot Act expanded the scope of the authorized use of wiretaps to account for the realities of terrorism. Unlike (for example) gambling investigations, such crimes as chemical weapons–related offenses, the

---

3   Related reforms were also invaluable, repealing the laws that had barred criminal investigators from sharing with intelligence agents the fruits of grand-jury proceedings and criminal wiretaps.

use of weapons of mass destruction, the killing of Americans abroad, terrorist financing, and computer fraud were *not* legal grounds for wiretapping. Now they are.

♦ This latitude was applied also to "roving wiretaps." For years, criminals have exploited telecommunications technology, notably by constantly switching cell phones to evade wiretap surveillance. Congress nearly twenty years ago authorized wiretaps in criminal investigations that targeted *persons,* rather than telephone numbers. Until the Patriot Act was adopted, however, intelligence agents investigating terrorism and espionage under FISA were denied this roving wiretap authority.

♦ The Patriot Act also revamped other telecommunications-related techniques. It made evidence derived from broadband (primarily cable) Internet access available on the same terms as records from dial-up communications service providers.

♦ The act also closed other gaping e-mail loopholes, such as enabling grand juries to subpoena payment information, in addition to the customer's name, address, and length of service (the only information allowed under prior law). This makes it possible to trace terrorists (and other criminals) who routinely use false names and temporary e-mail addresses.

These modifications reflect basic common sense. If we are to prevent terror attacks, they are vital.

Yet, the Patriot Act has been the subject of tireless, savage, and fundamentally misleading criticism. Such criticism is best illustrated by two targeted provisions: the so-called library records provision and sneak-and-peek search warrants.

A Sensible Approach to Library Records

The dust-up over government access to library information is truly a manufactured controversy. For one thing, libraries are not mentioned anywhere in the pertinent Patriot Act provision. Moreover, law enforcement has been authorized for decades in ordinary criminal cases to subpoena library records (along with any other business records). This has not translated into any noticeable impact on Americans' reading habits.

All the Patriot Act did was make business records (including those maintained by libraries) available on roughly the same terms in national security cases as they have long been in criminal cases. The reason for this should be obvious: It makes no sense to enshrine libraries as safe havens for terrorist planning.

In fact, as we now know, many of the September 11 hijackers used American and European libraries for preparation in the run-up to the attacks. Relevant literature evidence (such as bomb manuals and jihadist materials) has been a staple of terrorism prosecutions for more than a decade.

Privacy extremists of organizations like the American Civil Liberties Union (ACLU) have nonetheless reacted to the Patriot Act's much-needed business records law as if the Gestapo had seized office in the United States.

Common Sense Regarding "Delayed Notifications"

Similarly, the Patriot Act did not—as its critics would have us believe—create new and unsavory "sneak-and-peek" warrants. It does, however, allow agents to search premises but delay notification of the search to subjects of a terrorism investigation.

The Patriot Act's notification provision is no different in principle from the legal notice that was previously required to be given to persons intercepted in a court-ordered wiretap. In such situations, notification of the target has routinely been delayed for weeks or months after the eavesdropping ends. Doing so can be absolutely critical to the arrest and prosecution of suspected perpetrators: Delayed notification allows the government to complete its investigation without giving the subjects the sort of heads-up that would certainly cause them to flee or destroy evidence.

What the Patriot Act did, in the so-called sneak-and-peek arena, was to establish consistent standards that the federal courts must follow in determining whether to permit delayed notification. Previously, a hodge-podge of different rules was applied in various jurisdictions. This is precisely the sort of fairness and equal protection Congress *should* provide—yet, it has been criticized sharply for doing that in the Patriot Act.

The True Agenda of the Patriot Act's Critics

With regard to both the business records and delayed notification sections of the Patriot Act (among others), the stance taken by the ACLU and like-minded critics seems to have an ulterior motive. They are not only opposed to such legislation in the Patriot Act, they also appear intent on reopening settled case law regarding the use of these authorities with respect to crimes unrelated to terror.

Unfortunately, many of the most crucial Patriot Act improvements, including the dismantling of the Wall, are slated to expire (or "sunset") at the end of 2005 if they are not renewed before then. Congress is now considering legislation that would make permanent most (or virtually all) such authorities. If we are to be on a War Footing—and if we are to have any chance of disrupting terrorists before they can strike—the Patriot Act must be made permanent.

The Patriot Act as a whole infringes only modestly on our civil liberties and only to the extent absolutely necessary. We need to keep in mind that, if these precautions should fail to prevent some further terrorist attack, we are likely to see impassioned demands for greater security measures, at the expense of our freedoms. In the hope of avoiding such an outcome, we need to make sure the Patriot Act remains in place and effective.

2. *"Profiling"*

Profiling is the practice of taking into account certain relevant background information (for example, demographic data, nation of origin, religious affiliations, etc.), among other data, to help narrow the search for and evaluation of potential terrorists. Opposition to its use in an appropriate fashion by law enforcement in time of war reflects the triumph of political correctness over common sense.

The U.S. government has gone to absurd lengths to avoid acknowledging that our enemy is the political movement known as militant Islam. We are unjustified in assuming that, by acknowledging this reality, we will offend *all* Muslims, rather than just the Islamists and their vocal allies.

This self-defeating caution is greatly compounded by the government's refusal to adopt an approach known to emergency medical personnel as "triage": the strategic application of limited resources, allocated with a view to saving the most lives. That is, after all, precisely what profiling is about.

It is certainly true that the occasional Islamic militant (for example, British shoe-bomber Richard Reid and the "American Taliban," John Walker Lindh) may not be obviously Muslim or of Middle Eastern or North African descent. But it is silly to conclude, therefore, that a helpful and fairly accurate profile cannot be developed.

This mixes apples and oranges. First, we are not proposing to target people for investigation in the absence of a known crime or any basis for suspecting a specific crime other than race or ethnicity. It is certainly appropriate, however, to take into account in investigations of known and ongoing crimes the characteristics inextricably tied to that crime. Indeed it would be ridiculous and irresponsible not to do so.

Ethnic considerations have in fact long been factored into criminal investigations: Italian heritage in mafia investigations; Irish heritage in the probe of New York City's "Westies" in the 1980s; Colombian nationality in drug cartel cases; Chinese heritage in investigations of Tong activity; and so forth. We can readily see that it would violate the Constitution's proscription against unreasonable searches to target, say, one or two elderly black women in a mafia case, simply in order to demonstrate that Italian men had not been singled out.

Second, a profile is not a judgment of guilt or even an *accusation* of guilt. It is merely an investigative tool. It enables law enforcement to organize suspicions and to allocate resources rationally; that is, in a manner related to a known threat.

Such practices are not foolproof, as those who use profiling recognize. Its point is not to cast aspersions. Rather, it is to improve the odds of thwarting an attack whose repercussions could be catastrophic. This approach is absolutely essential to any strategy aimed at *preventing* a strike rather than prosecuting the guilty after the victims have been slaughtered.

There is no getting around this striking fact: In the ongoing war, operatives who have carried out strikes, in the United States and worldwide, are overwhelmingly young Muslim males, especially of Middle Eastern and North African descent. That does not mean every individual—air traveler, subway passenger, or visitor to a building—who falls into that profile is a terrorist. Nor does it deny that individual *behavior* is the most important attribute to monitor.

Not every terrorist will fit the profile. But to deny police the ability to take such straightforward identifying information into account—and, in so doing, to waste precious resources by focusing attention on people unlikely to be terrorists—amounts to *inviting* attack.

3. "Material Support" to Terror

Perhaps the most vital law-enforcement initiative of the post–September 11 era has been a newly assertive use of a *pre*–September 11 law: legislation enacted in 1996 and aimed at criminalizing material support to terrorists.

The theory behind this law is exquisitely simple. The use of terrorism to achieve political or social goals is unacceptable—period. Therefore, any organization that engages in terrorism forfeits any right to legitimacy or government assistance, no matter what socially beneficial services it might also offer.

This distinction is vital because terror groups like Hezbollah and Hamas incorporate components that purport to engage only in political and public welfare activity (as opposed to acts of violence). Even Osama bin Laden has understood the goodwill value of spending on education and public welfare, to ingratiate himself with his hosts in the governments of Afghanistan and Sudan.

Regrettably, material support laws have also come under attack by self-styled humanitarian activists. They assert a right to contribute financial and other assistance to what they deem to be First Amendment–protected activities of such organizations. Leaving aside the fact that foreign organizations have no rights under the U.S. Constitution, the error of this argument should be obvious.

- ◆ As we noted in Step 4, money is fungible. The contributor of funds, even if he honestly believes he is engaged in charitable giving, has no control over the receiver's actual use of those funds, including to support terror. Similarly, contributions may simply free up funds already in hand, to be used for terror-related purposes.
- ◆ Any assistance that strengthens a terror organization also makes it more efficient at the brutal business of killing. This is the end result of contributions that enhance its overall resources and its attractiveness to potential recruits.
- ◆ Finally, terrorism cannot be marginalized and eradicated if those who engage in it are legitimized. A legal regime that allows terror organizations to flourish—to masquerade as mere political entities that happen to be armed—is self-defeating.

Law enforcement alone cannot defeat our enemies. Military successes in killing and capturing terrorists since September 11 remain the chief reason why we have not suffered a domestic attack in the interval.

But our enemies will be far more formidable if they are afforded a supporting infrastructure and the latitude to operate inside the United States. Only law enforcement can deny them these advantages. It can only do that with the sort of forward-looking, proactive, and preventive strategy that is made possible by a permanent Patriot Act along with appropriate use of profiling and prohibitions on material support.

Preparing the Police for War at Home

The local police—who often represent the "point of the spear"—will need to be properly prepared to use these legal tools effectively. Police officers are in a position to be *first preventers* of terrorist attacks, and not just first responders after they have happened.

Bob Fromme is a North Carolina sheriff's deputy with a career's worth of experience and training as a local policeman. In 1995,[4] while working as an off-duty security guard, he took the initiative to investigate three men whose

---

4   For a detailed account of the investigation see, Tom Diaz and Barbara Newman, *Lightning Out of Lebanon: Hezbollah Terrorists on American Soil,* Ballantine Books, 2005.

suspicious behavior attracted his attention. They turned out to be part of the largest terrorist-financing ring in the country: smuggling cigarettes to raise millions of dollars for Hezbollah.

Former CIA Director R. James Woolsey made this point in testimony before the House Select Committee on Homeland Security:

> Only an effective local police establishment that has the confidence of citizens is going to be likely to hear from, say, a local merchant in a part of town containing a number of new immigrants, that a group of young men from abroad have recently moved into a nearby apartment and are acting suspiciously. Local police are best equipped to understand how to protect citizens' liberties and obtain such leads legally.[5]

Director Woolsey is not alone in this view. It is becoming conventional wisdom today that local public safety agencies are critical to defeating our terrorist enemies. In his former capacity as chairman of the House Homeland Security Committee, then-Rep. Christopher Cox observed: "The private sector, firefighters, police officers, emergency medical professionals and public works employees have all emerged as new stakeholders in U.S. national security."[6]

Equipping the Police

Recognizing the new role that local police must play in defending America is an important first step. The more difficult task, however, comes with identifying and adopting practical, cost-effective strategies for enabling police and related organizations to serve as the dominant preventers of terror attacks.

Local institutions need to adapt to the changed reality of domestic terror. Fortunately, many are. Several of the nation's leading police departments—most notably, New York and Los Angeles—are moving away from organizing their activities solely around reducing crime and prosecuting criminals. The prevention of terrorist attacks, although it does not necessarily lead to criminal prosecutions, is now considered a core function for these departments.

In the case of New York, a transformation of this magnitude required the leadership of Mayor Michael Bloomberg and NYPD Commissioner Raymond Kelly and the support of their fellow New Yorkers. The implementation of such needed changes elsewhere will likely require other local political leaders to also become engaged in placing their police departments and public safety agencies on a War Footing.

---

5   R. James Woolsey, Testimony before the House Select Committee on Homeland Security, June 24, 2004.
6   See the congressman's "Foreword" to *Winning the Long War,* by James Jay Carafano and Paul Rosenzweig, Heritage Books, 2005.

It will also require mobilizing their public. The importance of enlisting the American people in support of law-enforcement efforts is illustrated by the case of James Elshafay and Shawar Matin Siraj, arrested in 2004 for conspiring to bomb New York's Herald Square subway station, near the site of that year's Republican National Convention.[7]

Thanks to a citizen's call to a terrorist tip line, the NYPD had been alerted to Shawar Siraj's jihadist rhetoric. The decision to begin a preliminary investigation was made not on the basis of criminal allegations but rather on the basis of a normally protected activity: free speech. The investigators soon determined that Siraj frequently engaged in violent anti-American rhetoric; that he usually aired his views only to a select group of people he trusted; that he had a criminal record; and that he was in the U.S. illegally.

Armed with this additional information, the police initiated an undercover operation to discover whether Siraj and his associate, James Elshafay, were involved in a specific terrorist scheme. Their arrest, and the disruption of the planned attack, resulted from a timely shift in organizational thinking, combined with the input of informed citizens and good old-fashioned police work.

Organizing for Success

Although good police work is the foundation of an effective local prevention program, more is clearly required. Police units need to develop:

- the intelligence data about the potential for local Islamist operations.
- the individual and collective skills needed to utilize such data.[8]

To be sure, individual cops use intelligence every day. The problem is that each individual officer tends—like Detective Fromme—to be his or her own intelligence collector, analyzer, and prioritizer. Given the magnitude of the potential threat, we need to ensure that the most efficient possible use is being made of these police officers.

Making the most of our police forces requires three mutually reinforcing initiatives:

1. Executive-level decision makers must receive timely information and analysis so that they are able to provide effective guidance to direct the activities of tactical units.

---

7   Craig Horowitz, "Anatomy of a Foiled Plot," *New York Magazine*, December 6, 2004. Available at http://www.newyorkmetro.com/nymetro/news/features/10559/index.html.

8   See Jerry H.Ratcliffe, "The effectiveness of police intelligence management: A New Zealand case study." Available at http://jratcliffe.net/conf/Ratcliffe%20(in%20press)%20NZ%20case%20study.pdf. Dr. Ratcliffe presents a clear description of and persuasive argument for intelligence-driven policing.

2. Tactical commanders—who are typically responsible principally for crime reduction—have different intelligence needs. They must have intelligence products that help them provide the right information to patrol officers and to deploy their resources most efficiently.

3. Individual officers must be able to act as informed observers and to report what they learn, with an understanding that this information improves the ability of senior executives to plan and provide future guidance.[9]

The contrast between such a three-part approach and the one that typically operates in law enforcement today is underscored by the case of Diana Dean, the U.S. Customs inspector who in 1999 thwarted the Millennium Bomber, Ahmed Ressam, in his planned attack on Los Angeles at the turn of the century. Inspector Dean's trained instincts discerned that this individual seemed nervous enough to warrant further investigation.[10]

As with Bob Fromme's intervention with the Hezbollah ring, success occurred in this case solely because an individual, veteran law-enforcement officer's suspicion was aroused. It did *not* result from an orderly process designed reliably to detect, intercept, and defeat our enemies.

In fact, in both of these noteworthy cases, key ingredients for an orderly intelligence management process were missing:

♦ There was no senior-level law-enforcement executive able to visualize the criminal threat environment or to issue guidance to shape and focus the operations of subordinate commanders.

♦ There was no analytical team in place, responsible for providing periodic criminal threat assessments for the senior-level executive, with daily intelligence summaries for the shift leader.

♦ Nor was there a shift leader prepared to combine such an intelligence summary with knowledge of the local environment to brief individual officers in the unit.

---

9   See James Q. Wilson and George L. Kelling, "Broken Windows: The police and neighborhood safety," *The Atlantic Monthly*, March 1982. "Broken Windows" theory challenged police to create orderly social environments by addressing signs of disorder, such as broken windows, graffiti, panhandling, and public intoxication. Attacking disorder created environments hostile for criminal activity and resulted in decreasing incidents of crime. NYPD, among others, adopted the principles of this theory and pioneered CompStat, an information management system that collects timely and accurate information on criminal activities and holds individual precinct commanders responsible for involving the community, applying problem-solving techniques, and achieving measurable outcomes. See also, "Hard Won Lessons: Problem-Solving Principles for Local Police," May 2005. Available at http://www.manhattan-institute.org/pdf/scro02.pdf.

10 Hal Bernton et al., "The Crossing," *The Seattle Times*. Available at http://seattletimes.nwsource.com/news/nation-world/terroristwithin/chapter12.html.

♦ Street officers had not been properly briefed to understand Islamic fundamentalism and terrorist tactics.[11]

In both of these cases, it was sheer luck that experienced law-enforcement officers with good instincts were at the right place at the right time. We simply cannot afford to rely on luck in the face of determined and deadly foes, armed with a sophisticated understanding of our vulnerabilities and how to exploit them. The New York Police Department clearly appreciates that reliance on good fortune is not enough. The department has striven to put in place the sort of process outlined above, by

♦ developing robust intelligence and analytical capabilities.
♦ educating its officers regarding Islamic fundamentalism and terrorist tactics.
♦ assigning 150 detectives to the Joint Terrorism Task Force (with additional detectives assigned to overseas locations).
♦ developing multiple programs to educate and engage the public.

Most police departments lack the resources to develop such an extensive all-crimes intelligence infrastructure, let alone to adopt the rest of New York's comprehensive program. This reality requires that multiple jurisdictions (state, local, and, where appropriate, tribal) cooperate and share resources. The private sector, which has massive experience in establishing cooperative business relationships, also has much to offer in this regard.

Engaging the Public

As we have seen, private citizens also have a role to play in making success less reliant on luck. By empowering our citizens to become informed observers, we can dramatically increase the ability of law enforcement to collect and act in a timely way upon relevant information.

Local law enforcement has vast experience in developing and effectively using Neighborhood Watch programs. To help put our country on the needed War Footing, we must now harness this capacity by networking these groups into a national neighborhood watch.

Such networks can be used to attack both crime and terror, which often overlap. The vast numbers of eyes and ears that can be brought to bear in this

---

11 Bob Fromme originally thought he was witnessing members of a Latin drug gang laundering the proceeds of a narcotics enterprise. Diana Dean and her team originally thought they had uncovered an attempt to smuggle drugs across the U.S.-Canadian border.

fashion can be a powerful force multiplier for the authorities, but citizens need to be attuned to the threat and informed as to how they can take action.

For most citizens, the appropriate action is to report the information to a tip line or an intelligence center that is capable of "fuzing" it—that is, of processing the raw intelligence and disseminating analyzed products quickly to operators in the field.

Ensuring that the public knows how to report information is only half the equation, however. The other half is knowing what type of information to report. Terrorist attacks do not occur in a vacuum. They require planning, materials, and often some form of authorization.

Given these factors, we must equip the American people to do more than just report "suspicious behavior." Public employees, business people, and other members of the community must be helped to become *educated* observers of suspicious conduct. On the basis of a careful study of terrorist tactics, the authorities need to educate citizens about how a terrorist might exploit their own community program, business activity, or government service.

The point is not to encourage people to become spies on their neighbors but rather to sensitize them to the sorts of signals of incipient attacks they may encounter in the course of their normal daily activities.

A national neighborhood watch network could be created at low cost by leveraging already existing organizations. The LAPD, for example, has tapped into existing business and security organizations to conduct vulnerability assessments and share information.[12] NYPD detectives regularly communicate with business groups in New York City and disseminate industry-specific threat information. For example, real estate agents have been briefed on the particular features al-Qaeda operatives have been trained to look for when renting an apartment.[13]

Practically every local community in the United States has such business, community, and security-minded groups. The key is to educate the members of such groups (and for those members to educate themselves) so they will have a better understanding of what is suspicious conduct and will know how to report it. A good starting point is the work of LAPD's Chief Bill Bratton, who is taking the lead in creating a network of major city police forces to share intelligence, as well as the burdens of improving collective capabilities.[14]

---

12 "Hard Won Lessons: Problem-Solving Principles for Local Police," May 2005, p. 15. Available at http://www.manhattan-institute.org/pdf/scro02.pdf.
13 Police Commissioner Raymond W. Kelly, Testimony before the House Judiciary Subcommittee on Crime, Terrorism and Homeland Security, November 20, 2003.
14 John Broder, "Police Chiefs Moving to Share Terror Data," *The New York Times*, July 29, 2005.

Since September 11, we have not suffered another terrorist attack against the homeland. Local communities, with their unique assets and potential, can be decisive in continuing this trend. By establishing local intelligence infrastructures and involving an informed citizenry, local communities can begin to realize their potential value as stakeholders in U.S. national security.

Preparing our Community Leaders Before Disaster Strikes

The disastrous storms that ravaged the Gulf States in fall 2005 have made one thing very clear: The lives and fortunes of perhaps millions of Americans may be saved or lost in catastrophic events. The prospect of an influenza pandemic adds further urgency to doing what we can to mitigate such losses.

The outcome of a major natural or terrorist-induced disaster depends in no small measure on two factors: (1) How well has emergency planning been conducted *prior* to the event? (2) How well prepared are the public and its leaders—at all levels—to implement these plans?

Arguably, the most important contributor to getting these two factors right is the level of training leaders have in disaster preparedness and crisis management. And the single most effective way of providing such training before catastrophe strikes is through *simulation*: exercises that play out crisis scenarios in order to refine the skills of those who must contend with them.

It is not enough to use such simulations to train first responders, however. Long before Hurricane Katrina came ashore in September 2005, such training had been available to police, firefighters, and other personnel in line to cope with a major storm threatening New Orleans and other vulnerable parts of the Gulf States region.

Unfortunately, the leaders who would have to make key decisions did not receive the same instruction and familiarization with the emergency plans. Neither did they receive the specialized training that leaders need. As a result, these leaders were not ready when the big storm arrived. Such an oversight is analogous to sending trained soldiers to be commanded by untrained officers. Who would want to follow an untrained leader into battle?

Just as we expect our commanders to know how to develop an effective strategy, to adapt to changing circumstances, to coordinate with other units, and to make good decisions under fire, we should expect the same of our civilian leaders.

Take Me to Your Leader

Such leaders include the large group of people whose decisions and leadership affect a community's survival in a crisis. The obvious officials are the mayor, the police chief, the fire chief, and the head of emergency services. The group also includes representatives of the FBI, the National Guard, and, where appropriate, the Coast Guard.

Other members of the community leadership team who should receive crisis simulation training include the governor, county health officials, and state police, as well as the directors of such critical infrastructure as gas and electric utilities, the water system, the airport, the railroad, mass transit, hospitals, and telecommunications. Still other candidates include school district officials who decide how to safeguard children in crisis situations; company executives who decide what their employees should do; and the trucking managers who decide when and how to transport critical supplies.

Such leaders represent more than just a large group. It is a group with unique attributes: Their decisions affect each others' portfolios; they depend on each other; and they normally do not have a clear hierarchy. The complexity—and the necessity—of training community leaders as *a team* is demonstrated by the following facts.

- Most community leaders serve more than one constituency. For instance, decision makers at an electric utility have to worry about *all* the communities connected to the power grid, not just the one affected by the crisis. They may choose to cut power to one community rather than risk blacking out all of them. Thus, it is critical for the group to understand each other's jobs so they will not make assumptions about what will or will not happen in a crisis.
- Community leaders' decisions have a ripple effect. A big-company executive may decide to send his employees home during a crisis, unintentionally snarling traffic and blocking emergency vehicles and possibly trapping his people in harm's way.
- Such leaders may never have met each other prior to a crisis, yet they must be able to work as an effective team amid relentless chaos, lack of information, and desperate time pressure. In an emergency, community leaders will have to coordinate across different areas (for example, police, fire, utilities, hospitals) and different levels of government (local, state, and federal). That is why it is critical for them to train beforehand as a team.

◆ Leaders accept extraordinary responsibility. In their hands are the fates of large numbers of Americans. Therefore, they must have the best pre-crisis training we know how to provide.

Dealing with crises is different from dealing with routine events or even emergencies. Crises bring unique challenges that require unique training. Because crises are uncommon or unprecedented, there are no instruction manuals and no experts who have done-it-a-hundred-times-before to tell leaders how to cope with them.

What is needed is training that goes beyond drills and manuals to teach the first-rate decision-making and leadership skills that lead to creative solutions when there is no manual. This kind of leadership does not come naturally. It must be learned, and it is far preferable that it be learned *before* a crisis, not in its midst.

Crisis Simulations

The best training is inexpensive, quick, rich in feedback, and realistic.

◆ *Inexpensive* does not mean low quality. It means training where the *price of mistakes* is low. All of us make mistakes as we gain experience. The idea is for leaders to make their mistakes during training, where no one will suffer the consequences.

◆ *Quick* does not mean rushed. It means *efficient*. We do not have the luxury of spending years training a leader, especially given the rapid turnover in many posts.

◆ Training is *rich in feedback* if it helps participants learn by connecting actions to results. We all need feedback to know if our communication and decisions were effective, and we all benefit from expert teachers and coaches who provide honest, constructive advice.

◆ Exercises can be *realistic* without exactly reproducing real-world conditions. They must, however, simulate an environment that matches the intensity, chaos, speed, information, emotions, and challenges that the leader will face in an actual crisis.

Such training allows leaders the opportunity to learn crisis response the easy way. The alternative—on-the-job training in the midst of a disaster—is likely to be horrifically expensive and tragically late.

People learn more from experience than from lectures. That is why simulations—in which real people with real responsibilities wrestle with realistic crisis scenarios—work so well.

The most powerful element of such an exercise may be what *does not* happen. In an intellectual discussion or an academic debate, people tend to be complacent or to deny that a problem exists. But complacency and denial simply are not options in a realistic simulation. People have to deal with the problem confronting them, and even experts learn from the experience.

Finally, participants in such simulations find it difficult afterwards to dismiss the danger they had to contend with in the simulation. An appropriate analogy is the sort of changes people make in their lives after a near-death experience—without the associated danger and trauma.

The following description is just one part of an actual scenario used recently to train the mayor and other leaders in a major American city. The participants learned firsthand about decision making in the midst of chaos and confusion, where nothing was known with certainty and a city was in "real" danger.

> You are the mayor. A bomb has exploded on a bridge, as cars and a train passed over it. The explosion also severs electricity, gas, and fiberoptic lines that use that bridge to serve your community.
>
> Vehicles and their occupants fall into the river and onto the river banks. Firefighters and police swarm to the site, followed by emergency medical personnel. A victim is trapped underneath a car. He is bleeding to death. The only way to get him out is to amputate the limb that is caught under the car. Medics are preparing to do exactly that.
>
> Then, the police discover a suspicious box nearby. It could be another bomb. Terrorists have been known to plant secondary bombs, specifically designed to kill the crowds and first responders that arrive on a disaster scene.
>
> Do you let the medics stay on-site so they can extricate the trapped person? If you do and if the suspicious box turns out to be a bomb, many people will die. If you tell the medics to evacuate, the trapped person will surely die, and the suspicious box may turn out to be harmless. What would you do? If it's bomb, it could go off any second. If you call for more information, the bomb (if it is a bomb) could go off while you wait. *Decide!*

The Impact of Training on Leaders

A leader who has experienced a realistic simulated crisis is more likely to stay calm, focused, and effective in a real crisis than is a leader facing such conditions for the first time. Many leaders have developed decision-making and leadership skills that work well during normal times.

What few leaders have is well-developed decision-making and leadership skills for times of crisis, simply (and fortunately) because actual crises are rare. So, if we want leaders to be experienced in handling crises, we need to simulate the sort of conditions—pressure, chaos, emotion, confusion, life-and-death choices—that they might face in real life.

Simulations can not only help leaders respond effectively in real crises, they can also help *prevent* crises, by identifying vulnerabilities that leaders can repair.

On May 25, 1979, American Airlines flight 191 crashed on takeoff at Chicago's O'Hare International Airport. The DC-10 lost its left engine, after which the aircraft rolled to the left, stalled, and crashed. All 271 people on board the plane lost their lives, as did two people on the ground.

According to the National Transportation Safety Board, the aircraft wasn't doomed because it lost the engine. It was doomed because it lost the engine *and the flight crew didn't know what was wrong.*[15] Lacking that information, they couldn't diagnose or work around the problem. Better knowledge might have made a difference.

> During the investigation, the NTSB asked 13 qualified pilots to fly various [simulated] takeoff profiles. 70 takeoff simulations were flown. All crashed the airplane when flying the crash profile. Several pilots, when left to their own devices, and with extensive knowledge of the events, managed to control the airplane, nonetheless, by recognizing the initial roll and applying full opposite aileron and significant rudder, and lowering the nose to gain air-speed. All pilots who received appropriate feedback, via a functioning stickshaker, and who increased their airspeed to stay above the stickshaker value—168 knots—saved the airplane.[16]

The simulations helped uncover ways in which one disaster might prevent others in the future, notably by designing aircraft to give more information to the flight crew.

Several other real benefits are derived from training leaders to contend with crises *before* they occur:

---

15 From National Transportation Safety Board report, available at http://yarchive.net/air/airliners/dc10oohareocrash.html.

16 Ibid.

- Decision-making and leadership skills are *transferable*. If a leader learns how to make good decisions under pressure in one kind of crisis, he or she can apply that skill in a different setting and circumstance.
- Leaders move from job to job and from community to community. The more we train, the more an entire nation benefits.
- Super Bowl performance only comes from players who practice together. When a community's leadership team trains together, they build the relationships and trust they need to work together. They even learn who they can count on—before they have to count on them.
- The impact of actual crises can be reduced. For instance, in the chaos of the simulated terrorist bomb on the bridge, real leaders lost track of important communications between the city and the state. As a result, badly needed aid from the state did not arrive for hours. Knowing about that weakness, they were prepared to take action (as simple as assigning an aide to manage those communications) that would prevent the same mistake in a real-life crisis.

Of course, even the best simulation-based training cannot guarantee that leaders will make all the right decisions or that all crises will have happy endings. In any crisis situation, leaders must make decisions with incomplete or inaccurate information, and they don't have infinite resources to deploy. But proper training does greatly increase the odds that leaders will decide wisely. Better decisions generally translate into saving more lives, livelihoods, and homes.

Posse Comitatus

Posse comitatus is the federal law that, in general, prohibits the use of the military as a domestic police force.[17] The recent experience of crisis management in dealing with hurricanes Katrina and Rita has led to questions about the practical and legal implications of this prohibition.

Even communities that have well-trained leaders and an informed public are going to need additional help when subjected to the sort of massive devastation that was inflicted on the Gulf States by powerful storms in fall 2005—to say nothing of a widespread outbreak of contagious avian influenza or some other pandemic or an attack involving the use of weapons of mass destruction. In such circumstances, the U.S. military can and must play a role.

In the aftermath of hurricanes Katrina and Rita, however, questions have been posed about precisely what that role should be. For example, should the

---

17 *Posse comitatus* is codified at Section 1385 of Title 18, United States Code.

armed forces be permanently assigned responsibility for domestic disaster relief? And, even if they are given a more limited assignment—for example, in dealing with specific, extraordinary emergency situations on a case-by-case basis—is there a need for a change in the statute governing military participation?

The short answer to both questions is "No." Under the Constitution and federal law, there is plenty of discretion for a president confronted with a truly catastrophic situation to deploy the military to keep order and protect the general welfare. In fact, Article IV of the Constitution guarantees "a Republican Form of Government" to each of the states. It commits the federal government to protect them against both "Invasion . . . and . . . domestic violence." Moreover, if an outbreak of domestic violence is in prospect, Article IV empowers the president to respond unilaterally if Congress cannot be convened in time to authorize such an intervention.

The Constitution is, of course, the supreme law of the land. No statute, including the posse comitatus law, can override its commands, which do not merely permit but actually *compel* the executive branch to act when public safety is gravely imperiled.

In point of fact, however, there is no tension between posse comitatus and the president's constitutional responsibilities. The statute makes it a crime willfully to use the armed forces "as a posse comitatus or otherwise to execute the laws."[18] But the statute contains an important qualification: "except in cases and under circumstances expressly authorized by the Constitution or Act of Congress" (see also Step 7). Thus, the law explicitly honors the Constitution's formula, respecting the president's duty to act, and Congress's prerogative to legislate accordingly, in times of domestic crisis.

In short, there is no need to modify posse comitatus. We do not, and *should not*, want our armed forces doing any more on the home front than to provide for limited assistance where absolutely necessary. Quite aside from concerns about the undesirable intrusion of the military in civilian functions of government, we can ill afford—especially in time of war—to squander the armed forces' unique abilities and resources on the sorts of emergencies that are the normal responsibility of state and local authorities.

The rule of thumb should be that only the president can make a declaration of martial law and thus confer on the military the principal responsibility for emergency management and remediation. Unless and until such a declaration is mandated, the job should remain the responsibility of civilian authorities.

---

18 The statute only refers to "the Army or the Navy," but the principle is understood as embracing all the armed services.

To enhance civilian capacity to meet an emergency, consideration should be given to making the Federal Emergency Management Agency (or, more likely, some reconfigured successor) into a true *operating* agency rather than merely a coordinating one. To perform such a function, that agency will require its own logistical and other assets. Ideally, these would be prepositioned around the country and available for redeployment on short notice.

In fact, a small-scale program along these lines currently exists, with gear stored at nine sites, ready to be manned and rolled out on six hours' notice. It would be prudent to enlarge and dedicate this program to enable substantial capability to be brought to bear within six to ninety-six hours. This would also further reduce the need to rely on scarce military resources for such domestic emergency relief purposes.

What Needs to Be Done

This chapter details many useful initiatives. Perhaps the most important responsibility of the American people, however, is to participate in the process by which we select our elected leaders, from the local to the federal levels. Similarly, the boards of hospitals, utilities, and other private-sector ventures have a special responsibility in naming their executive leadership. They need to be mindful that their managers may, on some fateful day, shoulder a responsibility far greater than the organization's quarterly bottom line.

If we can entrust our security and the stewardship of crises to people who are seasoned, competent, and effective leaders, we will do much to ensure that they perform well if and when a terrorist attack or natural disaster strikes.

Whatever the abilities and skills of our leaders may be, however, we should be certain that they have specialized training in emergency response. Toward that end, as our part in putting our communities on a War Footing, each of us should undertake the following steps:

1. **Urge community leaders to get simulation-based training** in programs that build decision-making and leadership skills. Rather than rehearsing an emergency checklist, these exercises should include "curve balls" that provide the unpredictable demands typical of real crises. Leaders should be able to make mistakes in the training in the hope that they will not make the same mistakes in real life. In particular, they should be encouraged to train together as a team and to include representatives of government and businesses who must work together in a crisis.

2. **Create a network to share information with neighbors** regarding who has special skills or special needs and how to contact each other in an

emergency. In addition to properly trained leaders, having citizens who are familiar with and trained in emergency procedures is essential if our communities are to be as prepared as possible for terrorist attacks or natural disasters.

3. **Encourage community leaders to interact with constituents** about emergency preparedness and training. They should be asked the following sorts of questions:

   - How well do you understand the key vulnerabilities and interconnections within our community and in relation to actors outside our community (government, infrastructure, business, etc.)? How well do you understand the cascading effects of your decisions and of decisions made by others?
   - Are our community's plans and drills realistic for complex crises that can have long-term effects, such as natural disasters, radiological attacks, or pandemics? Do you limit those plans and drills to simple effects at a single location?
   - In an emergency, do you know how to communicate effectively with those who need to know, including the public, the media, infrastructure owners, private businesses, and others who take part in coping with the emergency? How will you communicate if the power goes out or telephones stop working?
   - What vulnerabilities have you discovered that would put our community at risk in different kinds of crises? What are you doing to repair those vulnerabilities? How can we, the people, help?
   - Do you know the exact steps to take to call for assistance from other levels of government? Have you trained with other parts of the government to ensure you and they are in synch?
   - Do our leaders, and others in interconnected areas, practice in a realistic process that simulates the pressure and chaos you are likely to face in a real crisis? Have you done that kind of training as a team? How recently? What action did you take as a result of the training?
   - Do you only practice established plans and routines or do you also practice, as a team, improvising solutions for new and unanticipated situations?
   - Have you brought in experts to validate our community's planning and training? Have you communicated your approach to

planning and training to build confidence in your leadership? Do you think you have told us, your constituents, what we need to know and how we can help if a crisis should hit?

All these steps—making the Patriot Act permanent, responsibly using pro-filing, counteracting material support to terrorist organizations, equipping our police officers and our communities to be better informed and more effective in preventing attacks, and preparing ourselves and our leaders to deal with disaster should it come—are necessary to protect our homeland as best we can, in the face of the threat posed by the Islamofascists and their allies. Doing anything less is not an option.

STEP 6

Counter the Mega-Threat: EMP Attack

With Contributions from U.S. Rep. Curt Weldon and U.S. Rep. Roscoe Bartlett

I f Osama bin Laden's al-Qaeda—or the dictators of North Korea or Iran—had the ability to destroy America as a superpower, would they be tempted to try?

Wouldn't that temptation be even greater if that result could be achieved with a single attack, involving just one nuclear weapon, perhaps even one of modest power and relatively unsophisticated design?

And, what if the attacker could be reasonably sure that the United States would not know who was responsible for such a devastating blow?

Unfortunately, that scenario is not far-fetched. This kind of attack might be what one (or more) of our enemies *already has in mind for us.*

A Blue-Ribbon Warning

This is not empty speculation. It is the conclusion of a report issued in 2004 by a blue-ribbon commission created by Congress. The commission found that a single nuclear weapon, delivered by a ballistic missile to an altitude of a few hundred miles over the United States, would be "capable of causing catastrophe for the nation."

How is that possible? By precipitating a lethal electromagnetic pulse (EMP) attack.

In 2000, concerned about EMP technology, Congress created the "Commission to Assess the Threat to the United States from Electromagnetic Pulse Attack" (the EMP Threat Commission, for short). In its final report,[1] presented in summer 2004, the panel warned that terrorists could indeed execute such an attack by launching a small nuclear-armed missile from a freighter off the coast of the United States.

The ingredients for an EMP attack may be already within reach.

◆ Al-Qaeda is known to have a *fleet of freighters.*

◆ One of those freighters could easily be outfitted with a short-range *ballistic missile* capable of getting a nuclear weapon to almost any point in the airspace above our country.

◆ Thousands of *Scud missiles* exist around the world, and they are said to cost less than $100,000 to purchase from willing suppliers like North Korea. (In December 2002, a North Korean ship was intercepted, temporarily, as it prepared to deliver twelve Scud missiles to Yemen.)

◆ North Korea has also declared its willingness to sell *nuclear weapons* to terrorists.

◆ Iran has demonstrated it has the *capability to launch* a Scud missile from a vessel at sea.

Ship-launched ballistic missiles have a special advantage. The "return address" of the attacker may be difficult to determine, especially if the missile is a generic Scud-type weapon, found in many countries' arsenals.

But even though all the tools needed for this nightmare scenario could be in the hands of terrorists already, and even though a high-altitude EMP attack could be considered the ultimate "weapon of mass destruction," little has changed in our level of preparedness or even our policy debates. EMP is still rarely mentioned in discussions of the WMDs we need to worry about.

We need to start worrying.

An Atmospheric Tsunami

A nuclear weapon produces several different effects. The best known are the intense heat and hyperpressures associated with the fireball and the accompanying blast.

But a nuclear explosion also generates massive outputs of other kinds of energy. These include the creation of intense streams of x-rays and

---

1   The unclassified executive summary of the commission's report may be viewed at
    http://empcreport.ida.org.

gamma-rays. If those are unleashed outside the earth's atmosphere, some of them will interact with the air molecules of the upper atmosphere.

The result is an enormous pulsed current of high-energy electrons that will interact, in turn, with the earth's magnetic field.

In an instant, an invisible radio-frequency wave is produced—a wave of almost unimaginably immense intensity, approximately a *million times* as strong as the most powerful radio signals on the earth. The energy of this pulse would reach everything in line of sight of the detonation. And *it would do so at the speed of light.*

The higher the altitude of the weapon's detonation, the larger the affected area would be. At a height of three hundred miles, for example, the entire continental United States would be exposed, along with parts of Canada and Mexico.

As the fireball expands in space, it would also generate electrical currents on earth—ultra-high-speed electromagnetic "shock waves" that would endanger much of our technological infrastructure. Such high-speed currents would disable, temporarily or permanently,

- extended electrical conductors, such as the electricity transmission lines that make up our power grid.
- any unprotected computers and microchips.
- all the systems that depend on electricity and electronics, from medical instruments to military communications.

  As the EMP Threat Commission put it: The electromagnetic fields produced by weapons designed and deployed with the intent to produce EMP have a high likelihood of damaging electrical power systems, electronics, and information systems upon which American society depends. *Their effects on dependent systems and infrastructures could be sufficient to qualify as catastrophic to the nation.* [Emphasis added.]

The systems at risk from EMP include:

- electronic control, sensor, and protective systems of all kinds
- computers and cell phones
- cars, boats, airplanes, and trains
- the infrastructures for handling electric power, telecommunications, transportation, fuel and energy, banking and finance, emergency services, and even food and water.

A One-Two-Three Punch

Following rapidly on this electromagnetic tsunami, there would be a "medium-speed component" of EMP. It would cover roughly the same geographic area as the first, "high-speed" component, though its peak power level would be much less.

This medium-speed component follows the high-speed component by merely a fraction of a second. It further damages the electric systems that are already impaired and exposed by the initial electromagnetic impact.

And finally, there is a third wave of EMP attack, the "slow component" produced by the continuing expansion of the fireball in the earth's magnetic field. This slow component—a pulse that may last just seconds or minutes—creates disruptive currents in electricity transmission lines, damaging the surviving electrical supply and distribution systems.

Unpredicted Test Effects

The destructive power of EMP effects was first glimpsed in the atmospheric nuclear tests of the Cold War era. The United States and the Soviet Union independently discovered the same phenomenon: a high-altitude nuclear explosion could damage or destroy electronic systems on the earth, with potentially devastating consequences for the targeted society.

- ◆ In 1962, the United States conducted a test called "Starfish," detonating a nuclear weapon about 250 miles above Johnston Island in the Pacific Ocean. The resulting EMP reached all the way to the Hawaiian Islands, a little over 700 miles away. There, on the far edge of the EMP field, the explosion extinguished streetlights in Honolulu, tripped circuit breakers, triggered burglar alarms, and damaged a telecommunications relay facility.
- ◆ The Soviet tests included a series of high-altitude nuclear detonations over South Central Asia. EMP from these tests damaged overhead (and even underground) electrical cables at a range of 375 miles, causing surge arrestor burnout, blown fuses, and blackouts.

The consequences of an EMP attack would of course be far more significant today, with so much of our infrastructure (civilian as well as military) dependent on electricity and electronics. The EMP Threat Commission estimated that it could take "months to years" to fully restore critical infrastructures after an EMP attack:

Depending on the specific characteristics of the attacks, unprecedented cascading failures of our major infrastructures could result. In that event, a regional or national recovery would be long and difficult and would seriously degrade the safety and overall viability of our nation. The primary avenues for catastrophic damage to the nation are through our electric power infrastructure and thence into our telecommunications, energy, and other infrastructures. These, in turn, can seriously impact other important aspects of our nation's life, including the financial system; means of getting food, water, and medical care to the citizenry; trade; and production of goods and services.

The recovery of any one of the key national infrastructures is dependent on the recovery of others. The longer the outage, the more problematic and uncertain the recovery will be. It is possible for the functional outages to become mutually reinforcing until *at some point the degradation of infrastructure could have irreversible effects on the country's ability to support its population.* [Emphasis added.]

What Is Being Done to Address the Danger?

An EMP attack potentially represents a high-tech means for terrorists to kill millions of Americans the old-fashioned way, through starvation and disease. Although the direct physical effects of EMP are harmless to people, a well-designed and well-executed EMP attack could kill—*indirectly*—far more Americans than a nuclear weapon detonated in our most populous city.

Dr. Lowell Wood of Lawrence Livermore Laboratory, a member of the EMP Threat Commission, has warned in testimony before Congress that an EMP attack could reduce the United States to a *pre-Industrial Age capacity*, in terms of its ability to provide vital food and water to its population.

In 1900, prior to widespread electrification of the United States, our country's population was less than one-third of its size today. An attack that destroyed our technological infrastructure would certainly decimate the population.

But if EMP is such a big threat, why have we not heard more about it? Why do we not hear discussions of how to reduce its potential impact on this country? In fact, the EMP Threat Commission was the outcome of four years of hearings and briefings, as a frustrated Congress tried to alert the executive branch to the danger of EMP attack.

Their efforts seemed futile. In 1997, Gen. Robert Marsh (then-chairman of the Commission on Critical Infrastructure Protection) told the House Armed Services Committee:

> [W]e consider a terrorist acquiring a nuclear weapon, and positioning it at the high altitude necessary for generation of an EMP burst that would debilitate our infrastructures, to be a very remote possibility. . . . Such an event is so unlikely and difficult to achieve that *I do not believe it warrants serious concern at this time.* [Emphasis added.]

In contrast, the testimony Congress received from other sources strongly suggested that such a devastating attack was neither unlikely nor difficult to achieve. It seemed that there was, in fact, reason to be concerned that terrorists and rogue states might present an EMP threat to the United States.

Concerned members of congress received help from an unlikely quarter in May 1999, when Russia explicitly invoked the specter of an EMP attack on the United States. Vladimir Lukin (the chairman of the Duma International Affairs Committee) assured a delegation of American legislators that Russia was not helpless in the face of U.S.-led interventions:

> Hypothetically, if Russia really wanted to hurt the United States in retaliation for NATO's bombing of Yugoslavia, Russia could fire a submarine-launched ballistic missile and detonate a single nuclear warhead at high-altitude over the United States. The resulting electromagnetic pulse would massively disrupt U.S. communications and computer systems, shutting down everything.

This blunt statement succeeded in getting the attention of both parties in Congress. A second opinion was clearly needed. And on October 30, 2000, the EMP Threat Commission was established by law.

The EMP Threat Today

The EMP Threat Commission conducted a worldwide survey of foreign scientific and military literature to assess the knowledge and intentions of foreign states regarding an EMP attack. The survey confirmed that both the physics and the military potential of EMP are indeed widely understood in the international community.

The commission survey found that the following nations were knowledgeable about EMP: China, Cuba, Egypt, India, Iran, Saddam Hussein's Iraq, North Korea, Pakistan, and Russia.

The commission also learned that some foreign military experts regard EMP attack as a form of electronic or information warfare, not primarily as a form of nuclear war. One of China's leading military theorists has written:

> Information war and traditional war have one thing in common, namely that the country which possesses the critical weapons such as atomic bombs will have "first strike" and "second strike retaliation" capabilities . . . .
>
> As soon as its computer networks come under attack and are destroyed, the country will slip into a state of paralysis and the lives of its people will grind to a halt. (Su Tzu-Yun, *World War: The Third World War—Total Information Warfare*, 2001.)

In Iran—the most unabashed state-sponsor of international terrorism today—some theorists have argued that the key to defeating the United States lies in attacking its electronics. This is from an Iranian political-military policy journal:

> Once you confuse the enemy communication network, you can also disrupt the work of the enemy command and decision-making center.
>
> Even worse, today when you disable a country's military high command through disruption of communications you will, in effect, disrupt all the affairs of that country. . . . If the world's industrial countries fail to devise effective ways to defend themselves against dangerous electronic assaults, then they will disintegrate within a few years. . . . American soldiers would not be able to find food to eat nor would they be able to fire a single shot. ("Electronics to Determine Fate of Future Wars," *Nashriyeh-e Siasi Nezami,* 1999.)

And this implied threat may not be empty words. In addition to their successful ship-launched Scud missile test, the Iranian military has reportedly performed tests of its Shahab-3 medium-range ballistic missile in a manner consistent with an EMP attack scenario.

America the Vulnerable

The EMP Threat Commission noted (ominously, in this context) that "the U.S. has developed more than most other nations as a modern society heavily dependent on electronics, telecommunications, energy, information networks, and a rich set of financial and transportation systems that leverage modern technology."

Given our acute national dependence on such technologies, it is astonishing—and alarming—to realize how vulnerable they still are.

♦ Very little redundancy has been built into America's critical infrastructure.

   To give just one example, there should be a parallel "national security power grid," built with greater resiliency than the civilian grid.

♦ America's critical infrastructure has scarcely any capacity to spare in the event of disruption, even in one part of the country, let alone nationwide.

   Remember the electrical blackout that crippled the northeastern United States for a few days in 2003?

♦ America is generally ill prepared to reconstitute damaged or destroyed electrical and electricity-dependent systems.

The aftermath of Hurricane Katrina is a powerful reminder that America has for many years neglected civil defense preparedness. The lingering effects of that cataclysmic storm have exposed the vulnerability of our highly efficient, but not always resilient, economy.

A Tempting Target

The technological advances that make us an unequaled military and economic superpower are also the source of our gravest vulnerability.

In a world wracked by terrorists and their state sponsors, America's strength has become a tempting target. And EMP technology may represent an irresistible opportunity.

An EMP attack would target the very source of our technological achievements—the electronic circuit—as a way of bringing us to our knees. And it would do it by unleashing its own massive storm, in the form of a kind of rogue electromagnetic current.

This tactic perhaps has a special appeal for the Islamofascists. They are stridently contemptuous both of our man-made sources of power and of the sorts of democratic, humane, and secular societies that these sources help make possible.

Our enemies are undoubtedly also aware of these additional tactical considerations:

♦ An EMP attack could severely degrade our ability to retaliate, even if we could be sure who was responsible.

◆ Determining responsibility would be much more difficult if electrical systems, telecommunications, and other infrastructure were disabled.

◆ Although U.S. forces deployed overseas might avoid damage in such an attack, the systems that transmit their orders and sustain their operations would almost certainly be disrupted.

◆ Overseas forces might also be targeted by EMP strikes in their theaters of operations.

Our Unprepared Military

This danger is all the greater because many of our military systems are arguably as vulnerable as our civilian technologies.

With the end of the Cold War, the U.S. Defense Department shied away from spending the funds necessary to shield equipment from electromagnetic pulses. Moreover, the Pentagon rapidly lost its capacity to understand and address EMP (particularly during the Clinton presidency), as EMP simulators were mothballed or even dismantled.

And, inevitably, the cessation of underground nuclear testing meant that the national nuclear laboratories could no longer provide our armed forces with *the most reliable means* of assessing the EMP vulnerabilities—and the available safeguards—for their advanced weapons, sensors, telecommunications gear, and satellites.

Finally, even those military systems that were protected against traditional EMP effects might be unable to withstand the more intense electromagnetic effects generated by nuclear weapons specifically designed to maximize such effects. Without a robust program for assessing such advanced designs (one that may well require nuclear testing), we are unlikely to be able to quantify such threats, let alone to protect even our military resources against them.

What Needs to Be Done

EMP attack poses a clear and present danger to our national security, our technological society, and our democratic and cosmopolitan way of life. We have no choice but to take urgent action to mitigate this danger.

Fortunately, the EMP Threat Commission has presented a blueprint for protecting both U.S. military forces and the U.S. homeland from EMP attack. The blueprint involves a comprehensive approach. If implemented, it could greatly reduce our vulnerability to the catastrophic effects of an EMP attack in a reasonable period of time (perhaps three to five years) and at relatively modest cost.

The EMP Threat Commission's plan includes three focused efforts.

1. **Deter EMP attacks.** We must make it difficult and dangerous to acquire the materials to make nuclear weapons and the means to deliver them. We must hold at risk of capture or destruction anyone who has such weaponry, wherever they are in the world. Those who engage in or support these activities must be made to understand that they do so at the risk of everything they value. Those who harbor or help those who conspire to create these weapons must suffer serious consequences as well.

These measures will require the following:

♦ vastly improved intelligence
♦ the capacity to perform clandestine operations throughout the world
♦ assured means of retaliating with devastating effect after an EMP attack.

For this reason, among others, we must act now and adopt a program to ensure that our deterrent forces are safe, reliable, and credible.[2] We must also ensure the certain ability to command and control those forces.

A more controversial factor in deterrence is the timely communication (through private, if not public, channels) of the targets identified for potential retaliation—irrespective of whether a definitive determination can be made of responsibility for an EMP attack on this country.

2. **Defeat EMP attacks.** We must protect our critical military capabilities and civilian infrastructure from the effects of EMP attacks. This will require a comprehensive assessment of our vulnerabilities and assessment of the effectiveness of corrective measures. We must swiftly rebuild our neglected scientific and technical base for conducting and analyzing EMP tests of military and civilian equipment.

The EMP Threat Commission judged that, given the sorry state of EMP preparedness on the part of the tactical forces of the United States and its coalition partners, "it is not possible to protect [all of them] from EMP in a regional conflict." The commission recommended that priority be given to protecting "satellite navigation systems, satellite and airborne intelligence and targeting systems, [and] an adequate communications infrastructure."

The threat of EMP attack means that an effective ballistic missile defense system is all the more imperative. We know that a catastrophic EMP attack

---

2   For more on the need to restore the U.S. nuclear deterrent—and what it will take to do so—see Appendix II's contributions from Vice Adm. Robert R. Monroe, the former director of the Defense Nuclear Agency.

can be mounted only by putting a nuclear weapon into space over the United States. We also know that, as a practical matter, this can be done most surely and easily via a ballistic missile. It is imperative, therefore, that the United States deploy as quickly as possible a comprehensive defense against such delivery systems.

Fortunately, the fastest and most cost-effective way to get such a defense is at hand. We need to give the U.S. Navy's existing fleet of some sixty AEGIS air-defense ships the capability to shoot down short- to medium-range missiles— the kind that might well be used to carry out ship-launched EMP strikes.[3]

3. **Reduce our vulnerability to EMP attacks.** Finally, we must prepare for the consequences of an EMP attack in the event that deterrence and protection fail. This will require close collaboration between government *at all levels* and the private sector, which owns, designs, builds, and operates most of the nation's critical infrastructure.

We need to do a far better job of monitoring our infrastructure. We must be prepared to take corrective action should it be disrupted or destroyed by EMP attacks.

We must ensure that we have on hand, and *properly protected*, the equipment and parts needed to repair EMP-damaged systems. As the EMP Threat Commission observed, this is especially important for those components that are difficult or time-consuming to produce: "large turbines, generators, and high-voltage transformers in electrical power systems, and electronic switching systems in telecommunications systems."

Blueprint for Preparedness

The EMP Threat Commission plan goes on to provide detailed and in-depth recommendations for protecting the nation's critical infrastructures. Here are the highlights of the plan, as presented by the commission.

> **Electric power grid.** It is impractical to protect the entire electric power system from damage by an EMP attack. There are too many components of too many different types, manufacturers, designs, and vulnerabilities within too many jurisdictional entities, and the cost to retrofit is too great. . . . However, by protecting key system components needed for restoration, by structuring the network to fail gracefully, and by creating a comprehensive prioritized recovery plan for the most critical power needs, the risk of an EMP attack having a catastrophic effect on the Nation can be greatly reduced.

---

3   See Appendix III for more on the steps needed rapidly to deploy effective sea-based missile defenses.

Telecommunications. Effective mitigation strategies include a combination of site-hardening and installation of protective measures [against the fastest and most intense burst of EMP energy]. [We must] improve the ability of telecommunications to withstand the sustained loss of utility-supplied electric power. . . . [We should also] conduct exercises that test and provide for improved contingency operations, assuming widespread multi-infrastructure degradation.

Transportation. The ability of the major transportation infrastructure components to recover depends on the plans in place and the availability of resources—including spare parts and support from other critical infrastructures upon which transportation is dependent. . . .

[We must] perform test-based assessments of railroad traffic control centers and retrofit modest EMP protection into these facilities, thereby minimizing the potential for adverse long-term EMP effects. . . .

[We must] initiate an outreach program to educate state and local authorities and traffic engineers on EMP effects and the expectation of traffic signal malfunctions, vehicle disruption and damage, and consequent traffic congestion.

[We must] work with municipalities to formulate recovery plans, including emergency clearing of traffic congestion and provisioning spare controller cards that could be used to repair controller boxes. . . .

The Department of Homeland Security should coordinate a government program in cooperation with the FAA to perform an operational assessment of the air traffic control system to identify a "thin-line" that provides the minimum essential capabilities necessary to return the air traffic control capability to at least a basic level of service after an EMP attack.

Food and Water. Federal, state and regional governments should establish plans for assuring that food is available to the general population in case of a major disruption of the food infrastructure. Planning to locate, preserve, deliver, distribute, and ration existing stockpiles of processed and unprocessed food—including food stockpiled by the Department of Agriculture, Department of Defense, and other government agencies—will be an important component of maintaining the food supply. Planning to protect, deliver, and ration food from regional warehouses, under conditions where an EMP attack has disrupted the power, transportation, and other infrastructures for a protracted period, should be a priority.

Because there is so much to do in all of these areas, it would be wise to take one further critical step: **Extend the life of the EMP Threat Commission** for four additional years. This would ensure that Congress, the relevant departments and agencies of the U.S. government, and the private sector can continue to benefit from this invaluable "second opinion" on the EMP threat and on progress being made to protect the country against it.

We Have Been Warned

The members of the EMP Threat Commission—who are some of the nation's most eminent experts in the field of nuclear weapons design and effects—have rendered a real and timely public service. In view of the dire warnings they have issued, there is no excuse for our continued inaction.

But the inescapable fact is that—although the Department of Defense has recently issued its own assessment, which is said to confirm the findings of the EMP Threat Commission and to endorse its recommendations—the commission's report has received little serious attention to date from the White House, the Department of Homeland Security, the Congress, or the media. Allowing Americans to remain ignorant of the EMP danger and the urgent need to address it ensures that we will remain tragically unprepared for a danger as serious as any we have ever faced.

And by remaining unprepared for such an attack, we are surely inviting it.

The good news is that steps can be taken to mitigate this danger and perhaps to prevent an EMP attack from occurring. The bad news is that there will be significant costs associated with those steps, not only in monetary terms but also in terms of controversial policy decisions.

We have no choice, however, but to bear these costs. The price of continued inaction could be a disaster of infinitely greater cost and unimaginable hardship for this and future generations of Americans.

STEP 7

Secure Our Borders, Secure Our Country

With Contributions from Rosemary Jenks, Jim Staudenraus, Amanda Bowman, and Colleen Gilbert

S teps 5 and 6 offered ways in which America can be better prepared to contend with—and prevent—future, potentially devastating attacks on this country. We cannot hope to protect our homeland, however, unless we take steps to remedy our porous borders, improve dysfunctional immigration policies and procedures, and create systems to ensure the authenticity of identity documents.

These problems were among the defects documented by the staff of the National Commission on Terrorist Attacks upon the United States ("The 9/11 Commission") in a stunning report issued just over a year ago. "It is perhaps obvious to state that terrorists cannot plan and carry out attacks in the United States if they are unable to enter the country . . . [yet] border security still is not considered a cornerstone of national security policy."[1] The commission called on the president and the Congress to close the many loopholes in U.S. immigration law that were exploited by the September 11, 2001, terrorists—and by other terrorists before them.

The Problem Is Political

Unfortunately, neither the president nor the Congress has taken to heart the commission's fundamental finding, that immigration enforcement is critical

---

1   Preface, "9/11 and Terrorist Travel: Staff Report of the National Commission on Terrorist Attacks upon the United States," National Commission on Terrorists Attacks upon the United States, July 2004. Available at http://www.9-11commission.gov/report/911ReportoExec.htm.

to our national security. Unless the U.S. government can control entry to our borders, identify and track visa applicants, and address the problem of illegal immigrants, Americans will be no safer than on September 10, 2001.

As it happens, Congress has already enacted most of the legislation needed to secure America against hostile immigration. The laws we have, however, are not being enforced. The trouble is that national security requirements are regularly trumped by the demands of special interests, which include the cheap-labor lobby, ethnic advocacy groups, some religious organizations, and influential immigration lawyers.

As a result of such pressure, federal agencies refrain—even today—from enforcing all the immigration laws. These agencies tend to focus their enforcement efforts on statutes that can yield positive publicity and offer the public an unwarranted sense of security.

It is obvious (as the commission staff observed) that terrorists operating outside this country cannot carry out attacks on our territory if they cannot enter it. It is equally clear, however, that even well-designed laws will not suffice to keep terrorists out if they can be easily evaded. Similarly, closing loopholes—as the commission recommended, and we endorse—will do little good if the underlying legislation is not properly enforced.

Step 7 of the War Footing therefore calls for:

♦ full enforcement of existing laws relating to border security, immigration, and identity documentation .

♦ elimination of legal loopholes in the areas of illegal immigration, legal immigration, and secure documents.

The "Secure America" Pledge

The first step in achieving better enforcement and corrective legislation must be to create a new political reality—namely, a counterweight to the influential special interests whose priorities take no account of national security.

Opinion polling consistently shows that the majority of Americans, regardless of demographic, ethnic, economic, geographic, sex, and age distinctions or political party affiliation, oppose illegal immigration and want it stopped.[2] The 2004 vote on Arizona's Proposition 200 is the latest indication that the opposition to illegal immigration is real and can be translated into

---

2   For example, see "Elite vs. Public Opinion: An Examination of Divergent Views on Immigration." Public opinion poll conducted by Chicago Council on Foreign Relations, October 2002. Available at http://www.worldviews.org/detailreports/usreport/html/ch5s5.html.

political power. Still, although a large and growing number of organizations are working to express this viewpoint, the necessary political "critical mass" has not yet been achieved on a national basis.

Take the pledge. The time has come for the American public to hold our elected representatives responsible for making the necessary changes in immigration policy, legislation, and enforcement. Toward that end, more than thirty organizations have come together to create the "Secure America" Pledge, a set of ten principles that *every politician in America should be asked to sign.* (The pledge is reproduced as Appendix IV, in a form ready for signature.)

The Secure America Pledge reads as follows:

1. The purpose of U.S. immigration policy is to benefit the citizens of the United States.
2. Because immigration policy can profoundly shape a country, it should be set by deliberate actions, not by accident or acquiescence, with careful consideration to ensure that it does not adversely affect the quality of life of American citizens and their communities.
3. Immigration policy should be based on and adhere to the rule of law. Immigration laws must be enforced consistently and uniformly throughout the United States.
4. Noncitizens enter the United States as guests and must obey the rules governing their entry. The U.S. government must track the entry, stay, and departure of all visa holders to ensure that they comply fully with the terms of their visas or to remove them if they fail to comply.
5. The borders of the United States must be physically secured at the earliest possible time. An effective barrier to the illegal entry of both aliens and contraband is vital to U.S. security.
6. Those responsible for facilitating illegal immigration shall be sought, arrested, and prosecuted to the full extent of the law and shall forfeit any profits from such activity. This applies to smugglers and traffickers of people, as well as to those involved in the production, procurement, distribution, or use of fraudulent or counterfeit documents.
7. U.S. employers shall be given a simple and streamlined process to determine whether employees are legally eligible to work. Employers who obey the law shall be protected both from liability and from unfair competition by those who violate immigration law. The violators shall be subjected to fines and taxes in excess of what they would have paid to employ U.S. citizens and legal residents for the same work.

8. Those who enter or remain in the United States in violation of the law shall be detained and removed expeditiously. Illegal aliens shall not accrue any benefit, including U.S. citizenship, as a result of their illegal entry or presence in the United States.

9. No federal, state, or local entity shall reward individuals for violating immigration laws by granting public benefits or services, or by issuing or accepting any form of identification, or by providing any other assistance that facilitates unlawful presence or employment in this country. All federal and all law-enforcement agencies shall cooperate fully with federal immigration authorities and shall report to such authorities any information they receive indicating that an individual may have violated immigration laws.

10. Illegal aliens currently in the United States may be afforded a one-time opportunity to leave the United States without penalty and seek permission to reenter legally if they qualify under existing law. Those who do not take advantage of this opportunity will be removed and permanently barred from returning.

The implementation of these principles should involve the following steps, as part of a War Footing strategy.

Illegal Immigration

Illegal immigration into the United States represents an obvious threat to national security. Each year, the U.S. Border Patrol catches roughly *1 million* aliens attempting to cross illegally into the United States. That figure, of course, is just a fraction of the number who succeed in entering illegally: at most, only 15 to 20 percent of illegal aliens are actually intercepted, according to quasi-official estimates.

The vast majority of these illegal immigrants are Mexican nationals looking for work. Recently, however, the number of people designated as "Other-than-Mexicans" (OTMs) has skyrocketed, from some 37,000 in 2002 to more than 75,000 in 2004. And the number may double this year again: in the nine months between October 1, 2004, and July 12, 2005, the number of OTMs apprehended by the Border Patrol had reached 119,000.

These OTMs come from every country in the world—including from each and every one of the nations the U.S. government has designated as state sponsors of terrorism.

It is shocking to learn, therefore, that the policy of the federal government's Customs and Border Protection (CBP) has been to *release* OTMs if they are caught. To be sure, they are asked to return at a future date to be processed for removal, in accordance with what is known as the "catch-and-release" policy. Not surprisingly, however, the vast majority of them never show up for deportation; instead, they simply disappear into American society.

What Needs to Be Done

The most urgent priority is to secure our porous borders. A large part of the problem is the sheer volume of illegal aliens crossing our border each year, overwhelming the wholly inadequate number of CPB personnel assigned to prevent them from getting in.

Border Patrol resources, including personnel, have increased steadily over the years, but they are still far from sufficient. CBP has only 10,700 Border Patrol agents, tasked to guard 7,500 miles of land borders—twenty-four hours a day, seven days a week—against penetration by terrorists, criminals, and contraband. With three rotations per day, and normal absences for leave time and training days, the number of agents on the job at any given time is desperately small.

Similar understaffing afflicts the immigration and customs divisions, who are responsible for controlling 350 official ports of entry, including land crossings, seaports, and airports. The following steps need to be taken immediately:

1. Border Security

A. **Augment the Border Patrol.** The first, urgent task is to augment the Border Patrol and its sister agencies, either directly or indirectly. The fastest approach would be to bring in military personnel to augment the Border Patrol by helping to locate illegal entrants, and then monitor or detain them—or possibly assist in their arrest.[3]

---

3   As noted in Step 5, arguments that putting the military on the border to assist the Border Patrol would violate the prohibition on posse comitatus are misleading. The military would enforce no laws against U.S. citizens; it would be performing its original function of defending the country from invaders. Moreover, Congress has enacted a number of exceptions to the Posse Comitatus Act that have direct relevance for the use of the military in counterterrorist measures at the border:

  ♦   Counter-drug assistance (Title 10 USC, Sections 371-381).
  ♦   Assistance in enforcing prohibitions regarding nuclear materials (Title 18 USC, Section 831), when the Attorney General and the Secretary of Defense jointly determine that an emergency situation poses a serious threat to United States interests, beyond the capability of civilian law-enforcement agencies.
  ♦   Emergency situations involving chemical or biological weapons of mass destruction (Title 10 USC, Section 382); see http://www.northcom.mil/index.cfm?fuseaction=news.factsheets&factsheet=5#pca.

There are advantages to such a cooperative effort, on both sides. The Border Patrol would gain access to the military's superior technology, including unmanned aerial vehicles, detection devices, vision-enhancing devices, and so forth, accompanied by personnel trained in using them. The military would gain valuable training in virtually every type of terrain, on U.S. land borders traversing the arid deserts of Arizona, the frozen mountains of Montana, and the dense forests of Maine.

Interim assistance from the military would give us time: to recruit, hire, and train a sufficient number of new Border Patrol agents; to implement testing and training for the technological tools that will make these agents more efficient; and—most important—to build where appropriate permanent physical barriers to illegal immigration.

B. **"We need a fence."** High-tech security fences would make it vastly more difficult for illegal immigrants to transit our land borders. Even the existing, relatively primitive fences erected along stretches of our Mexican border have cut dramatically the number of aliens crossing illegally through that sector.

As long as there are gaps in the fence, however, the effect is largely to reroute the illegal immigrant flows to unfenced and generally barren border areas—often resulting in deaths from exposure in the harsh desert conditions. We will save lives, as well as protect our country, if we swiftly close these gaps and secure the entire southern boundary with a "fence," or, more accurately, a fifty-yard-wide, multilayered composite obstacle.[4]

Such a fence would include these features:

+ a ditch
+ coils of barbed wire
+ two tall, sturdy wire fences, with sensors to warn of any incursion
+ a patrol path for vehicles between the fences
+ a smoothed strip of sand that runs parallel to the fence, to detect footprints
+ closed-circuit TV cameras and motion detectors
+ up to two hundred legal crossing points to permit cross-border commercial, tourist, and legitimate commuting traffic.

The cost of this state-of-the-art barrier, along the two thousand miles of the U.S.-Mexico border, is estimated to be between $2 billion and $4 billion. Such an outlay, though large, would result over time in substantially lower manpower costs associated with monitoring the border. There

---

4   For more on this initiative, see the Let Freedom Ring Project's Web site: http://www.WeNeedaFence.com.

would also be lower costs in other areas, notably the social, economic, and national security implications associated with illegal immigration.

C. **Secure the Mexican border first.** Securing the Mexican border must be the immediate priority. After all, that is the route used to gain access to this country by the vast majority of illegal immigrants. There is evidence that would-be Islamist terrorists have targeted known smuggling operations across our southern frontier as a means of gaining entry into the United States. In February 2005, Adm. James Loy, the then-deputy secretary of the Department of Homeland Security, told Congress:

> Recent information . . . strongly suggests that al-Qaeda has considered using the Southwest Border to infiltrate the United States. Several al-Qaeda leaders believe operatives can pay their way into the country through Mexico and also believe illegal entry is more advantageous for operational security reasons.[5]

Another source of concern about the southern border is the fact that (as discussed in Step 9) Latin America is increasingly a locus of organizations and activity threatening to the United States.

For example, the so-called Tri-Border area of South America—the area where Argentina, Paraguay, and Brazil meet—has become a haven for illicit activities that generate billions of dollars annually, in money-laundering, arms and drug trafficking, counterfeiting, document falsification, and piracy. This region of Latin America also hosts a large community of Arab and Muslim expatriates, including nationals of countries known to sponsor terrorism. The Tri-Border region is thus a natural terrorist habitat, affording safe haven, sources of financing, access to illegal weapons and advanced technologies, easy movement and concealment, and a sympathetic host population. Ease of movement to and through Mexico gives such groups ready access to our southern border.

> We have Cold War mindsets that are not adequate for today. The United States thinks of Latin America as a benign backyard. They are wrong. It is a nightmare ready to go north, and the Americans don't understand that.
>
> —Robert Steele, USMC (Ret.), former deputy director, U.S. Marine Corps Intelligence, March 2003

D. **Do not neglect Canada**. The U.S. border with Canada is even longer, and far more open, than the one we share with Mexico. Unfortunately, it

---

5 Loy testimony before the Senate Select Committee on Intelligence, February 2005.

must also be considered a likely clandestine point for entry for terrorists. According to the Canadian Security Intelligence Service (CSIS), "With the possible exception of the United States, there are more international terrorist organizations active in Canada than anywhere in the world."[6]

In fact, Canada has long been home to front groups and supporters of some of the most violent terrorist groups in the world. These include al-Qaeda, Hamas, Egyptian Al Jihad, and various other Sunni Islamic extremist groups, as well as Hezbollah and other Shi'ite terrorist groups. Canada also has supporters of the Provisional Irish Republican Army (PIRA), the Tamil Tigers (LTTE), the Kurdistan Workers Party (PKK), and each of the major Sikh terrorist groups.

Canada's permissive asylum and refugee policies serve as the primary magnet for these terrorist groups and their supporters. The CSIS reports that terrorist groups operating within Canada use the country as a base for fund-raising, lobbying through front organizations, procuring weapons, and facilitating transit to and from the United States.

Under these circumstances, America must also make a concerted effort to help the Canadian authorities identify and neutralize such operations across the border, undertake systemic reform of its asylum policies, and take all practicable steps to monitor and secure our northern frontier.

2. Interior Enforcement

A. **Establish worksite enforcement.** All sides of the immigration debate recognize that jobs are the key to controlling illegal immigration. Most illegal aliens come to the United States seeking jobs. If they were not able to obtain jobs once they arrived—and could not get access to public welfare (see "Secure Identification," below)—they would have little choice but to leave. Many would choose not to come in the first place. As long as jobs are easily available, however, some illegal immigration will continue, regardless of what barriers or other measures are put into place to impede such flows.

The bottom line is that unlawful immigration provides ready cover for those coming with the intention to harm us. It is highly relevant to the War for the Free World that we find a way to turn off the jobs magnet for illegal aliens.

This is made more difficult because of the political realities that shape our immigration policy. The federal law that makes it illegal knowingly

---

6   "The Current Canadian Picture," Canadian Security Intelligence Service (CSIS), August 9, 2002.

to hire an unauthorized alien was *designed* to fail. Employers are allowed to accept from a prospective employee any of a number of easily forged documents as proof that they are legally eligible to work here. That being the case, it is rarely possible to prove that an employer *knew* the alien was illegal—making the law almost unenforceable.

B. **The "Basic Pilot."** The 1996 Illegal Immigration Reform and Immigrant Responsibility Act (IIRIRA) required the creation of several pilot programs that would allow employers to verify that a new hire was legally authorized to work. Of these experimental initiatives, only one is still in existence—the Basic Pilot, which verifies that the new hire's Social Security number and name and date of birth match according to the Social Security Administration's (SSA) records.

The Basic Pilot is an automated, online system that is simple to use and provides instant confirmation in 80 to 85 percent of all inquiries. (The remaining 15 to 20 percent take somewhat more time, because the new hire must be given an opportunity to correct any incorrect data that either the Social Security Administration or the Department of Homeland Security may have recorded.)

Currently, however, use of the Basic Pilot is *voluntary*, which means that honest employers who want to obey the law will use it, whereas those who want to continue employing illegal aliens will not. Such an arrangement places honest employers at an economic disadvantage, because their dishonest competitors are able to pay lower wages and benefits to illegal workers.

Congress must therefore make employers' use of the Basic Pilot program *mandatory* to level the playing field for employers. Curbing employment of illegal workers is the first, critical step toward encouraging the millions already here to return home and to discourage additional aliens from trying to sneak into the United States.

C. **Institute an effective, automated entry/exit system.** Well before the September 11 terrorist attacks, Congress noted the need for an automated, nationwide system to track foreign visitors and to prevent terrorists from entering through border checkpoints and ports. Nothing has changed, even though just such a system was required by IIRIRA in 1996—and even though the perpetrators of the September 11 attacks took lethal advantage of this deficiency.[7]

---

7   Janice Kephart, "Immigration and Terrorism, Moving Beyond the 9/11 Staff report on Terrorist Travel," Center for Immigration Studies, September 2005. Available at http://www.cis.org/articles/2005/kephart.html.

It is a fact that America's private sector tracks movie rentals and credit cards far more effectively than the federal government tracks the aliens who enter our country.

- In 2004, Americans rented and returned about 2.6 billion DVDs and videos.[8]
- Americans carry more than 300 million Visa branded credit cards, and every day of the year more than 200 million Americans make a credit card purchase with their Visa cards. Using advanced algorithms, constantly updated databases, and high-speed communications, each of these 200 million purchases is approved within seconds—and fraud is reduced to 0.05 percent to 0.07 percent.[9]

In the two pieces of legislation that were its principal responses to September 11—the Patriot Act of 2001 (see Step 5) and the Enhanced Border Security and Visa Entry Reform Act of 2002—Congress renewed its call for an automated entry/exit system. Such a system would help to address the challenges posed by *both* illegal and legal immigration.

The Department of Homeland Security has finally begun to deploy the *entry* portion of the system as part of the immigration inspection process for selected aliens. Known as the "United States Visitor Immigration Status Indicator Technology" (or US-VISIT), the system fingerprints and photographs arriving aliens and verifies that their biometric data match the biometric data stored on their visas.

Americans who have watched television images of foreign visitors being photographed and fingerprinted by U.S. officials might conclude that this system is helping to protect them from new waves of foreign terrorists who might be trying to gain access to this country in some illegal fashion. Regrettably, that is not the case. Despite an initial investment of almost $1 billion, US-VISIT is being implemented in a way that makes it virtually useless in terms of keeping terrorists out of the United States.

- Most visitors who enter at border crossings, as opposed to airports, are not screened at all under the system.
- Almost all Canadians and Mexicans, who make up about 80 percent of entrants by land, have been exempted from the system.

---

8   Video Software Dealers Association, Encino, CA. See
http://www.idealink.org/Resource.phx/vsda/pressroom/rev-trend.htx.
9   Website of Visa, USA Inc. San Francisco, CA, http://www.usa.visa.com.

These exemptions continue even after eight Canadian nationals were found by US-VISIT to have suspected links to terrorism. These Canadians were screened only because they tried to enter the United States *through airports*, rather than by land, where they would likely have been waived through.

♦ US-VISIT currently records only 22 percent of foreign visitors as they enter and an even smaller fraction of the aliens departing the country.

♦ The system is available only in *secondary* inspection stations, rather than primary inspection locations, so only those aliens who are referred for secondary inspection are processed through it.

The law mandating the creation of US-VISIT is clear. It requires that the entry into and the departure from the United States of *"every alien"* be recorded. That means that *every noncitizen*—not just every visitor or every non-Canadian or non-Mexican visitor—is supposed to be screened before he or she is admitted into the country. And the departure of every noncitizen should be confirmed.

The reasons for this broad application are obvious: (1) a biometric verification process is highly resistant to fraud or counterfeiting; and (2) recording entry and departure is the only way to address the estimated 40 percent of the illegal alien population who arrive on valid, short-term visas and stay past the expiration date.

D. **Take advantage of available force-multipliers.** Immigration and Customs Enforcement (ICE) is responsible for the enforcement of immigration laws in the interior of the United States. As such, their mission includes worksite enforcement, the removal of criminal aliens, antigang activities, and antismuggling operations. In addition, the agency is charged with combating marriage fraud, document fraud, and other types of immigration fraud. ICE also is responsible for removing from the United States the estimated 450,000 "absconders"—illegal aliens, ordered deported by the courts, who disappeared before they could be removed from the country. Among these absconders are an estimated 80,000 convicted criminals.

With approximately 2,000 immigration agents and fewer than 20,000 detention beds to accomplish all this, ICE is simply unable to perform its many vital functions. Fortunately, we can readily augment the manpower available for the ICE mission at relatively low cost by using other appropriate law-enforcement personnel and assets.

For example, there are 650,000 *state and local law-enforcement officers* across the country. Many of them come into contact with illegal aliens and other criminal aliens every day in the course of their duties. All law-enforcement officers have the inherent authority to enforce federal immigration laws, just as they enforce other federal laws. In fact, it is a *violation of federal law* for any state or local entity to adopt a "sanctuary" policy, formal or informal, that restricts an employee's ability to communicate or otherwise cooperate with federal immigration authorities.

E. **Make federal data available to other law-enforcement personnel.** If state and local authorities are to help ICE do its job, federal immigration authorities must provide them with relevant information. Data on illegal and criminal aliens must be made available to authorized personnel via the National Crime Information Center (NCIC) database. State and local police also need access to terrorist watch-list information so they can identify and arrest listed aliens and immigration absconders discovered during routine traffic stops and other enforcement activities.

Two notable incidents dramatize the need for better coordination:

- Mohammed Atta, the ringleader of the September 11 terrorists, had already overstayed an expired visa when he was ticketed in Broward County, Florida, in spring 2001 for driving without a license.
- Maryland State Police stopped September 11 hijacker Ziad Jarrah for a routine traffic stop—two days before September 11, 2001.

Had police had access to the information they needed to detain either or both of these terrorists, the entire plot might have unraveled. Instead, both were allowed to go on their way.

F. **The federal authorities must do their part.** If we are to ask state and local police to assist with enforcement of federal immigration laws, we must also require federal immigration authorities to respond when local authorities request assistance. Specifically, immigration authorities must be required either to take custody of aliens apprehended by local authorities or to reimburse local authorities for the costs of detaining such aliens.

Legal Immigration

Although illegal immigration is the most likely avenue for terrorists and other enemies to gain access to this country, we must also ensure that the legal immigration system functions to keep such individuals out. Obviously, the larger the number of visitors or would-be permanent residents, the more challenging the task of conducting background checks for terrorist connections or other criminal activity.

Today, these numbers are huge: around 1 million legal, permanent immigrants enter the country each year—about the same number as are caught coming here illegally, or unlawfully overstaying a temporary visa to settle in the United States. And another 25 million to 30 million foreigners enter with some kind of temporary status, including 20 million to 25 million tourists.

What Needs to Be Done

1. **As mentioned above, we must institute an effective entry/exit monitoring system.** An effective, automated system is needed to perform checks on *all* noncitizens, at *all* border entry points, to control both legal and illegal immigration.

2. **Perform rigorous security checks** *before* **issuing visas.** A key lesson of the September 11 experience is the necessity of proper vetting of visa applicants. This is a shared responsibility of the U.S. State Department, which processes visas at its offices overseas, and the U.S. Citizenship and Immigration Service (USCIS), which processes immigration applications filed from within the United States.

   The visa process includes fingerprints, photographs, and extensive background checks on all applicants, designed to reveal whether an applicant has a criminal record or known terrorist connections or otherwise presents a threat to national security. *These data searches are our best line of defense against the next attack on our homeland.*

   Unfortunately, in October 2005, a shocking fact was revealed: Of the four thousand USCIS adjudicators who process and approve visa applications, as many as one-third (thirteen hundred) *have no access to the databases* for the required background checks. Therefore, applications for green cards, citizenship, work permits, and change of status are routinely being processed by adjudicators who have no way of knowing whether the applicant might be a known serial killer or a terrorist.

   Equally troubling, a significant number of "national security" cases (that is, applications for which a records check has generated a national security "indicator"[10]) have been set aside by adjudicators for review. However, the adjudicator tasked with conducting the further review

---

10 A "national security indicator" means that the FBI, CIA, or some other agency has derogatory information about the applicant that is too sensitive to be posted in the database.

may also be *unable to access* the derogatory information. In other words, immigration decisions regarding the entry of potentially dangerous individuals are frequently made without an informed understanding of the actual risk factors.

In light of these revelations from USCIS, Congress should consider ways to correct what ails this agency. At the very least, access to the necessary information must be afforded to all personnel involved in determining visa applications. Other steps to reduce its workload may need to be considered as well. Most important, Congress must impress upon both the State Department and USCIS that visa-related background checks are integral to the security of the country.

3. **Stop the visa lottery from being a game of Russian roulette with terrorists.** In her extraordinary 2002 book, Michelle Malkin discussed one of the most lunatic aspects of our current, dysfunctional immigration system: the practice of holding "visa lotteries"—with no method of excluding terrorists from participating.[11]

For reasons described throughout this book, we have very good reasons to be alert to the danger posed by Islamists who seek to come to this country from terrorist-sponsoring or terrorist-friendly nations such as Saudi Arabia, Iran, Libya, Syria, and Yemen. But instead of restricting—or even scrutinizing—applicants from such states, U.S. immigration law includes a program that appears to be dedicated to providing visas to nationals from such terrorism-friendly places.

In fact, the visa lottery was created in 1990 as a way to "launder" the status of illegal aliens from Ireland. Today, it gives away fifty thousand visas each year through a *random* drawing. Arbitrary standards restrict the eligible pool to individuals (1) who are nationals of countries sending fewer than fifty thousand immigrants to the United States in the previous five years, and (2) who have either a high school education (or equivalent) or two years of work experience or training.

In 2004, about *one-third* of all lottery winners came from Muslim-majority countries. More than 20 percent of all immigrants entering via the visa lottery identified themselves as Muslims, as compared with 8 percent of the total number of legal immigrants.

A number of lottery winners have been involved in terrorism in the United States. Michigan sleeper cell member Karim Koubriti,

---

11 Michelle Malkin, *Invasion: How America Still Welcomes Terrorists, Criminals and Other Foreign Menaces to Our Shores*, Regnery, 2002.

convicted in summer 2005 on terrorism-related charges, was a lottery winner from Morocco. The most notorious lottery winner is Hesham Mohamed Ali Hedayet, the Egyptian immigrant who went to Los Angeles International Airport to kill Jews on July 4, 2002. Hedayet came to this country in 1992 on a temporary visa, became an illegal alien when he overstayed his welcome, was denied asylum, but eventually got a Green card when his wife won the visa lottery.

Ms. Malkin—who is one of our era's most courageous and thoughtful commentators on immigration and other public policy issues—offers a bold concept to address the visa lottery's potentially fatal shortcoming: "immigrant profiling," as a means of distinguishing between those "who want to live the American dream, rather than those who want to come here to dishonor our laws or even kill us" (for more on profiling, see Step 5).

4. **Exclude hateful, violent ideologues.** From colonial times until fifteen years ago, the United States allowed immigration officials to deny admission to aliens espousing ideologies incompatible with American principles. Foolishly—in the mistaken belief that the end of the Cold War meant the end of ideologically motivated warfare against this country—Congress in 1990 dropped ideological grounds as a basis for either excluding visa applicants or deporting aliens once here.

In a recent analysis of this issue, Dr. James Edwards writes:

> The United States has a legitimate right to exclude from her borders foreigners whose main purpose is propaganda or to undermine US policy. This country certainly has a right to bar those aliens predisposed to promote or advance radical ideologies that are inimical to American principles. [F]or a foreigner to serve as a propagandist, a purveyor of hate and violence and sedition, on American soil serves no valid intellectual or political or public purpose.[12]

In the wake of attacks on its soil, Great Britain has initiated a series of measures aimed at preventing Islamofascist operatives and front groups from further exploiting its traditions of religious tolerance and its lax immigration policies. The United States must now do likewise, restoring our traditional

---

12 James Edwards, *Keeping Extremists Out: The History of Ideological Exclusion, and the Need for Its Revival,* Center for Immigration Studies, September, 2005.

principle of ideological exclusion by drawing a line between legitimate religious activities and terrorist indoctrination avowing our destruction.

Secure Identification

Until the attacks of September 11, a driver's license was simply a document kept in the wallet to be thought of pretty much only at renewal time. Since September 11, however, these little cards have been recognized as something else altogether. They are weapons in the War for the Free World—and a dangerous Achilles' heel for the security of our homeland.

Licenses and the September 11 Terrorists

For the September 11 terrorists, the driver's license was the ID card that gave them access to their precision-guided munitions—American Airlines Flight 11; United Airlines Flight 175; American Airlines Flight 77; and United Airlines Flight 93. Because they carried driver's licenses, the nineteen terrorists walked onto those planes with few questions asked.

The hijackers' ability to board those planes using driver's licenses was only half the story. The terrorists had numerous legitimate and phony driver's licenses, obtained from states all over the country.[13] They had exploited various jurisdictions' lax standards for documentation and the absence of any centralized database that might flag unlawful duplication. Some licenses were simply forged, a practice some states have refused to make more difficult.

Armed with these IDs, the murderers of September 11 were able to operate below the radar of law enforcement as they prepared and implemented their attacks. Not surprisingly, there is evidence that other terrorist organizations—most notably, Iranian-backed Hezbollah, which is estimated to have cells operating in ten American cities—have similarly become expert at obtaining driver's licenses to cloak their activities here.

Today, driver's licenses make possible:

- access to sensitive government and commercial facilities, such as the Capitol building or the New York Stock Exchange.
- access to commercial aircraft, like those seized on September 11.

---

13 For example, "...the 9/11 Commission's counsel told the Senate Judiciary Committee of al-Qaeda operative Nabil Al-Marabh, who sneaked illegally over the Canadian border in mid-2001 and was found to have received five Michigan licenses in 13 months, plus licenses from Massachusetts, Illinois, and Florida." Mark Kirkorian, *A REAL Solution, The Safe Side of the ID Debate*, Center For Immigration Studies, March, 2005. Available at http://www.cis.org/articles/2005/mskoped32205.html.

◆ bank accounts, to launder money and conceal terror-related financial transactions.
◆ the purchase of guns and ammunition.
◆ the rental of vans and small trucks (of the sort used to atatck the World Trade Center in 1993 and the Murrah Building in Oklahoma City in 1995).
◆ the charter of small aircraft at private airports.

In short, driver's licenses are the keys to navigating in contemporary American society, institutions, and enterprise. We cannot afford to allow such keys to fall into the hands of people bent on our destruction.

The 9/11 Commission and the Real ID Act

It was clear to the 9/11 Commission that, with fifty states having different standards for driver's licenses—some of them wholly inadequate—a *federal* solution was needed. In its report to Congress, the commission recommended bluntly: "Secure identification should begin in the United States. The federal government should set standards for the issuance of . . . sources of identification, such as driver's licenses."[14]

It was a logical—and obvious—solution. The prosaic driver's license had clearly become a *national security* issue, an area in which the states have no direct responsibility. And some states had shown little inclination to exercise due care to ascertain the identity—let alone the legal status—of those to whom licenses were being issued.

The commission rightly recognized that with state-issued driver's licenses, America can be only as strong as its weakest state. If just a single state were to continue handing out licenses without verifying applicants' identities, the entire nation would remain at risk.

This key security recommendation of the 9/11 Commission was finally adopted by Congress on May 10, 2005, in the Real ID Act. It passed overwhelmingly in Congress, despite a two-year campaign to defeat it. The opposition included, among others, the illegal alien lobby and the ACLU, which, with characteristic hyperbole, denounced this legislation as a step toward an Orwellian society run by the all-seeing, all-powerful Big Brother.[15]

---

14 Op. cit.
15 National Council of La Raza denounces passage of 'REAL ID ACT,' February 10, 2005, http://www.nclr.org/content/news/detail/29653/; American Immigration Lawyers Association (AILA), "REAL ID is Not Real Security," January 26, 2005, http://www.aila.org/content/default.aspx?docid=12196; ACLU, "Allies Oppose Sensenbrenner's Anti-Immigrant Bill; Mean-Spirited Measure Would Hurt Persecuted, Undermine Privacy," American Civil Liberties Union, February 9, 2005, http://www.aclu.org/SafeandFree/SafeandFree.cfm?ID=17446&c=206.

Important as this legislation is, it has several shortcomings.

♦ It gives states *three years* to meet the uniform, secure licensing standards expected shortly to be issued by the Department of Homeland Security. This delay affords a generous window of opportunity for terrorist organizations to exploit the identified vulnerabilities in various state systems.

♦ States do not have to comply with the law; it is *voluntary*. To be sure, if they chose not to implement the Real ID Act, their residents' licenses will not be accepted as a form of federal ID. That means that license holders from those states will not be able to fly on commercial airlines without producing additional documentation. Still, such states would remain very weak links.

Regrettably, some states are resisting the Real ID Act, often claiming (1) that its documentation requirements are too onerous on citizens and (2) that the paperwork involved is too costly for already overstretched state budgets.

1. **Too burdensome on drivers?** This argument is absurd. Real ID's standards will not impose an appreciable hardship on would-be drivers.

   ♦ Applicants will have to provide their state motor vehicle administration with a Social Security number, which will be verified against a federal database (a practice already required in thirty-six states).

   ♦ A digital photograph will likely be taken, as required for all U.S. passports.

   It may take a few extra minutes to process a license application, but these are reasonable inconveniences to prevent these valuable IDs from facilitating terrorist activities.

   Most Americans appreciate that the inconvenience is fully warranted. In an August 2005 national survey, commissioned by the Coalition for a Secure Driver's License, more than two-thirds of respondents supported implementation of the provisions of the Real ID Act. And a full 84 percent said they would be willing to stand in line a little longer or pay a little extra to accomplish that.[16]

2. **Too costly for states?** The opposition of state leadership clearly goes beyond the issue of cost. Even before the Department of Homeland Security had issued its specific recommendations, some state governors and legislators were vehemently protesting.

---

16 Coalition for a Secure Driver's License, http://www.securelicense.org/site/
PageServer?pagename=pollhighlights.

♦ Democratic New Mexico Governor Bill Richardson threatened to file a class action on behalf of his and other states to block Real ID from being implemented.

♦ The Republican-controlled Montana legislature passed a resolution saying that its state will refuse to comply with the act.

The "Terminator's" sensible view. One individual who clearly understands the security implications of state-issued identity documents is himself a legal immigrant and an American-by-choice. In his first two years as governor of California, Arnold Schwarzenegger has acted to remove from the books a driver's license law that contained loopholes that illegal aliens, criminals, and terrorists could exploit while vetoing two similarly flawed bills.

> This bill . . . could undermine national security efforts to identify individuals who pose enormous risk to the safety of Californians. I have repeatedly stated that *the ability to verify documents used to establish an identity must include a way to determine whether an individual is who he or she purports to be and must include a criminal background check.* [Emphasis added.]
>
> —Governor Arnold Schwarzenegger,
> vetoing SB60, October 7, 2005

If New Mexico and Montana should fail to implement a secure system for issuing driver's licenses, the weakest link will be very weak indeed. America will remain vulnerable to a well-understood terrorist tactic—one that has already been used, to deadly effect. Our state officials must heed this statement of the 9/11 Commission: "For terrorists, travel documents are as important as weapons."[17]

What Needs to Be Done

1. A sound national standard for driver's licenses must be quickly adopted and implemented by every state in the Union.
2. Similar efforts must be undertaken to validate the authenticity of the "feeder" documents used to obtain driver's licenses, such as passports and birth certificates.
3. An electronic birth/death registry is needed to prevent the fraudulent use of Social Security numbers and the issuance of identification documents

---

17 Congressional Testimony by Assistant Secretary of State for Consular Affairs Maura Harty before House International Relations Committee, Washington, DC, August 19, 2004.

in the name of deceased individuals, using innovative biometric technologies as appropriate.

4. All levels of government need to stop recognizing consular documents (such as the Mexican *matricula* card) as a valid form of ID in the United States. These are readily issued with little or no documentation and are easily counterfeited in any case.

In all these aspects of home security—legal and illegal immigration and documentation—we have allowed the integrity of our systems to be seriously eroded.

♦ Complacent politicians are content to leave statutes unenforced.
♦ State and local leaders deliberately undermine the federal legal code.
♦ Officials pay lip service to border security (or posture by declaring meaningless "states of emergency") while doing everything possible to subvert sensible immigration policies.
♦ Bureaucrats choose to ignore violations of those laws they do not like.
♦ Licensing authorities heedlessly credential people without knowing their true identity.

The cumulative effect of all these shortcomings has been to leave the country vulnerable to the activities of terrorists, who would exploit our civil liberties in order to vanquish them (see Step 5). By implementing the many recommendations that make up Step 7 of the War Footing, we can begin to protect against the threat to our constitutional freedoms and society from those who want to come to this country to do us harm—or that have already done so.

PART IV
Waging the "War of Ideas"

There has been more *talk*, with less *action*, about waging the "war of ideas" than for any other aspect of this conflict. Most people acknowledge it has to be a part of the war effort. Secretary of Defense Donald Rumsfeld famously warned that if we don't do a better job on this front, our Islamofascist enemies are going to be producing jihadists faster than we can kill them.

Some people believe we *are* doing something about the war of ideas. They note the president's recent appointment of his long-time aide and confidante, Karen Hughes, to a senior State Department post with responsibility for "public diplomacy." Since assuming these responsibilities in September 2005, Undersecretary Hughes has indeed made a point of reaching out to Muslims at home and abroad, with a view to retooling America's image and improving its relationship with the Islamic world.

Unfortunately, these measures—even if properly conceived (as they rarely are)—are woefully inadequate to the task at hand. The bottom line is that the United States and freedom-loving people everywhere, Muslims as well as non-Muslims, are confronting at present very dangerous and determined adversaries. These foes are driven by a fervently embraced ideology, made more aggressive by its supposed God-given mandate. They have been developing and establishing the instruments for indoctrination and recruitment for decades. They are deadly serious—not just about winning "hearts and minds," but about *winning, period*

We must be no less serious about defeating them at the ideological level than at every other level. This section focuses on three ways in which that must be done.

♦ Step 8 helps explain the nature of wars of ideas and the instruments of political warfare needed to wage and win them. It describes what has worked in the past and missteps that have been made that have set back our cause. And it lays out specific initiatives that can, and must, be taken now if our ideas are to triumph over theirs.

♦ Step 9 lays out the various theaters in which we must mount appropriately tailored initiatives in the war of ideas. At the moment, these can be political warfare campaigns, *not* military ones. If we are unwilling or unable competently to mount such campaigns, however, we are likely to find ourselves fighting the old-fashioned sort of war—quite possibly on terms that are neither at our initiative and advantageous to us nor assured of success.

We describe in this step challenges to American security and interests that are emerging not just in the obvious place, the Middle East, but also in every other major region of the world: Asia, Africa, Latin America, Russia, and Europe. We must understand the rise of Islamofascism in each of these places. We also need to recognize the emergence of other potential adversaries, most of whom are allied with or at least making common cause with the Islamists. These steps are necessary if we are to mobilize the War Footing effort needed to ensure we survive and prevail in not only the current struggle but also in those that lie ahead.

♦ Step 10 identifies resources that are either not being properly brought to bear in the war effort or that are, to varying degrees, *compounding* the other problems we face. These include:

- *Enlisting the State Department.* As long as America's diplomats are not put on a War Footing in support of the commander in chief's strategies and policies, the coherence and effectiveness of both will continue to be undermined. Despite the appointment of the president's trusted foreign policy counselor, Condoleezza Rice, as secretary of state, the record suggests that Foggy Bottom is still not with the program. This situation has already been tolerated for far too long. It can no longer be accepted if we hope to survive and prevail.

- *Marginalizing the UN.* The "world body" has never lived up to its founding promise—to be an engine for protecting and promoting freedom around the world within a "well-ordered system of sovereign states." Instead, for nearly all of its institutional life it has been, at best, ineffectual. At worst, it has been rabidly anti-American and a vehicle for agendas hostile to our interests and those of liberty more generally.

The UN's bureaucrats, and many of its members, make no secret of wanting to diminish U.S. sovereignty and freedom of action and ultimately to supplant it with some sort of "world government." Neither America as we know it nor our cherished liberties will long endure such an arrangement, especially in the face of those determined to destroy both.

- *Obtaining academia's support.* American taxpayers pay roughly $120 million annually to academic institutions to ensure that the nation has a highly trained professional cadre of regional experts and linguistic specialists. Their abilities to make developments abroad understandable—both literally and figuratively—can be instrumental to the success of the war effort.

  Regrettably, we have far less to show for this investment than we should, and far less than we need. In fact, for too long our government has allowed these vast sums to be worse than wasted. They have been expended in ways that have left the country with a serious deficit of proficient translators and experts who are deeply knowledgeable about foreign regions and who will unapologetically and unequivocally favor *our side* in the current struggle with Islamofascism and its friends. This bizarre situation is but one example of serious problems afflicting U.S. higher education—one that needs to be corrected as a matter of the utmost importance to the security of the nation.

STEP 8

Wage Political Warfare

With Contributions from Dr. J. Michael Waller, Alex Alexiev, and Caroline B. Glick

I n a recent policy address,[1] President George W. Bush discussed what is motivating the onslaught of terrorist attacks in Europe, Asia, and the Middle East.

> Some call this evil Islamic radicalism; others, militant Jihadism; still others, Islamofascism. Whatever it's called, this ideology is very different from the religion of Islam. This form of radicalism exploits Islam to serve a violent, political vision: the establishment, by terrorism and subversion and insurgency, of a totalitarian empire that denies all political and religious freedom.
>
> Some might be tempted to dismiss these goals as fanatical or extreme. Well, they *are* fanatical and extreme—and they should not be dismissed. Our enemy is utterly committed. As [the Jordanian terrorist Abu Musab al-] Zarqawi has vowed,[2] "We will either achieve victory over the human race or we will pass to the eternal life." And the civilized world knows very well that other fanatics in history, from Hitler to Stalin to Pol Pot, consumed whole nations in war and genocide before leaving the stage of history. Evil men, obsessed with ambition and unburdened by conscience, must be taken very seriously—*and we must stop them before their crimes can multiply.* [Emphasis added.]

---

1 Speech delivered at the National Endowment for Democracy, October 6, 2005. Available at http://www.ned.org/events/oct0605-Bush.html.
2 One issue to be addressed in formulating a political warfare strategy is whether senior officials should cite individual terrorists by name, thus possibly enhancing their stature.

President Bush clearly understands that this War for the Free World is fundamentally *political* in character. If we are to defeat our enemy's totalitarian ideology, it will not be enough to marshal the tools laid out in the preceding chapters—the array of energy, financial, legal, and security measures. We must integrate these measures within an overall strategy of *political warfare*, a form of war that specifically attacks the ideological and psychological factors that motivate our enemies.

Political and psychological warfare strategies are designed to undermine and divide the enemy: splitting apart and peeling away the enemy's support base; denying the enemy the social support infrastructure that shelters its forces, funds its operations, and provides its cadres; pitting enemy factions against one another; and discrediting the ideological belief system that legitimizes its cause.

Political Warfare Works

Since the Revolutionary War, America has had considerable experience with political warfare. Samuel Adams, Benjamin Franklin, and George Washington practiced it with skill against the British. Various presidents, particularly Harry Truman, Dwight Eisenhower, John F. Kennedy, and Ronald Reagan, advocated and used political warfare as normal tools against the ideological warfare of the Soviets.

In fact, the Reagan administration devised a strategy to help destroy the totalitarian adversary whose global ambitions last threatened the Free World—the Soviet Union.[3] The principal reason for the victory of the Free World over the Soviet empire was the dramatic response of the citizens of that empire—including many of the ruling elite—to Mr. Reagan's sustained political warfare initiatives and the erosion of their confidence in the Soviet ideology.

America has also been at the losing end of political warfare. The North Vietnamese defeat of the United States was not a triumph of battlefield accomplishments; rather, they successfully attacked our political will, convincing the American people that the war in Vietnam could not be won—and that the fight could be abandoned without long-term consequences. This success has inspired our enemies in the present War for the Free World; it represents a strategy they explicitly are seeking to emulate.[4]

---

3   See Norman A. Bailey, *The Strategic Plan that Won the Cold War: National Security Decision Directive 75*, The Potomac Foundation, 1999.

4   See intercepted letter from Ayman Zawahiri to Abu Musab Zarqawi, July 2005, Office of Director National Intelligence, News Release No. 2-05. Available at http://www.ndi.gov.

The Islamists' political warfare strategy has another crucial target: their potential supporters in the Arab world, and Muslim communities elsewhere. The goal is to persuade this audience that their interests are best served by supporting, or at least not opposing, the jihadists. Beheadings, successful acts of terror, progress in imposing Shari'a—all trumpeted by al Jazeera and other "independent news networks," which are essentially organs of enemy propaganda—are tactics to demonstrate that Islamofascism is the way of the future.

Unilaterally Disarmed

Despite the obvious importance of the political/ideological warfare component in the current conflict, the United States has, to date, scarcely engaged in it. The fact is, we have *unilaterally disarmed* in this arena of the battle space.

To be sure, President Bush and his administration have made a political measure—promoting democracy—a central feature of American strategy in this war. As he put it in the same October 2005 speech to the National Endowment for Democracy:

> Our strategy . . . is to deny the militants future recruits by replacing hatred and resentment with democracy and hope across the broader Middle East. This is a difficult and long-term project, yet there's no alternative to it. Our future and the future of that region are linked. If the broader Middle East is left to grow in bitterness, if countries remain in misery, while radicals stir the resentments of millions, then that part of the world will be a source of endless conflict and mounting danger, and for our generation and the next.
>
> If the peoples of that region are permitted to choose their own destiny, and advance by their own energy and by their participation as free men and women, then the extremists will be marginalized, and the flow of violent radicalism to the rest of the world will slow, and eventually end. By standing for the hope and freedom of others, we make our own freedom more secure.

But the contrast between *real* political warfare and this sort of effort to promote the benefits of democracy calls to mind Mark Twain's observation that there is a considerable difference between "lightning and a lightning bug." We must certainly continue to hold out to the people of the Middle East, and other regions under assault from Islamofascism, the democratic ideal of self-rule under accountable and peaceable governments. But we must also use *political techniques* to defeat enemies who are determined to supplant democratic government and values throughout the Free World.

The U.S. government is scarcely organized for this purpose. In summer 2003, the government's top "war of ideas" experts played a first-ever "strategic communications" war game—and quit halfway through, because everything was so dysfunctional.[5] Although the CIA's clandestine service has recently been authorized to stand up a strategic influence unit, its checkered past, and the depletion long ago of its skilled political operatives, means that today it has neither the staff nor the tasking to wage political warfare on a global strategic level.

Strangled in the Crib

The first effort since September 11, 2001, to constitute an institutionalized political warfare capability—an organization created by Secretary of Defense Donald Rumsfeld in October 2001 and called the Office of Strategic Influence (OSI)—was itself the target of a two-fisted political attack, *by one of Mr. Rumsfeld's own senior staff.*

The history of the OSI is instructive. It was launched in October 2001 as a component of a broader, government-wide strategic communications campaign, specifically to assist government agencies in crafting policy regarding the military aspects of information operations. Its initial plans included operations to counter Iranian government propaganda in Afghanistan, Saddam Hussein's propaganda throughout the Middle East and South Asia, and disinformation from radical Islamist clerics.

The new office also planned to establish access to information for those in regions dominated by enemy propaganda, such as the jihadist schools of Pakistan—the most fertile recruiting fields for terrorism. Its concept of operations included unique and innovative approaches, developed both internally and with outside experts whose creativity was unhampered by the stifling constraints of bureaucracy.

Some in the Pentagon's civilian and uniformed hierarchy, however, felt threatened by the sort of wide-ranging mandate, out-of-the-box thinking, and bureaucratic agility Secretary Rumsfeld had wisely seen fit to encourage in the OSI team. On February 13, 2002, an OSI official reported to a senior official in the Pentagon chief's office:

> We've had considerable resistance to our plans from the staff within the Pentagon itself. There is an inability to recognize

---

5   David E. Kaplan, "Hearts, Minds, and Dollars," *US News & World Report*, April 25, 2005, p. 24.

influence campaigns directed at the terrorists' support and recruitment as a legitimate military function. The most resistance comes from Public Affairs and the General Counsel, who seem to have forgotten that five months ago an airliner crashed into our building killing nearly 200 people! I would characterize their objections as *looking for reasons not to do something* instead of helping us to proceed.[6]

The bureaucrats won. Pentagon spokeswoman Victoria Clarke had opposed the OSI from its inception, and she succeeded in sabotaging the project by informing the *New York Times* (incorrectly) that OSI planned to plant lies in the foreign media. American journalists seized upon the *Times* report to suggest that the effect, whether intended or not, would be to disinform this country's press as well.

Clarke then compounded the damage done by her false allegations by directing, in her capacity as the assistant secretary of defense for public affairs, that OSI officials not try to set the record straight, thus ensuring that all the news coverage and commentary would be onesided and negative. Within days, the organization's reputation had been so badly compromised in the press that it had to be shut down. The episode made this vital mission so politically radioactive that no comparable effort has subsequently been launched to perform it.

The Limitations of "Public Diplomacy"

In the absence of a real political warfare program, the United States has been condemned to pursue a far more limited effort known as "public diplomacy." This is at best a poor substitute for political warfare and potentially even counterproductive. For one thing, it tends to conceal the fact that we are failing to mount a proper political warfare program.

For another, conducted in isolation, it pursues objectives largely irrelevant to the conduct of the war. Public diplomacy tends to imply that the reason we are in this war is because people do not know or understand us. In fact, Islamists hate us and our civilization because they *know* where we stand and the values we represent—values that they believe must be destroyed to bring about their millenarian utopia.

Even when they are well conceived and well executed, however, public diplomacy strategies will be a long-term effort. This is in their nature, given the reliance they place on such instruments as international media programming,

---

6   Internal Pentagon memorandum dated February 13, 2002; made available to the authors on an off-the-record basis.

exchange visits of political and cultural figures, humanitarian and development assistance, training future leaders, and so forth. Such efforts may take years (or even generations) to build reserves of trust and goodwill between the United States and foreign populations. And we do not have the luxury of time, as we contend with the threat posed by Islamofascism and its allies.

Getting It Backward

Moreover, a public diplomacy strategy that is not clearly thought through will seize on goals that are vague or irrelevant. Currently, the underlying theme is "Why do they hate us?" when it ought to be "What is wrong with *them*?"

This is by no means a matter of empty semantics. The latter question implies a serious attempt to come to terms with the ideas and factors that motivate our enemies—without which winning an ideological war is all but impossible. The former question is grounded in the seriously flawed implicit premise that, if they hate us, it must surely be our fault.

We find precisely this flawed logic in some statements of public diplomacy advocates. The 2003 report of a State Department committee, chaired by retired Ambassador Edward Djerejian, squarely blamed U.S. policies in the Middle East for 80 percent of the anti-American hostility in the region.[7] Followed to its logical conclusion, such a position leads to exonerating Islamist extremism and terrorism, justifying the vicious anti-American propaganda in the Middle East, and blaming America first. It is analogous to asking the victim of domestic abuse what she did to provoke the assault.

Furthermore, American public diplomacy was seriously impaired by the loss of an independent communications office, when the U.S. Information Agency (USIA) was folded into the State Department under the Clinton administration. The result was a general downgrading (and underfunding) of the effort to communicate America's policies and messages to the world. The activities that survive are no longer implemented by professional USIA officers but by career diplomats, who are typically less enthusiastic about promoting abroad American values and exceptional success as a role model (for more on the Foreign Service culture, see Step 10).

---

7   Edward P. Djerejian, Chairman, *Changing Minds, Winning Peace: A New Strategic Direction for U.S. Public Diplomacy in the Arab & Muslim World.* Washington: Report of the Advisory Group on Public Diplomacy for the Arab and Muslim World to the Committee on Appropriations, U.S. House of Representatives, October 1, 2003 (see also Step 10).

What Needs to Be Done

The United States needs to take a number of steps, urgently, to inaugurate a program of political warfare.

1. **Stop evading the issue.** No government strategy to date for the so-called War on Terror has included political warfare as an explicit element of the American arsenal.[8]

2. **Devise, staff up, and begin executing a political warfare strategy.** Countering the Islamofascist ideology must be its near-term focus.

3. **De-legitimize Islamist extremism in the eyes of Muslims, and especially its potential supporters.** We need to show that, although violent Islamism is certainly a problem for us in the West, it is a vastly greater problem for the Muslim community.

   ♦ **Challenge the Islamists on religious grounds.** Many Muslim leaders teach the message of civility and tolerance, and their voices need to be amplified. We can help call attention to contradictions between Islamism and the Koran, on such matters as prohibitions of violence against Muslims; relations between Muslims and "people of the book" (Jews and Christians); the ban on compulsion in religion; the doctrine of jihad; the rules of war; killing of innocent civilians, prohibition of suicide, and so forth.

   ♦ **Expose economic disaster.** There is ample evidence that Islamism, and its imposition of Shari'a law, results in crippling limitations to economic development, and thus to the socioeconomic well-being of Muslims. Relevant cases are Pakistan, Iran, Sudan, and Nigeria.

   ♦ **Celebrate educational opportunity.** Radical Islam has a strongly negative effect on educational standards because of its narrow emphasis on Koranic instruction which fails to equip graduates with any practical job skills, destining them for jihad or unemployment. Where Islamists hold sway, an erosion in quality similarly afflicts what had been *secular* educational systems.

     There is evidence, moreover, that with the proliferation of madrassa education, functional illiteracy is spreading, and literacy rates for women are stagnating. Any serious effort at political

---

8   Even the influential Defense Science Board, in its 2004 study on "Transition to and from Hostilities"—which devoted more attention than any other government agency to strategic communication—failed to include political warfare as a component.

warfare must emphasize the immense costs to societies that do not fully use the talents of half of their population.

♦ **Emphasize progress.** Shari'a-ruled countries exhibit a strong bias against science and technology education, to the huge detriment of their economic development. The 2004 UN Report on Arab Human Development shows that the Arab world has yet to join the Industrial Revolution—let alone the *Information Revolution*—and that it neither produces much scientific literature nor carries out real research.[9] A successful political warfare strategy must highlight this key failure by documenting the numerous religious prohibitions and restrictions on scientific and technological pursuit imposed by Islamist ideology.

♦ **Enshrine human rights.** The regular and officially sanctioned abuse of basic human rights in Shari'a-dominated countries is yet another glaring Islamist misdeed that needs to be exposed. Such abuse includes the widespread judicial and customary discrimination and outright mistreatment of women, from uncivilized practices such as forced marriages to truly inhumane treatment such as genital mutilation and "honor" killings. Virtually all of these extreme Islamist tenets and practices stand in direct contradiction to the UN Universal Declaration of Human Rights—an international human rights standard to which all of the Shari'a-dominated countries nominally adhere.

4. **Use legislative vehicles for political warfare.** Congress has an important role to play. The groundbreaking 1972 Jackson-Vanik Amendment made favorable trade relations with the Soviet Union contingent on its permitting free emigration. Under the leadership of the remarkable Sen. Henry M. Jackson, this legislation proved to be a powerful congressionally created political weapon, one that was used to decisive effect in de-legitimizing totalitarian Soviet Communism.[10] Sanctions legislation and assistance to democratic opposition movements can serve a similar purpose in the War for the Free World.

5. **Use our strengths.** The good news is that Americans are among the world's experts at political warfare. The bad news is that *we mainly use it against each other*: after all, the strategies and tactics of any hard-fought election campaign are precisely the stuff of applied political warfare.

---

9   2004 Arab Human Development Report: Towards Freedom in the Arab World. Available at http://www.rbas.undp.org/ahdr2.cfm?menu=12.

10 See Robert Kaufman, *Henry M. Jackson, A Life in Politics*, University of Washington Press, 2000.

The talent, creativity, ingenuity, and, yes, ruthlessness of top-flight political campaign strategists of both parties should be mustered for the purpose of fighting our enemies and helping our friends rather than fighting each other. The model for such an effort is the "dollar-a-year man," the highly skilled private-sector leaders who volunteered their services to the government to assist in the World War II effort. With this kind of help, we could quickly be well on the way to building a formidable and effective national political warfare capability.

6. **Invest in the instruments of political warfare, including public diplomacy.** Public diplomacy, intended to influence perceptions, attitudes, and actions abroad is as a form of political warfare. We have been dramatically underfunding an important area of natural American expertise and capability: multimedia communications aimed at foreign audiences. As part of our War Footing strategy, we must stop nickel-and-diming our international broadcasting operations. All too frequently in recent years, we have increased transmission to one region at the expense of reducing it to another.

An immediate and sweeping ramp-up of our international broadcasting capabilities is needed to provide high-quality programming:

- **Voice of America;** "free radios"; new services like Radio Sawa and Al Hurra; and support for the extremely effective private-sector broadcasts (for example, those beamed into Iran from Los Angeles) and other more innovative vehicles (including, where appropriate, sometimes covertly sponsored ones).
- **A range of formats** (television, satellite, AM/FM or shortwave radio or both, and the Internet).
- **Operating twenty-four hours a day,** seven days a week, where needed.
- **Serving, at a minimum, every country** currently or potentially under assault from Islamism.

The cost of such an ambitious undertaking—though appreciably greater than the stingy investment we are making in international communications today—pales by comparison with the costs of military warfare. The investment will be well repaid if it helps us protect and expand the Free World against the Islamists and their friends, without resorting to further use of military force.

7. **Use the Internet as a tool of political warfare.** In particular, the power of creative Web sites, Webcasting, and blogging should be aggressively exploited.

8. **Strengthen the CIA clandestine services, and authorize and fund them for long-term strategic political warfare.**

9. **Grant the Department of Defense the primary responsibility for political warfare.** Just as the State Department leads in public diplomacy, the "warfare" side of communications is legitimately a Pentagon function and must not be assigned to our diplomats.

10. **Don't forget political warfare in non-Islamist areas.** The United States must combat adversarial political warfare wherever it arises, even in countries traditionally considered friendly. Despite their differences, the United States and Germany continue to have strong political, economic, cultural, and military ties. Yet the Socialist/Green coalition ruling Germany during the first years of the war went out of bounds in its differences with U.S. policy—to the point of deliberately undermining American security interests for the sake of political gain in domestic elections. When politicians cross the line between opposition and sabotage, the United States must have capabilities to battle them politically.

11. **Reinforce and strengthen our friends.** By demonstrating that there are not only consequences for opposing us, but also real and tangible benefits from supporting us, we can maximize the chances of our success. Critical in this regard is the American commitment to the continued survival of one of the most exposed countries of the Free World: Israel.

    The political warfare of our enemies attempts to erode American support for the Jewish state, promoting the idea that if the United States would only abandon Israel, we would have no further problem with the Islamists. As we argue in Step 9, such a retreat would simply embolden our adversaries and reduce our allies' confidence in us—to say nothing of the impact on uncommitted parties. We should refrain from taking actions that undermine the security of the Jewish state, whether by pressing for further Israeli concessions to jihadist Palestinians or indulging in symbolic gestures designed to appease Arab public opinion.

Winning a political war is, in the end, a question of credibility. When nations stand firm for what they claim to believe in, they are perceived as credible. When they appear unwilling to stand firm—regardless of their rhetoric—they are vulnerable to their enemies' more decisive use of political warfare.

With the fate of the Free World hanging in the balance, we cannot be (or be perceived to be) weak and irresolute. Toward this end, we must wage political warfare effectively, convincingly, and decisively.

STEP 9

Launch Regional Initiatives

As an essential component of America's War Footing, political warfare must be waged in specific regional initiatives aimed at defeating the Islamofascists, neutralizing their supporters and strengthening our true allies in defense of the Free World.

The initiatives discussed in Step 9 are political and ideological rather than military, but they reflect a core strategic understanding that we are confronting a sustained and many-tentacled attack. The United States must adhere to an offensive rather than a defensive strategy if it hopes to survive and prevail in this war.

There are a host of measures that can and must immediately be undertaken, literally all over the world, that do not require the use of American armed forces. In fact, if we wish to avoid calling on the U.S. military for further missions, these actions will be essential—in the Mideast (and its periphery) and in Africa, Asia, Latin America, Russia, and Europe.

If we fail to undertake such regional initiatives, it is almost certain that new threats to the Free World will arise in many (or all) of these quarters. The cost of dealing with such threats after they have fully emerged, measured in both blood and national treasure, may be very high. These sorts of initiatives must therefore be urgently integrated into America's strategy for winning the War for the Free World.

A. Defend and Foster Freedom in the Middle East and Its Periphery

With Contributions from Lt. Gen. Tom McInerney, USAF (Ret.), Maj. Gen. Paul E. Vallely, USA (Ret.), Alex Alexiev, Kenneth R. Timmerman, Dr. Michael Rubin, Caroline B. Glick, and Christopher Brown

---

Any discussion of regional initiatives against terrorism must begin with the Middle East. Unlike some recent discussions of the Middle East, however, this will not be a list of potential targets for hypothetical American military strikes. Instead, it is designed to provide a truly strategic examination of the threat we face from several of the regimes in this general region and the framework for applying the *political* warfare strategy outlined in Step 8.

A comprehensive history of this region, or even a proper examination of the current social, political, and religious situation there, is well outside the scope of this book. However, the brief overview provided here concerning the most strategically important states in the region and nearby should suffice for the current purpose: to help Americans understand the imperative to place our country on a true War Footing and how to prevail in the current global conflict.

Iran

It is surprising to most terrorism experts that, even after four years of a global war on terror, there has yet to be any serious national debate about the need and the means to confront Iran. Consider the following:

◆ Prior to the attacks of September 11, 2001, Iran was responsible for the deaths of more than fifteen hundred Americans—more than any other state sponsor of terror or terrorist organization in history.[1]

◆ The U.S. Department of State has designated the government of Iran as the "the most active state sponsor of terrorism."[2]

According to press accounts, a report by the Israeli secret service estimates that Iran has "invested more than $10 million to encourage terrorist activity against Israel."[3]

Iran is responsible for developing Hezbollah in Lebanon, contributing training, equipment, funds, and political support. Hezbollah is by far the best organized and best developed terrorist organization in the world and the only such organization that exercises physical control over an international border (between Lebanon and Israel). Hezbollah has, moreover, followed in the footsteps of its Iranian patrons in developing strategic ties with Hugo Chavez of Venezuela and others in Latin America (see Part C of this step).

◆ There are many indicators that Iran is connected to al-Qaeda, both ideologically—despite their religious differences, they share a commitment to radicalized political Islam—and operationally.

◆ Finally, there is the matter of Iran's acquisition of nuclear weapons and ballistic missiles.

"Death to America"

The birth of the current Iranian regime is best remembered by Americans for the sacking of the U.S. embassy in Tehran and the subsequent hostage crisis that occurred early in the 1979 revolution. The new president of Iran, Mahmoud Ahmadinejad, was in fact one of the leaders of the student group responsible for seizing our embassy.

It is often forgotten, however, that the Iranian revolution was originally composed of three factions: the democratic nationalists; the Soviet-backed Marxists; and the Islamists, inspired by the radical Shi'ite Ayatollah Ruhollah Khomeini. The democratic forces were quickly marginalized and then violently eliminated by the joint forces of the Marxists and the Islamists—and soon afterward, the Islamists did the same to the Marxist forces. Hence, what

---

1   Rohan Gunaratna, *Inside Al-Qaeda: Global Network of Terror*, Berkley Publishing Company, 2002, p. 197.
2   See http://www.state.gov/s/ct/rls/45392.htm.
3   Uri Dan, "Terror Trail of Cash Leads to Iran, Saudis," *New York Post* online edition, October 1, 2005.

began as a broad-based revolution comprising many factions morphed into "the *Islamic* revolution." Its transformation and success have become inspirations for Islamist movements around the world, including Sunni variants such as al-Qaeda.

Triumph of the Jihadists

Khomeini soon put into place his ideology of Velayat-e Faqih ("Governance of the Jurist"). In practice, this meant that the supreme leader (then Khomeini, currently Ayatollah Khamenei) would exercise absolute control of the Iranian government (see Figure 1). Iranian elections include only candidates preapproved by the supreme leader, through the Council of Guardians; claims of democracy in Iran are a sham.

The direct exercise of power by the clerical leaders of Iran is in fact heretical to the teachings of traditional Shi'a Islam. *For this reason, Khomeini created a program to spread his own version of Islamist ideology*, and to impose it on others using violence in the form of terrorism. This instrument enabled the regime first to consolidate power within Iran and then to seek power elsewhere, beginning with Lebanon.

Iran in Lebanon. In April 1983, an Iranian intelligence operative named Imad Mugniyeh organized an attack that blew up the U.S. embassy in Lebanon, killing 63 people. In October of the same year, Mugniyeh orchestrated another suicide truck attack, this time targeting the Marine barracks housing part of the U.S. peacekeeping contingent, killing 241 U.S. servicemen.[4] Almost simultaneously, another truck bomb exploded at the headquarters of French paratroopers.[5] A third suicide truck attack, against the Italian headquarters, was apparently thwarted by the dispersal of Italian forces.[6]

Interestingly, the use of simultaneous attacks was a signature technique of Mugniyeh (and the Iranian-backed Hezbollah terrorist organizations) throughout the 1980s; only later, beginning with the attack on U.S. embassies in East Africa in 1998, did the technique become associated with al-Qaeda. This similarity was no accident: beginning at least in 1993, al-Qaeda operatives were receiving terrorist training from Iran, through Mugniyeh himself.[7]

---

4   Rex Hudson, "The Sociology and Psychology of Terrorism: Who Becomes a Terrorist and Why?" Federal Research Service at the Library of Congress, September 1999, Washington, DC.
5   Rohan Gunaratna, *Inside Al-Qaeda Global Network of Terror*, Berkley Books, 2002, p. 196.
6   Ibid.
7   For an in-depth look at the ties between al-Qaeda and Iran, see Christopher Brown, "Ties That Bind: Iran and Al-Qaeda," Hudson Institute Briefing Note, July 5, 2005.

Figure 1. Iran: Governing Institutions[1]

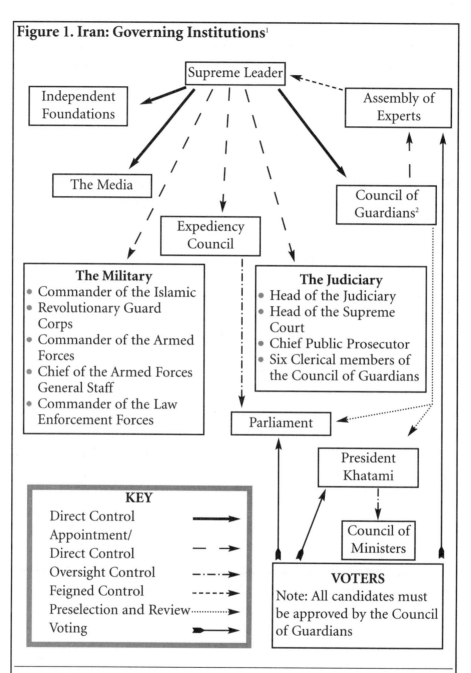

1   Adapted from: Wilfried Buchta, Who Rules Iran? The Structure of Power in the Islamic Republic, Washington Institute for Near East Policy, 2001.

2   The Council of Guardians (1) preselects and approves all candidates for all elections; (2) reviews all laws passed by parliament and decides whether these are compatible with the Holy Law of Islam; and (3) interprets the constitution.

This orchestrated onslaught was rewarded. The multinational military forces were withdrawn in the same year.

The Islamist perpetrators were powerfully affected by the success of these attacks and their results. Take, for example, the subsequent Iran-sponsored truck-bomb attack in June 1996 on U.S. forces housed in the Khobar Towers in Saudi Arabia. The attack killed 19 U.S. airmen. Upon learning of its success, the commander of the Iranian Revolutionary Guards told his son that Islamic Republic leaders expected that this would compel the United States to withdraw from the Persian Gulf. "If we kill just one US soldier, the others will withdraw," he predicted, explicitly invoking the Lebanon experience.[8]

Iran versus the Free World

As these episodes make clear, Iran began to wage war against America more than three decades ago and has drawn inspiration ever since from our retreat from Lebanon. It continues to threaten us and our interests in many ways.

- Iran directly supports most of the Shi'ite-based political movements in Iraq and their militias. Indeed, Iran largely created the revolt in Najaf fomented by the radical Shi'a cleric Muqtada al-Sadr. (Al-Sadr's troops were reportedly trained at camps inside Iran.[9])
- The Iranians are actively supporting the flow of money, weapons, and people not only across the Iran-Iraq border but also through Syria as well.
- Iranian intelligence and other elements are working to destablize the pro-Western government in Afghanistan and the regime of Gen. Pervez Musharaf in Pakistan.
- Iran is the patron of Hezbollah, its radical Shi'a terrorist proxy that seeks to deny freedom to the people of Lebanon and threatens American and Israeli interests and assets.
- Despite differences on some religious points, Iran also directly supports the despotic regime in Syria, as well as such Palestinian terrorist groups as Hamas, Islamic Jihad, and Fatah. Iran is dedicated to helping Hamas emerge as the dominant power in the Palestinian areas as an ally with the shared goal of destroying Israel.
- There are many indicators that Iran is actively supporting al-Qaeda's operations inside Iraq, led by the Jordanian terrorist Abu Musab

---

8   Kenneth R. Timmerman, "Unlimited Offense: Iran's Response to the Missile Threat," Paper presented at *Military Strategy in the Age of Ballistic Missiles*, co-sponsored by the U.S. Army War College, the Jewish Institute for National Security, and the Boeing Corporation, February 23, 1999, Washington, DC.

9   "Iran's Al-Quds Corps Chief Reportedly Admits Providing Facilities to Al-Zarqawi," *Al-Sharq Al-Awsat*, August 11, 2004.

al-Zarqawi. The chief Iranian terrorist operative, Mugniyeh, has reportedly recommended coalescing the operational forces of al-Qaeda with other groups inside Iraq.[10] The regime in Tehran is also providing safe haven to al-Qaeda members and leaders inside Iran.[11]

♦ Significantly, Iran has never renounced its stated ambition to spread its Islamic Revolution throughout the Persian Gulf.

A Nuclear-Armed Iran

The most ominous development, however, is Tehran's increasingly blatant disregard of its obligations to remain a non-nuclear weapons state under the Nuclear Non-Proliferation Treaty. In the context of its aggressive program for refining and deploying ballistic missiles for the delivery of nuclear arms (and possibly other weapons of mass destruction), and given the mullahs' oft-stated determination to destroy America and Israel, this posture must be viewed as extremely dangerous.

The latest U.S. National Intelligence Estimate (NIE) on Iran, leaked to the media in August 2005, states that the Islamic Republic is unlikely to produce the fissile material it needs for a nuclear weapon until "early to mid-next decade."[12] If correct, this time line would indicate that a nuclear-armed Iran is at least five to ten years away—a sufficiently disturbing prospect.

But administration officials who track Iran's nuclear programs provide evidence that this time line is far too optimistic. The NIE estimate was influenced by the defensive mindset of the intelligence community, which was severely criticized for *overestimating* Iraq's WMD capabilities in 2003 (see Step 2).[13]

Since late 2002, a great deal of information about Iran's previously clandestine nuclear programs has become known. Following revelations by an Iranian opposition group, the International Atomic Energy Agency (IAEA) demanded that Iran allow international inspectors to visit undeclared sites (in Tehran, Isfahan, and Natanz) where the regime had launched a massive program to enrich uranium.

Communist China's bait-and-switch. Particularly problematic is the nuclear-related facility that the United States attempted (as early as October 1997) to prevent Iran from building with Chinese help—successfully so, we thought initially. Indeed, the Clinton administration publicly stated that

---

10 Ibid.
11 Robert Windrem, "Al-Qaida finds safe-haven in Iran," *MSNBC News*, July 24, 2005.
12 Dafna Linzer, "Iran is judged 10 years from nuclear bomb," *The Washington Post*, August 2, 2005.
13 Jed Babbin, "Midwives to nuclear terror," *The American Spectator*, August 15, 2005; "The Post's dubious slant on Iran," *The Washington Times*, August 8, 2005; Kenneth R. Timmerman, "Nuclear dance of 1,000 veils," *The Washington Times*, August 5, 2005.

China had agreed to cancel its plans to build the "hex" plant in Iran, in exchange for a U.S. agreement to sell nuclear power technology to the PRC.[14]

Once the American government declared the "case closed," however, the Chinese proceeded to *deliver the design information* for the entire facility to the Iranians—including, according to former State Department official Robert Einhorn, blueprints of equipment critical to the operation of the plant.[15] The Iranians were then able to build the facility themselves, while China ostensibly adhered to its agreement with the United States.

As a result of these sustained efforts, Iran is probably in a position to acquire nuclear weapons within a short period of time. (Some believe they may already have done so by purchasing them on the black market.) Especially in light of the mullahs' stated willingness to "share" their nuclear technology with other Islamic countries, the threat from Iran and its activities must be viewed as a ticking time bomb—and perhaps a mortal danger.

What do we do about the Iranian threat?

Détente Is Not an Option

It is vain to hope that the existing mullahocracy will become more moderate while its power to inflict violence on others increases. The regime has tolerated no substantial political or legal reforms but rather has used misleading rhetoric to clothe one of the world's most destructive regimes with a veneer of respectability.

Former president Mohammed Khatami—once the great hope of anti-regime elements in Iran and of many of their friends elsewhere—repeatedly made clear that he favored "democracy," but not in the traditional Western sense of that word. For example, while serving as a deputy in the Iranian parliament prior to becoming president, Khatami wrote in the official daily, *Keyhan,* that, because ordinary people cannot comprehend God's will, the full privileges of democracy should only extend to those with clerical education.[16] He has never repudiated this view.

In fact, during his eight-year presidency, Khatami failed to implement a single substantive reform. Cosmopolitan Iranian diplomats and reformists may enjoy some stature in Western circles, but true power inside Iran continues to

---

14 Kenneth R. Timmerman, "China backs off from Iran—maybe," The Iran Brief, November 10, 1997.

15 Einhorn was assistant secretary of state for nonproliferation. His comment on Isfahan can be found in Kenneth R. Timmerman, *Countdown to Crisis: The Coming Nuclear Showdown with Iran,* Crown Forum, 2005, p 159.

16 Ladan Boroumand and Roya Boroumand, "Illusion and Reality of Civil Society in Iran: An Ideological Debate," *Social Research,* Vol. 67, No. 2.

reside in an unelected supreme leader, who wields ultimate power over every aspect of Iranian policy, including the military.

Attempting to bribe or appease Tehran is not a viable alternative, either. Western think tanks, foreign policy and trade experts, and past and present government officials periodically propose "engaging" the Islamic Republic.[17] There is just one problem: Islamofascists in Iran, like their counterparts elsewhere, are deeply uninterested in peace with the West. They wish to destroy us. Their leaders have made clear that the sole purpose of negotiations with us is to buy time to realize their nuclear ambitions and to advance their jihad.[18]

Even as the European Union has sought to purchase a negotiated end to the Iranian nuclear weapons program—reluctantly supported by a Bush administration, for want of a better plan—the Islamists in Tehran have been holding their ground. The mullahs' oppression of civil society in Iran is as intense as ever. The media, for example, is under excruciating pressure from the regime: during the past five years, Iranian authorities have closed more than fifty newspapers. According to Reporters Sans Frontières, the Islamic Republic has the second-greatest number of imprisoned journalists in the world.

Indeed, far from changing Iranian behavior, the so-called EU 3 initiative (so named for its architects: Britain, France, and Germany) merely serves to convince the mullahs that they can act without consequence. It is instructive that executions in Iran have risen proportionally with European trade. Under Khatami, capital punishment ballooned. Iranian newspapers regularly announce public executions, including those of minors.[19]

Despite all this, a fragile civil society has managed thus far to survive the brutal dictatorship of the mullahs. Students, journalists, lawyers, businessmen, and others have created pockets of resistance. They speak on behalf of the millions of their countrymen who are too cowed by the regime's terror and repression to express their opposition openly.

What Needs to Be Done

These Iranians are desperately crying out for secular government. We should heed their call and adopt a comprehensive strategy designed to help them

---

17 See, for example, Suzanne Maloney, *Iran: Time for a New Approach*, Council on Foreign Relations Press, 2004. Maloney, until recently a Middle East policy advisor for ExxonMobil, has now taken up a position on the State Department's policy planning staff as an Iran expert, where she has helped to sabotage the Bush administration's efforts to bring real pressure to bear on the Iranian regime (see note 21).

18 Hosein Musavian, Chief Iranian Negotiator on Nuclear Affairs, appearing on Channel 2, Iranian TV, August 4, 2005 (translated and reproduced by the MEMRI TV Project).

19 For example, *Jomhuri Islami*, February 14, 2004; *Sharq*, February 18, 2004; *Jomhuri Islami*, February 25, 2004.

bring down an Islamist regime that poses a mortal threat to them and to us. Some essential components of such a strategy are the following:

1. **Make freedom in Iran America's declared policy.** It must become the official policy of the government of the United States to *support regime change in Iran*. We must abandon approaches that rely on voluntary behavior modification on the part of the mullahs—a stance they correctly regard as a sign of our weakness.

2. **Do as Reagan did.** We must seek to delegitimize the Tehran regime in every possible venue. A key part of Ronald Reagan's strategy against the Soviet Union was to deny it legitimacy by, among other things, properly calling it "the Evil Empire." The same must now be done with the Islamist regime in Iran.

3. **Pursue two tracks.** The new policy would have both economic and political elements:

   - **Economic warfare.** An economic offensive would include key steps that the American people can promote, such as the energy security initiative (Step 3) and the divest terror strategy (Step 4).
   - **Political warfare.** The United States must wage total political war against the Islamofascists in Tehran, both inside Iran and from the outside. This war should be designed to keep the Iranian regime off balance (including, where necessary, through the use of covert means), with the ultimate goal of undermining its control.

   By exacerbating the mullahs' internal problems, we would also ease the burden of citizens of Iraq, Afghanistan, Lebanon, and Israel, who are currently under assault from Iran and its proxies.

4. **Support resistance movements.** An important part of such a proactive strategy must be an immediate commitment of significant financial resources to help prodemocracy groups in Iran. The Iran Freedom Support Act, introduced by U.S. Sen. Rick Santorum in February 2005, would authorize the president to spend $10 million to support the resistance. This is a good start—but something closer to $300 million will be needed. Such a substantial expenditure would be fully justified if it would help rid the world of one of its most dangerous regimes without recourse to war.

   These funds need to be spent effectively: an earlier appropriation of $3 million to promote pro-democracy groups inside Iran was still unexpended in July 2005 because of the adamant opposition of a single, low-level State Department officer named Suzanne Maloney.[20]

In particular, we need to provide resistance groups with training in the tactics and tools of nonviolent conflict. One place to do so would be through the creation of independent trade unions in Iran. Like the Communist government in Poland, the Islamic Republic seeks to regulate and control all union activity. Unions can be powerful catalysts for liberty by channeling public discontent into irresistible forces for change.

5. **Develop intensive public diplomacy and strategic communications.** The president should appoint a U.S. ambassador to the *people* of Iran, based in Washington, D.C. This ambassador would convene an Iranian-style *majlis*, or national congress, composed of respected leaders of various Iranian communities:

   * Well-known exiles who have been working against the regime for more than two decades.
   * Young people who led the student uprising of July 1999 or more recent protests and had to flee Iran.
   * Representatives of pro-democracy groups inside Iran should also be sought out and, if possible, enabled to participate safely.

   This initiative must involve a no-holds-barred campaign to counteract the regime's influence throughout the region and beyond. That will require greatly expanding the public and private means of communicating directly with the Iranian people, including U.S.-based Iranian expatriate radio networks (see Step 8).

   The United States and the Free World must also help the Iranian people make their voices heard by providing the technical means (such as digital video cameras and satellite phones) to show the world what is happening inside Iran. In our cable news–driven policy debate, if an event is not seen on television, it is widely considered not to have happened.

6. **Confront Iran's nuclear threat.** Last, but hardly least, the United States must come to grips with the reality of Tehran's incipient nuclear weapons program. The Board of Governors of the IAEA agreed in September 2005 to refer Iran's violations of its nuclear safeguards agreements to the UN Security Council for further action—but this is by no means the end of the story. We must expect

---

20 The role played by Ms. Maloney in blocking the prodemocracy grants was detailed by J. Michael Waller of the Institute on World Politics. See "Junior State Department official and Kerry partisan blocks Iran democracy funds," available at http://fourthworldwar.blogspot.com/2005o07o01ofourthworldwaroarchive.html.

abism is characterized by a nearly pathological hatred of all things
ot in keeping with its own view of Islam, as well as by an oppressive
dicial authority. This Islamofascist ideology is thus in conflict with
the entire world. The Saudi regime's efforts to spread its official
ation of Islam—together with its own excesses—is now threatening,
, to undermine its continued control of the kingdom.

ed Society

p contrasts among Saudi Arabia's five distinct geographic regions
official claims of homogeneity:

tral (Najd). This region, from which the royal family originates, is
locus of both the capital, Riyadh, and of the Saud family's politi-
religious strength (Hanbali Wahabism).

stern (Hijaz). This region contains the two holiest sites in Islam:
cca and Medina. It was ruled by the Hashemite tribe for approxi-
ely a thousand years, until it was conquered by the House of Saud
he 1920s. The majority of the population adheres to the relatively
derate Maliki/Shafi'i schools of Sunni Islam.

thern (Asir, Jizan, Najran). This region is perhaps the most eth-
lly, tribally, and religiously diverse population of Saudi Arabia.
majority of the population has tribal and religious ties not with
House of Saud but with neighboring Yemeni peoples. This is
re the central authority is perhaps the weakest and where much of
illicit arms trade and other smuggling occurs. (The bin Laden
ily originates from this region.)

tern (Al-Qatif, Al Ihsa). This region, where most of the oil is found,
me to the kingdom's Shi'as, who constitute the majority of the local
ulation.

thern (Al-Jawf, Al Hudud). Bordering on Jordan and Iraq, this area
diverse in its ethnic and religious makeup as the southern region,
ough not as populous.

tion to these geographical differences, the kingdom's population is
three religious camps. Roughly one-third are Wahhabi (mostly in
l region); one-third Shi'a (mostly in the oil-rich eastern region);
hird of other Sunni schools (scattered throughout the country, but
centrated in the western region).

yal family and the ruling elite within Saudi Arabia almost all come
Najad region. The Wahhabi clerical system, buttressed by oil revenues,

that China and Russia (and perhaps other:
delaying game in the UN as we saw in the c₂
is not on our side; we must develop politi
strategies to counter a nuclear-armed Iran.

In the best case, this political and econo
in helping the Iranian people bring about
start implementing it today, however, resu
some considerable period. The stakes are su
also be prepared to use military force—alor
practicable—to disrupt Iran's known and si

The United States can never win the Wa
as the most active state sponsor of terroi
unchecked its support of violence against fi
least, the emerging ones in Afghanistan an
allowed Iran's nearly three-decade war aga
unanswered. And, unless we deal with it (
future, we will be faced with a nuclear-arn
shown no reluctance to attack American (
ests throughout the world.

Saudi Arabia

Officially, Saudi Arabia is represented as a socie⌐
and single religious faith (namely, the state-spon
as Wahhabism). The kingdom projects also a cai
enlighted, relatively friendly despotism. If not (
have long found a level of comfort in this sort o⌐
not want to see an unstable regime sitting atop r⌐
oil reserves (see Step 3).

In fact, these claims are as substantial as a (
potential for leading the unsuspecting traveler ir
fact a nation of tribes, afflicted with the turbule
plexities that we associate with the Balkans.

The Saudi royal family has deployed its pecu
Islam as an instrument to seize, hold, and expa
its country's people (see Step 1). Dating back (
known as Wahhabism, is a relatively small spli⌐
perhaps 1 percent of one school of Sunni Islam.
sical scholars, Wahhabism is at best a small sect

Wah⌐
that are
clerical⌐
virtuall⌐
interpre
ironical

A Fract⌐

The sha
belie th⌐

◆ C⌐
   th⌐
   ca⌐

◆ W⌐
   M⌐
   m⌐
   in
   m⌐

◆ So⌐
   ni⌐
   Th
   th⌐
   wh
   th⌐
   fai

◆ Ea⌐
   is l⌐
   po⌐

◆ No⌐
   is a
   alt⌐

In ad⌐
split int⌐
the cent⌐
and one-
most co⌐

The r⌐
from the

forms the basis of their power and legitimacy within the kingdom. They remain, nonetheless, the minority tribal and religious grouping.

The Saudis' true power centers—and what gives them prominence on the world stage—are the oil fields in the eastern regions and the Hijaz, which contains Mecca and Medina. Control of these holy cities gives Wahhabism the veneer of religious legitimacy within the Islamic world.

In both of these regions, though, Wahhabism has been especially hostile toward the indigenous populations. This has, in turn, created a great deal of internal pressure that could endanger the hold of the royal family.

The Saudi Double Game

The royal family is itself divided into lineage groups. The two main factions within the five-thousand-prince Saudi royal family have pursued two very different policies to retain power, while other groups within the family ally themselves with one or the other faction. Even in an absolutist monarchy, threats from within and without create jockeying for power.

The principal rivalry is between King Abdullah—who has at least paid lip service to the idea of liberal, if limited, reforms—and his half brothers, known as the Sudeiris. The latter have aligned themselves closely with the most extreme Islamofascist Wahhabis.[21] Both sides, however, continue to make common cause with the Wahhabist clerics in the face of internal pressures.

Notable among such pressures are the increasing violent attacks within the country, engineered by al-Qaeda and its allies. These attacks vividly demonstrate how dangerous Islamist terror can prove to be even to one of its principal sponsors.

The Saudi royals are thus in a completely untenable position. The family is the primary supporter of the religious ideology of Islamofascism—providing funds, direction, intelligence, and diplomatic cover. At the same time, they must relentlessly pursue its domestic adherents, labeling them "deviant elements." In fact, the terrorists' only "deviation" appears to have been their decision to challenge the ruling family's grip on Saudi Arabia.

In short, the House of Saud labors mightily to spread an intolerant religious doctrine that manifests itself as a toxic and violent political ideology. It is blithely unconcerned about the violence thus generated—except when that violence occurs in the Kingdom of Saudi Arabia.

---

21 Michael Scott Doran "The Saudi Paradox," *Foreign Affairs*, January/February 2004.

What Needs to Be Done

As part of putting the United States on a War Footing, we—and other free-dom-loving countries—must stop indulging this intolerable hypocrisy.

The Saudis must be made to understand that we can no longer tolerate their active support for our enemies. They must take concrete steps to curb the further spread of Islamofascism and, specifically, they must end their material role in underwriting and otherwise enabling it.

Specifically, the Saudi government must take the following steps:

1. Incarcerate Islamist clerics and scholars who justify and espouse vio-lence against other Muslims and non-Muslims.

2. End state sponsorship of Wahhabi institutions outside of Saudi Arabia, whether direct or indirect (for example, through Saudi "charities," busi-ness fronts, etc.). Such institutions include entities that purchase, finance, or otherwise support Islamist mosques and madrassas, as well as branch offices of Saudi and Wahhabi "charities."

3. Close "the Islamic interests sections" in Saudi embassies and consulates around the world. These are essentially covert instruments used to sup-port Wahhabi proselytizing and recruitment.

4. End the publication and distribution, in the United States and elsewhere, of official documents advocating jihad, intolerance, or anti-Semitic and anti-Christian behavior.[22]

5. Stop the payments made by Saudi official and other Saudi-controlled sources to families of suicide bombers and to terrorist groups like Hamas and Palestinian Islamic Jihad.[23]

If these essential steps are not implemented, the Saudis must be put on notice that they will suffer serious consequences. In the face of continued unacceptable Saudi behavior, the United States must be prepared to impose the following sanctions:

♦ Reduce the status of bilateral diplomatic relations, up to the closure of missions in both countries.

---

22 See Freedom House's excellent January 2005 study of the jihadist publications placed in American mosques and Muslim schools by the Saudi embassy (Washington, DC). Available at http://www.freedomhouse.org/religion/publications/Saudi%20Report/FINAL%20FINAL.pdf.

23 For specific examples of Saudi payments to the families of suicide bombers and a more general overview of Saudi government support for worldwide jihad, see Kenneth R. Timmerman, *Preachers of Hate: Islam and the War on America*, Crown Forum, 2003, pp. 115–150.

- Place Saudi Arabia on the State Department list of state sponsors of terrorism. This would, among other things, bar U.S. military sales to the kingdom.
- Freeze Saudi assets in the United States.
- Work with Shi'ites in the oil-rich eastern region who seek to break away from Saudi Arabia.
- As a last resort, seize Saudi oil fields and other critical energy infrastructure.

The message should be clear. These are steps we do not wish to undertake. We are fully aware that the repercussions of any such sanctions could be traumatic for both nations—and the world beyond.

We also realize that Saudi oil is a critical ingredient not only in our economy but that of many others. This is one reason why we recommend in Step 3, as an urgent national priority, reducing our reliance on such imported oil and the attendant vulnerability to political blackmail.

We recognize, too, that the likes of Osama bin Laden or Abu Musab al-Zarqawi might come to power in Saudi Arabia if the current regime falls because of U.S. sanctions or otherwise. In that case, however, it would at least be unmistakably clear that Saudi Arabia is in enemy hands, in contrast to the current, delusional belief of the U.S. government that the Saudis are our close and fully cooperative allies in the War for the Free World.[24]

That is surely not the current reality. We can no longer afford to act as though the United States and Saudi Arabia share a true alliance on this central issue. Our future, and that of our children and grandchildren, requires us to take corrective action if the Saudis will not or cannot end their support for Islamofascism.

Pakistan

Even if the Saudis renounced Wahhabism tomorrow and stopped funding its mosques, schools, and other programs around the world, it may already be too late to make a difference in Pakistan. As discussed in Step 1, Pakistan has its own Wahhabist offshoot, called Deobandism. Founded by Wahhabi missionaries in Northern India in 1867, the Deobandi school is just as vitriolic as the Saudis in its hatred of all things that do not meet its standard of what is Islamic.

---

24 Note, for example, Under Secretary of State Karen Hughes' statement in September 2005: "I salute the Kingdom's efforts to work with us to combat terrorism. I am proud of the excellent relations between Saudi Arabia and the United States and the exceptional cooperation between the two countries. Despite occasional disagreements, we have much in common."

The Rise of the Islamists

The Deobandis have played a pivotal, if often unappreciated, role in the history of colonial India—and particularly in the partitioning first of modern India and Pakistan and then in separating what is now known as Bangladesh from Pakistan. They were responsible for creating the world's first truly Islamist political party, founded in 1941 in then-colonial India.[25] Called Jama'at-e-Islami, the party was founded by Sayyid Abul A'la Maududi Jama'at, arguably one of the most important Islamofascists of all time. His writings had a direct impact on Islamism worldwide through his influential followers.

- Hassan al-Banna, founder of the Muslim Brotherhood.
- Ayatollah Seyyed Ruhollah Khomeini, founder and chief ideologue of the modern Islamist state of Iran.
- Syed Qutb, chief theologian of the Muslim Brotherhood, author of *Milestones*, and one of Islamism's key ideologues.
- Al-Faridah al-Gha'ibah, author of *The Neglected Duty* and a key founder of the Takfir wa'l-Hijra movement within the Muslim Brotherhood.
- Abdullah Azzam, one of bin Laden's primary theological inspirations, founder of Hamas and one of the original founders of al-Qaeda.
- Hassan Al-Turabi, founder of Sudan's National Islamic Front and the man who invited bin Laden to set up his operations there.
- Mullar Muhammad Omar, leader of the Taliban movement.
- Ayman al-Zawahiri, a leader within the Takfir movement and a second in command of al-Qaeda.
- Omar Abdul Rahman, spiritual guide to Ayman al-Zawahiri, currently in U.S. federal prison for planning and assisting in acts of terrorism within the United States.

The influence of Maududi and his Jama'at-e-Islami organization was particularly great in his country of origin, which came to be known as Pakistan. And, with Saudi help, both the party and the ideology have expanded their reach dramatically over time, most notably in the Pakistani government.

The Islamist "Death Spiral"

One indication of this growing influence is the equivalent status now assigned to degrees from madrassas (Islamic schools), placed on a par with secular academic programs for gaining admission into the military, intelligence service,

---

25 Although the Muslim Brotherhood was founded in 1928 by philosophical cousins of the Wahhabis in Egypt, it was originally intended not as a political party but as a social movement with a political agenda.

and civil service. This equivalence, in turn, has fundamentally altered Pakistan's society over the years—and especially its governing institutions. It has also done potentially irreparable damage to the country's economy, given the narrow religious and ideological scope of the madrassa education.

As a result, what was once among the most promising of developing nations has been reduced by Islamofascism to seemingly unending poverty and despair.

The grim economic realities feed into the death spiral typical of Islamist societies. Young people are subjected to what amounts to ideological indoctrination, in Koranic madrassas and, recently, in formerly secular public schools. As discussed in Step 1, they graduate ill equipped for employment other than to pursue jihad at home or abroad (in Kashmir, Afghanistan, India, and, most recently, Britain). The economy continues to nose-dive, creating still fewer alternatives to the opportunities afforded by terrorist recruiters.

Jama'at-e-Islami's current theologian is Khurshid Ahmad. Although virtually unknown to most American policy makers, he is one of the most influential contemporary Islamist ideologues. In a 2002 book titled *Amrika: Muslim Dunya ki Bey-Itminan* (America and Unrest in the Muslim World), Ahmad suggested the need for a Sino-Islamist alliance against the United States.

Even though many experts tend to dismiss the possibility of such an arrangement between atheistic Communist China and the Islamofascists, if the Islamists have taught us anything during this War for the Free World, it is that the only real limit to our enemies' malevolence is their own imaginations. We need to recognize, more specifically, that China has played a central role in assisting in the development of Pakistan's nuclear arsenal, which role dates back to the 1970s (see Part C of this chapter).

What Needs to Be Done

Pakistan's leader, Gen. Pervez Musharaf, has taken some steps that have been helpful to the war effort, notably by arresting foreign al-Qaeda members (see Step 1). But America's long-term security, as it relates to a nuclear-armed, Islamist-dominated Pakistan, cannot be based solely on a relationship with that country's current president. Furthermore, given the pace and extent of radicalization of the military and security organizations within Pakistan, it is very much an open question who the country's next leader will be and whether he will have a favorable or hostile attitude toward the United States.

In particular, there are many uncertainties about Pakistan's national commitment to a final victory by the Free World over Islamofascist groups like al-Qaeda. Quite apart from the ideological solidarity felt by many Pakistanis for their soulmates, there are tangible economic, political, and military benefits for a destitute country to be on the front lines of this war.

Nonetheless, several steps need to be taken while the opportunity exists.

1. Cut off Saudi funding for Islamist operations in Pakistan, as an essential first step.
2. Support a serious effort by General Musharaf to rebuild—outside of the government's control—Pakistan's former civil and democratic society.
3. Press for a government-wide effort to purge itself of Islamists, including a serious examination of the military and intelligence organization and a reversal of the practice of installing officers and officeholders who lack a truly secular education.
4. Finally, in Pakistan, as elsewhere, a proper U.S. political warfare strategy must be designed and implemented to counter the domestic appeal of the Islamist message (see Step 8).

Turkey

During the Cold War, the United States and its European allies had no more important strategic partner than Turkey. If anything, Turkey's role in the War for the Free World could be even more vital were it to serve as a democratic Muslim bulwark against Islamofascism. Yet, we now seem poised to lose that ally.

In a process with parallels to Pakistan (and reminiscent of other totalitarian hijackings of democratic governments), an fascistic takeover is under way in Turkey. It is being orchestrated by the Islamist AK Party (AKP), led by Prime Minister Recep Tayyip Erdogan, who is systematically turning his country from a secular democracy with a Muslim society into a state governed by a radical Islamic ideology hostile to Western values and freedoms.

The evidence of such an ominous transformation is not hard to find.

♦ Turkey is awash with billions of dollars of what is known as "green money," derived apparently from funds withdrawn by Saudi Arabia and other Persian Gulf states from the United States after September 11. U.S. policy makers are concerned that this unaccountable cash is being laundered in Turkey and used to finance businesses and generate new revenue streams for Islamist terrorism. It is certain at least that Erdogan's Islamist agenda is being lubricated by these resources.

♦ Turkey's traditionally secular educational system is being steadily supplanted by madrassa-style "imam hatip" schools and other institutions, where students are taught only the Koran and its interpretation according to the Islamists. The prime minister is himself an imam hatip school graduate and has championed lowering the age at which children can be subjected to this form of radical religious indoctrination, from twelve years old to four. In 2005, 1,215,000 Turkish students are expected to graduate from such schools. As we have seen elsewhere, the products of such schools emerge ill equipped for anything besides implementing the Islamist program of Erdogan's AKP.

♦ Tens of thousands of these madrassa graduates have already received government jobs, replacing experienced, secular bureaucrats with ideologically reliable theo-apparatchiks. In addition, an estimated four thousand madrassa graduates have packed Turkey's secular courts, in effect transforming them into instruments of Shari'a religious law.

♦ Religious intolerance is also on the increase. The one-third of the population known as Alevis observe a strain of Islam that retains some of the pre-Islamic traditions. Regarded as "apostates" and "hypocrites" by Sunni fundamentalists, they are subjected to increasing discrimination and intimidation. Other minorities, notably Turkey's Jews, are apprehensive of receiving the same treatment.

♦ In the name of internationally mandated "reform" of Turkey's banking system, the government is seizing the assets and operations of banks run by businessmen associated with the political opposition, even in the face of successive rulings by Turkey's supreme court explicitly disallowing one such expropriation.

♦ The AKP-dominated parliament has enacted legislation modeled after Nazi Germany's "kinship laws"—statutes that allow even distant relatives of business owners to be prosecuted for the proprietors' alleged wrongdoings. Among the beneficiaries of such shakedowns have been so-called Islamic banks tied to Saudi Arabia, some of whose senior officers now hold top jobs in the Erdogan government.

♦ By expropriating assets—or threatening to do so—the government has managed effectively to take control of the Turkish media. One conglomerate friendly to the Islamists now owns upward of 90 percent of the nation's press outlets. Combined with the increasing self-censorship of reporters, the result has been to deny prominent vehicles for the expression of mainstream views opposing the government.

♦ Thanks in part to Erdogan's domination of the press, Turkey has seen an inflaming of public opinion against President Bush and the United States. In 2005, a novel describing a war between America and Turkey and the nuclear destruction of Washington became a runaway best-seller, even in the Turkish military.

- ♦ The Islamists have also made substantial inroads in the Turkish armed forces—traditionally the guarantor of the secular, pro-Western Muslim state created by modern Turkey's founder, Mustafa Kemal Ataturk.

  - • The army must increasingly fill its ranks with conscripts who are products of an Islamist-dominated educational system.
  - • With Erdogan's "zero-problem" policy toward neighboring Iran and Syria, the Turkish military no longer provides a check on the regional drift toward Islamism.

What Needs to Be Done

1. As elsewhere in the Mideast and its periphery, the United States must help those moderate Muslims and others in Turkey who are bravely resisting the Islamists and their policies of political repression, religious intolerance, and economic impoverishment.
2. Turkey would also benefit, in the long run, from a cutoff of the green money and other subversive funding from Saudi Islamists. Turks would be better able to resist the Islamofascist onslaught if the United States begins to wage effective political warfare on behalf of freedom, in Turkey and in the region.
3. The West, however, has one other extraordinary opportunity to have an impact on Turkey's future course. Millions of Turks want to become part of the European Union, recognizing that membership will open up enormous economic and other opportunities.

   The Europeans should make it clear that Erdogan's Islamist takeover makes Turkey's EU bid a nonstarter. The AKP program will render Turkey ineligible for membership on the grounds that it will inevitably ruin its economy, radicalize its society, and eliminate Ankara's ability to play the constructive role made possible in the past by Turkey's geographic position in the "cockpit of history." Such a message could prove decisive in pulling Turkey back from the abyss and restoring to the Free World a valued ally.

Israel

An ally no less critical to the War for the Free World—and similarly on the front lines of that conflict—is the Middle East's only genuine democracy: Israel.

Some have mistakenly claimed that the Islamists' hostility toward the United States is due to America's support for Israel. According to this theory, if America would only abandon the Jewish State, the Muslim world's hostility toward this country would dissipate.

The facts are very different. As we have seen in Step 1, like all other totalitarian ideologies, Islamofascism needs a scapegoat to account for failures within the communities it seeks to dominate. For the Islamists, Israel provides one near at hand. But make no mistake: the Islamists' ultimate enemy is the one nation most capable of thwarting their designs—the United States of America. For example, in the notorious October 26, 2005, address given by Mahmoud Ahmadinejad, the Iranian president not only called for Israel to be wiped from the map, he also declared: "Is it possible for us to witness a world without America and Zionism? But you had best know that this slogan and this goal are attainable, and surely can be achieved."[26]

Indeed, it is not Israel that is labeled the "Great Satan" by the Islamists. That distinction is reserved for the United States. Israel is rather seen as a creation of the West, as a nation used by the United States to control the entire region; it is therefore referred to as the "Little Satan."

Both Islamists and secular Arab dictatorships throughout the Middle East have cultivated this preposterous claim for decades, as an excuse for the failure of the Arab countries to provide for their own people. This is one of the reasons why many Arab leaders have no interest in a permanent solution to the Palestinian-Israeli conflict.

The fact is that Israel is an *asset* in this war, not a liability. It is in a unique position to assist the United States in surviving and prevailing.

What Needs to Be Done

1. As a relatively young, but highly advanced state, Israel is an example of what is possible in the region for a free and democratic nation. Unless and until Iraq provides an Arab example,[27] Israel remains the only nation in the Middle East that demonstrates what people can do if afforded political and economic freedom. The United States should highlight this model, as a contrast to the dismal fate of countries subjected to Islamist misrule (see Step 8).

2. Thanks to Israel's geographic location and experience, it is in a unique position to provide both a physical platform for American operations and—one of the most important resources for this war—human

---

26 See http://www.memri.org/bin/openerolatest.cgi?ID=SD101305 and http://www.isna.ir/Main/NewsView.aspx?ID=News-603386

27 As discussed in Step 2, the enemies we are fighting in Iraq today are making such a determined effort to sabotage democracy there precisely because it would fundamentally undermine their entire ideological claim and discredit their vision.

intelligence (see Step 2). For instance, since its founding, Israel has been fighting for its very survival against many of the same forces we now face. As such, they have developed sources and methods of intelligence gathering that can be simply invaluable. In addition, for decades their security and intelligence services have had to be intimately familiar with Arabic.[28] The fact that Israel shares our Western values and interests makes it possible for us to take full advantage of such help.

3. Finally, Israel is an island of democracy surrounded by varying shades of tyranny. At a time when we are trying not only to defend the Free World but also to expand it, America's interests are best served by firmly aligning ourselves with the forces of freedom and democracy throughout the world, including in Israel.

In Step 2, we discussed the necessity of ensuring that freedom is consolidated in Iraq and the calamitous implications of abandoning that effort. It would be even more damaging for the United States to acquiesce in—let alone preside over—the dismantling of an *existing* outpost of the Free World. Such a step would be more than a tragedy for the Jewish State. It would also be a body blow to America's own security. Having finished off the "Little Satan," emboldened Islamist terrorists would surely come gunning for the "Great Satan."

Few countries, in the Mideast or elsewhere, have more to offer the United States as it moves onto a War Footing than the tiny state of Israel, a nation that has had to remain on such a footing ever since its founding fifty-seven years ago.

---

28 In the United States prior to September 11, 2001, there was not much demand for specialists in Arabic. The resulting shortfall in reliable, competent translators is one of our most acute counterterrorism challenges (see Step 10).

B. Counter the Islamofascists and their Friends in Africa

With Contributions from Christopher Brown and David McCormack

A t the dawn of the Cold War, even the most forward-thinking analyst could not have predicted the role that Korea (much less Cuba, Vietnam, Nicaragua, or Afghanistan) would play in the unfolding confrontation between the United States and the Soviet Union. Foreign policy experts in the latter 1940s were largely preoccupied, understandably, with the future of postwar Europe; nevertheless, entire regions that were at that time "off the radar" would prove to be pivotal.

Similarly, few policy makers today recognize the large role that Africa will play in the War for the Free World—in spite of some notable warning signs.

- One of al-Qaeda's first major strikes was the murderous attack on U.S. embassies in Kenya and Tanzania in 1998.
- Osama bin Laden found safe haven in Islamist Sudan from 1991 to 1996, before reestablishing his operation in Afghanistan.
- Al-Qaeda and other terrorist organizations are widely believed to be involved in the "blood diamond" trade in Angola, Sierra Leone, Liberia, and the Congo, as a means of both laundering money and financing their operations.[1]

These indicators are just a few of the "dots" that we need to connect if we are to understand the enemy's strategy for Africa.

---

1 Jeff Miller and Jeanette Goldman, " 'No' Court for Taylor, NBC Links Diamonds to Terror," *Rapaport News*, July 21, 2005.

South Africa: The Rudder of Africa

A strategic understanding of Africa must look beyond the micro-level—the fifty-four different nations, with more than one thousand languages and countless ethnic, tribal, cultural, and religious differences—to take a macro-level perspective. A strategic analysis must start with the Republic of South Africa, unquestionably the dominant actor on the continent due to its economic strength, military power, and rich natural resources. South Africa is central to any examination of contemporary Africa's strategic trends—and their worrying implications.

South Africa is a land of stark contradictions. Still recovering from decades of apartheid, it straddles, often uneasily, both the Western and the developing worlds. Yet, like a giant rudder, it sets the course that steers the entire continent.

Most Americans have forgotten (or never knew) that the current ruling party in South Africa, the African National Congress (ANC), was for most of its pre-government history a revolutionary organization that served as a front for Moscow during the Cold War. It was heavily supported by the Kremlin, as a means of undermining the West-friendly apartheid government of South Africa.

This background is relevant, even though the ANC is no longer in the opposition, let alone surviving in the bush as a revolutionary insurgency. In fact, the party now exercises virtually complete power in South Africa.

Still, the ANC's longstanding anti-U.S. orientation helps explain the domestic political and foreign policy activities of the current government. Unfortunately, under the influence of the ANC, Praetoria has steadily been moving South Africa—and hence the rest of Africa—away from the United States and toward ideologies and nations opposed to American interests.

Specifically, since the ANC came to power, South Africa has reached out to Communist China as well as to Libya, Iran, Syria, and other state sponsors of terrorism, including Fidel Castro's Cuba. These activities are not limited to the standard diplomatic relations. They involve a sustained effort to align the country and its people with those hostile to the United States and the Free World in the current global conflict.

Cause for Concern

Consider these worrisome recent developments in South Africa:

♦ The ANC has brought into South Africa an undetermined number of Cuban doctors.[2] As the foreign physicians embed themselves in the host

---

2   This move predated, and served as a model for, Fidel Castro's support for the increasingly authoritarian Chavez regime in Venezuela (see Section D of this step).

society, they serve as a vanguard for the host government's efforts to consolidate control, offering improved medical care in exchange for ever-fewer freedoms.

- The ANC is working on switching the international news feed on the three government-owned television channels—from CNN International to the English news service of al Jazeera.

- Two prominent organizations in South Africa are funded by and responsive to Iran: Qibla, a radical Islamist organization inspired by Khomeini's revolution, and People Against Gangsterism and Drugs (PAGAD), an increasingly violent Islamist vigilante group founded by Qibla as a self-contained system of social service and security.[3]

As long ago as 1996, South Africa's then-president Nelson Mandela was asked about reports that Iran was providing financial support to the Qibla and, by association, the PAGAD movement. He replied: "I am not aware of the Islamic Republic [of Iran] funding Qibla. If they do so, *there is no reason why we should complain. . . .* Any particular party or group is entitled to raise funds wherever they want."[4]

- While Mandela was downplaying Tehran's connections to Islamists in South Africa, PAGAD was signing an agreement of cooperation with the Iranian intelligence ministry.[5] This agreement turned PAGAD into the eyes and ears of Iran in southern Africa in 1996, just as al-Qaeda was being expelled from the Sudan.

- In addition to PAGAD's Iranian connection, the organization may also have established direct ties with al-Qaeda. In September 1999, Khalfan Khamis Mohamed, an al-Qaeda operative involved in the Tanzania attacks, was arrested in Cape Town, where he had been living openly since the bombings.[6]

- Members of MAGO (Muslims Against Global Oppression), a PAGAD front organization, bombed the Cape Town Planet Hollywood in January

---

3   See: "South Africa: Iranian agents accused of training Islamic terrorists," *London Daily Telegraph* December 8, 1996; "Islamic militants threaten war against government," *Agence France Presse*, August 12, 1996; and Christopher Brown "PAGAD & Qibla: The Terrorist Connection in South Africa," *Hudson Institute Briefing Note*, August 29, 2004.

4   "Mandela condemns US attacks on Iraq, affirms support for Iran," *Agence France Presse*, October 13, 1996.

5   Con Coughlin, "South Africa: Iranian agents accused of training Islamic terrorists," *London Daily Telegraph*, December 8, 1996.

6   One bit of good news is that Muhamed was arrested in a joint U.S.-South African operation, extradited to the United States in October 1999, and convicted for his part in the Tanzania murders of embassy personnel and locals. Jerry Seper, "U.S. vet admits helping terrorist," *The Washington Times*, October 21, 2000.

1999. The pretext was retaliation for the largely symbolic American strikes in the Sudan and Afghanistan, launched in response to the bombing of the two U.S. African embassies six months before.

♦ Two South Africans were recently deported from Pakistan because of their association with an al-Qaeda operative—a Tanzanian citizen named Ahmed Khalfan Ghailani who had purchased the truck and bomb-making material used in the Tanzania attacks and who had been captured in Pakistan.[7] The two South Africans have not been charged with anything, nor has there been an explanation of what they were doing in Pakistan in the company of a known al-Qaeda member.

♦ The ANC recently undermined joint U.S.-U.K. efforts to counter the increasingly capricious despotism of Zimbabwe's Robert Mugabe. Particularly ominous was the statement by the new deputy president of South Africa, Phumzile Mlambo-Ngcuka, that the ANC should pursue some of what have proved to be Mugabe's most dangerous and disastrous policies.[8]

This was not empty talk: In May 2005, the party successfully used the courts to block a South African newspaper from publishing a report on illegal transfers of funds from the state-owned oil company to the ANC's accounts.[9] Such behavior calls to mind an old saying: If you want to know where South Africa will be in ten years, look at where Zimbabwe is now.

The Libyan Connection

Of special concern is the rapprochement the ANC government has engineered with Muammar Gadhafi's Libya. Given its geographic location and traditional orientation, most people associate Libya with Arab North Africa or the Middle East. In recent years, however, a strategically momentous shift has occurred in Tripoli.

Gadhafi has been thwarted in his dream of being the next great pan-Arab leader. So, he has looked southward instead, in the hope of casting himself as the dominant force in Africa.

Toward this end, Gadhafi has reached out to his ideological soulmates throughout Africa. Preeminent among them is the ANC. The two governments

---

7   Paul Haven, "Pakistan: South Africans plotted attack," Associated Press, August 5, 2004.
8   Basildon Peta, "We should learn from Mugabe, says South Africa's deputy leader," *The Independent*, August 12, 2005.
9   Andrew Meldrum, "Court gag on South Africa 'oilgate' report," *The Guardian*, May 28, 2005.

have now joined forces in the tradition of other radical leftist governments around the world. An immediate goal of both nations has been to take control of regional organizations. The result has been an emerging north-south axis running from Tripoli to Cape Town, seeking to dominate the African Union and the continent.

The United States is very poorly positioned to counter this ominous strategic development, thanks to its own efforts at rapprochement with Gadhafi. This is a policy shift intended to "reward" the Libyan dictator for his recent purported "change of heart": ostensibly, Gadhafi decided after the liberation of Iraq to terminate his weapons of mass destruction programs and to end his ill-concealed support for terror.

It is unclear whether Gadhafi has actually had anything like a change of heart with respect to WMDs. What *is* certain is that he recognized that his regime's survival might depend on convincing the United States that he had, in fact, abandoned such programs. With Saddam gone, he feared, he might be the next despot in the U.S. crosshairs.

Ever the pragmatist, the Libyan dictator has tried to parlay this opening into a restoration of relations between Tripoli and Washington—and, especially, an end to the crippling American economic sanctions on his country.

This may be an instance of the United States enabling a despot to live to terrorize another day. Thanks in part to our long-standing sanctions, the Libyan economy is a shambles, with more than 30 percent of the population unemployed. Most probably, Gadhafi abandoned a weapons program that he could no longer afford; in response, the United States has begun easing its economic sanctions and rehabilitating Libya's leader. By so doing, U.S. policy has undermined the regime's democratic opposition within Libya, as well as the Libyan exile community.

This rapprochement is especially regrettable because Gadhafi's promises to end his support of terror ring hollow indeed. Even after his "change of heart," the United States obtained evidence of Gadhafi's involvement in a new plot: he had ordered the assassination of the then-crown prince (now king) of Saudi Arabia, in retaliation for a personal insult at a meeting of the Arab league.[10] The organizer of the plot was reported to be the head of Libya's foreign intelligence service, Musa Kusa—the same official designated to serve as Libya's point of contact for sharing intelligence with the United States.[11]

In spite of this pattern of duplicity, there is talk of further rewards for Gadhafi: the lifting of all sanctions, removal from the state sponsors of terror

---

10 Ibid.
11 Ibid.

list, and inclusion of Libya in the American-backed Trans-Sahara Counter-Terrorism Initiative. Few measures are more likely than the latter to compromise the operational security and the moral integrity of that program—especially given the despot's ongoing, aggressive efforts to promote Islamofascism and terrorism.

The Best Hope for Africa: Kenya and Nigeria

The best hope for countering the South African-Libyan axis is to strengthen the two African states with the potential to serve as counterweights: Kenya and Nigeria.

- ◆ Both Kenya and Nigeria are recognized by their neighbors as linchpins in the security architectures of their respective regions, East and West Africa.
- ◆ Both are functioning, if young, democracies; both are well-positioned economically, with the second- and seventh-largest GDPs, respectively, in the sub-Saharan region.
- ◆ The governing parties in both countries have proved to be allies of the United States, most noticeably through their support for American initiatives in the so-called War on Terror.

Despite these positive factors, Nigeria and Kenya are also both under sustained assault from Islamofascists and their supporters—from within the two countries' respective borders, from elsewhere on the continent (in particular, Libya and South Africa), and from outside (notably, Saudi Arabia, Iran, and Pakistan).

Sub-Saharan Africa is an extremely tempting target for the Islamist agenda. Its Muslim population of about 250 million offers a massive base from which to draw support. Its natural resources are immense. And, because of the almost complete neglect of this region in Western security circles, the Islamists have been able to develop their footprint there while operating in relative obscurity.

In addition, the subcontinent's budding democracies are largely powerless to fend off Islamist challenges to their authority. Porous borders, steady flows of illicit arms, and weak and corrupt political and financial institutions create an ideal operating environment for Islamists.

With Saudi Arabia leading the way over the past forty years, tens of billions of dollars have been poured into the region in support of these ideologues' activities. Often this is accomplished through nominally nongovernmental organizations, such as the Riyadh-controlled Muslim World League. According to Saudi sources, more funding for activity in Africa is provided to the Ministry of Islamic Affairs than to Saudi ambassadors.[12]

As is true elsewhere around the world, this money funds (among other things) radical mosques and madrassas and training for African clerics in extremism (see Step 1). In this way, *the Islamists are steadily eliminating the tolerant and moderate traditions of African Islam*—traditions that have historically contributed so much to the region in the areas of education, commerce, and government.

Taking hold in their stead is a volatile mix of the various strains of Islamist ideology taught in the regions' Wahhabi, Khomeini, and Deobandi schools. Given the context of endemic poverty, despotic and corrupt repression, vicious tribal sectarianism, periodic droughts and famines, and rampant health crises (especially the spread of the AIDS virus), the African stage is set for almost limitless jihadist recruitment.

The Shari'a Gambit

The numerous terror groups operating in the region are the most conspicuous manifestations of the Islamist advance. The primary method employed by Islamists in their takeover of Africa is less obvious, however. Whereas some seek armed revolution, others employ the more sophisticated political and social warfare techniques developed by Hezbollah in Lebanon and the Muslim Brotherhood in Jordan and Egypt.

These Islamofascists are using a more gradual, but no less insidious, means to come to power, usually tailored to exploit local conditions. The most commonly employed tactic is to try to establish Shari'a law at the regional level, creating a separate legal system for Islamic communities. The resulting opposition is then skillfully portrayed by Islamists as infringing upon "Muslim rights," and the Islamists themselves as the legitimate defenders of these "rights." This role, of course, enhances the influence of the Islamists, relative to the more moderate Muslims.

Nigeria. The Shari'a gambit has proved particularly successful in parts of Nigeria, where Islam claims 60 million adherents (roughly half the total population). In the shake-up that followed liberation from military rule in 1999, twelve predominantly Muslim states in northern Nigeria took advantage of the central government's weakened position to institute Shari'a and other Islamist social policies.

---

12 David B. Ottoway, "U.S. eyes money trails of Saudi-backed charities," *The Washington Post*, August 19, 2004.

The Islamist agenda in Nigeria has achieved frightening progress in the following areas:

♦ Segregation by sex on public transportation.
♦ A ban on alcohol, regardless of a citizen's faith.
♦ The institutionalization of corporal and capital punishment—including flogging and death by stoning.
♦ The forced teaching of Arabic.
♦ Compensation of Islamic preachers out of state funds.
♦ A deadly outbreak of polio that spread to several neighboring countries and some non-African Muslim countries, carried by pilgrims to Mecca. (Nigerian imams, alleging an American plot to sterilize Muslim women and infect their children with AIDS, had suspended inoculations with U.S.-supplied vaccines.)

If the Islamofascist agenda in Nigeria succeeds in its larger aims, the country will emerge as two separate societies: one Islamist and the other non-Muslim. Even worse, the widening imposition of Shari'a could trigger a civil war, possibly resulting in the forced imposition of Islamofascist rule over the entire country.

Kenya. Across the continent in Kenya, similar forces are at work among the Muslim population (at roughly 10 percent of the total, some 3 million people). Kenyan Islamists have focused on demanding that Kadhi (Islamic) courts be recognized in the national constitution, now being drafted. If they succeed, segments of Kenyan society would be governed by Shari'a, with predictable implications for further separatism and, in due course, sectarian strife.

As divided nations, democratic Kenya and Nigeria will be unable to provide effective African leadership—let alone counter the influence of Libya and South Africa. We must take prompt and effective measures to defeat the destabilizing Islamist agenda, not only in these two countries but also throughout Africa.

What Needs to Be Done

The U.S. policy posture in Africa today is reminiscent of the British policy of the mid-19th century that came to be known as "Masterful Inactivity"—a hands-off attitude that, in the end, facilitated Russia's conquest of almost all of Central Asia. For us to persist in such a posture today would be bad news not only for our own interests in the continent but also for the peoples and nations of Africa.

The United States has recently begun taking some steps in the right direction, though much remains to be accomplished.

1. **Support the Trans-Sahara Counter-Terrorism Initiative (TSCTI).** The TSCTI—partnering the United States with nine African countries—provides an excellent basis for helping those in Africa who aspire to freedom to build a comprehensive security framework. Launched in June 2005, TSCTI brings to bear the resources of the departments of Defense (with notable leadership from the European Command's Gen. James Jones), State, and Treasury, together with the U.S. Agency for International Development.

   This initiative will offer not only expanded joint military training and border control programs. It will also monitor money-laundering, provide developmental assistance aimed at promoting good governance, and encourage the growth of civil society. TSCTI's relatively small budget of $100 million per year will likely prove insufficient. Importantly, however, if countries like Libya are allowed to participate, *the program will be utterly compromised.*

2. **Develop public diplomacy.** Despite the positive recognition through TSCTI that a comprehensive approach is needed to tackle Islamism in Africa, the United States is continuing to fail miserably on another front: public diplomacy. Unfortunately, as we have seen in Step 8, this problem is not confined to the African continent. But it is particularly acute there.

   America's chief mechanism for promoting public diplomacy in Africa is the Voice of America, with 40 million listeners in Africa (out of VOA's total worldwide audience of 96 million). Yet, only 7 percent of VOA's budget ($11.5 million/year) is directed toward Africa. This effort warrants massive expansion.[13]

3. **Redirect official development assistance funds.** Public diplomacy and initiatives (such as TSCTI) can be funded without an increase in spending, by redirecting funds from official development assistance (ODA). These government-to-government outlays have largely been squandered by corrupt and unaccountable regimes. As a result, despite decades of such aid, the average African is poorer today than in 1970.

4. **Invigorate state-to-state diplomacy.** Combat the Islamist phenomenon by focusing on choking off radical Islam's authority and popularity.

---

13 For more on the ways in which the United States must use communications technologies to wage political warfare, see Step 8.

As discussed elsewhere in various contexts, both in this and other chapters, this will require, among other things, applying pressure to states outside of Africa—most especially, Saudi Arabia—that export Islamism to the region. Similarly, pressure should be applied on African governments contributing to the democracy deficit that makes Islamism's offer of empowerment alluring to frustrated populations.

5. **Engage the battle.** More than anything else, the United States and its people must recognize that we have long been targets in ideological wars for the hearts and minds of Africans. We have so far been largely unengaged in this battle, even though it has cost us dearly, both in terms of our strategic position and American lives.

    In order for the United States to win on this front of the global conflict in which we are embroiled—an outcome vital to our long-term strategic interests—we must recognize the need also to place our efforts in Africa on a true War Footing. This will require applying the nation's full political warfare arsenal and, as appropriate, its military capabilities to what Clausewitz called the enemy's "center of gravity." That means not only addressing the Islamofascists' bases of operation and support but also the ideology with which they are threatening the lives and prosperity and the people of Africa, as well as our own.

C. Thwart China's Ambitions for Hegemony in Asia and Beyond

With Contributions from Al Santoli and Lt. Col. Gordon Cucullu, USA (Ret.)

T he War for the Free World would be sufficiently complicated and challenging for America and other freedom-loving peoples if all we had to worry about were the Islamofascists and their state sponsors. Unfortunately, Communist China has chosen this moment to emerge as a "peer competitor"—a Pentagon euphemism for potential enemy.[1]

Our strategies for contending with the worldwide challenges posed by totalitarian Islamism will increasingly have to take into account, in Asia and elsewhere, an unappetizing reality. The Free World must deal simultaneously with China, with its immense and still-growing financial strength, its rapidly building and ever-more-offensively oriented military, and its increasingly ill-concealed global ambitions.

China's strategy appears to aim at displacing the United States as the world's preeminent economic power and, if necessary, at defeating us militarily. Although conflict with China may yet be avoidable, the Chinese government appears to believe otherwise and is apparently preparing for war in Asia and globally. In pursuit of this objective, Beijing is making common cause with the Islamist imams of Iran, the Wahhabis of Saudi Arabia, and the mullahs of Sudan. They are also embracing virtually every one of freedom's other foes from Hugo Chavez in Venezuela to the military junta in Burma, from Kim Jong-Il's North Korea to Fidel Castro's Cuba.

---

1   It is important to state plainly that our foe is the *government* of China, and not the Chinese people, who have no voice in their country's policies—domestic or international.

We can no longer safely ignore these developments. Neither can we bank on constraining the PRC's behavior through a strategy of "engagement"; that is, through bilateral trade relations (even on terms wildly disadvantageous to us), supposedly shared concerns about terrorism, or a purported mutual interest in a "nuclear-free Korean peninsula."

China's de facto alliance with the Islamists can best be understood in this light: It serves Beijing's strategy to support the Islamofascists' war against the West, as a way of bleeding and demoralizing U.S. forces in advance of a Sino-American conflict.

Part of a War Footing strategy thus requires a fresh appraisal of Chinese intentions, derived from a candid assessment of their conduct and their projected, as well as actual, capabilities. From such an assessment, the United States must develop initiatives within and beyond the Asian region to counter Communist China's agenda and thus protect the Free World from the PRC's emergence as one of the Islamists' most important anti-Western benefactors.

China Plans for War

Beijing's party cadres and military leaders have long been taught that war with the United States is "inevitable." Consistent with more than a decade of strategic writings,[2] Chinese diplomats who recently defected to Australia reported that the United States is routinely described in official circles as the "main enemy."

Here is another, appalling insight into the attitude toward us of the Chinese Communists. After September 11, 2001, Beijing sponsored official videos showing the collapse of the World Trade Center towers and the damage at the Pentagon, accompanied by the following commentary:

> This is the America the whole world wanted to see—blood debts being repaid in blood. . . . Look at the panic in their faces as they wipe off the dust and their once-strong buildings are just a heap of rubble. We will never fear these people again. They have shown themselves to be soft-bellied paper tigers—these Americans.[3]

Although the PRC is clearly preparing for such a war, the strategy they are pursuing appears designed—in keeping with the admonition of the ancient

---

2   See Michael Pillsbury, *China Debates, the Future Security Environment*, National Defense University Press, 2000; and *Chinese Views of Future Warfare*, National Defense University Press, 1998.

3   Cliff Kincaid, "Saving the United Nations from Itself," *USASurvival.org*, available at http://www.usasurvival.org/ck91202.shtml.

Chinese strategist Sun Tsu—to win if possible *without having to fight*. The following sections illustrate the many manifestations of this strategy.

A "First World" Military

China is engaging in a massive, high-technology, and offensively oriented military buildup—particularly of its missile, naval, and air forces.[4] The evident purpose is for the PRC to be able to project power credibly throughout East Asia. The most immediate objective appears to be to intimidate Taiwan into surrendering rather than trying to defend itself. This goal has been advanced in four ways.

- Earlier this year, Beijing went through the motions of adopting an "Anti-Secession Law," as an explicit warning to Taipei that it would use "non-peaceful means" in the event the island moved toward independence.
- The Chinese have made clear their ability to inflict mass destruction on Taiwan without warning. Toward this end, the PRC has deployed, among other offensive weapons, as many as 700 ballistic missiles aimed at Taiwan—with 150 more being added annually.
- The PRC is striving to deter the United States from dispatching carrier battle groups and other military assets to defend Chinese democracy on Taiwan by promising their certain destruction at the hands of superior numbers of increasingly sophisticated Chinese missiles, planes, and submarines.
- Using classic "United Front" tactics, mainland China is seducing Taiwanese politicians and businessmen to accept the inevitability of the PRC's takeover of the island.

The Moscow-Beijing Axis

Chinese military capabilities are being relentlessly enhanced by an ever-closer strategic partnership between Beijing and Moscow (see Section E of this step for a discussion of Russia). This arrangement has already equipped the People's Liberation Army (PLA) with advanced Russian destroyers, aircraft, missiles, radar, warhead designs, and other systems that, together, can now threaten U.S. forward-deployed forces, as well as American bases in Japan and elsewhere.

In 2005, Beijing and Moscow took this partnership one step further, by engaging in joint war games whose scenario clearly contemplated the two

---

4   Annual Report to Congress: The Military Power of the People's Republic of China 2005, Office of the Secretary of Defense, United States Department of Defense, available at http://www.defenselink.mil/news/Jul2005/d20050719china.pdf.

countries' forces taking on a military that looked a lot like ours. On August 15, 2005, the *Washington Post* reported: "Toward the end of the operation, the Russians will deploy strategic long-range bombers, which will fire cruise missiles at targets on the surface of the sea." That phase of the exercise could only have been directed at Free World naval forces, and most likely, those of the U.S. Navy.

By Hook and by Crook

China continues to mount the most comprehensive espionage and technology-theft program in the history of the world—involving untold numbers of overseas Chinese businessmen, students, tourists, and others, as well as professional collectors. According to a 1999 House select committee chaired by then-Congressman Christopher Cox, the PRC has had as many as *three thousand front companies* performing these functions in America alone.[5]

Chinese Hegemonism

China is behaving in an increasingly assertive fashion, globally and regionally—vis-à-vis not only Taiwan but also America's other traditional allies in East Asia.

China's "Near Abroad"

- Chinese submarines have begun encroaching on Japanese waters.
- The Chinese media has openly published a description of its military's warship patrols, and the ultramodern network of "fortresses of the sea" being built in the Spratley Islands, which are contested by neighboring countries.
- China has claimed Japan's Senkaku Islands outright. Should Japan begin to drill in areas of the East China Sea claimed by Tokyo, it could result in a shooting incident—or worse—even before China precipitates the coming crisis with Taiwan.

Enabling North Korea

China pays lip service to the need to denuclearize the Korean peninsula. Beijing has long been in a position to pressure Pyongyang into irreversibly dismantling its nuclear and missile arsenals.

The PRC supplies:

- roughly 90 percent of North Korea's oil.

---

5   The Select Committee on U.S. National Security and Military/Commercial Concerns with the People's Republic of China (also known as the Cox Commission), U.S. House of Representatives, May 1999.

♦ an estimated 40 percent of its food.

♦ about 35 percent of North Korea's foreign aid flows.

♦ strong military-to-military ties and arms transfers to North Korea.

The PRC has refused, however, to use its surely decisive economic and political leverage to disarm North Korea. Instead, China has used six-way negotiations to protect its North Korean client—at American expense. Beijing has declined to permit any form of economic sanctions to be imposed on North Korea for its covert nuclear weapons activities or to allow any effort to refer Pyongyang to the UN Security Council.

As a result, in the words of one observer, the PRC has induced the United States to go along with:

> A replay of the 1994 Agreed Framework under which Kim Jong-Il gets more foreign aid—including a "civilian nuclear reactor"—in return for the promise, but *not the reality*, of nuclear disarmament.[6] [Emphasis added.]

♦ **North Korea's threatening behavior.** Meanwhile, with China's unstinting support, North Korea is able to maintain its threatening conventional military force poised for a devastating attack on Seoul, located just a few miles south of the Demilitarized Zone. Kim Jong-Il's regime is believed also to be building up a horrifying arsenal of poison gasses, biological warfare agents, and, most recently, nuclear weapons.

   • According to substantiated accounts from defectors and refugees, political prisoners in the North's internal gulag have been used as test subjects for Kim Jong-Il's biological and chemical weapons programs. A former North Korean scientist described graphic tests on human beings in which chemical "suffocation, blister, and nerve agents" were used to "determine how much gas was necessary to annihilate the whole city of Seoul."[7]

   • Pyongyang's nuclear weapons program has benefited greatly from the proliferation made possible by the Pakistani counterpart program, long led by Dr. A.Q. Khan and supported by China. It is possible that the North Korean scientists have obtained sufficient data from Pakistani underground nuclear

---

6   Max Boot, "Project for a New Chinese Century: Beijing plans for national greatness," *Weekly Standard*, October 10, 2005. Available at http://www.weeklystandard.com/Content/Public/Articles/000/000/006/149ugqci.asp. A number of Mr. Boot's thoughtful suggestions are incorporated in the recommendations in this section.

7   "Human Guinea Pigs," *BBC News Newsnight*, July 27, 2004. Available at http://news.bbc.co.uk/2/hi/programmes/newsnight/3933727.stm.

tests (which they are believed to have observed) to permit their country to bypass explosive testing of the North's own weapons.

◆ **Buying South Korea.** Beijing has successfully played upon South Korean fears of the North and its desire to appease Kim Jong-Il to encourage Seoul's transformation from a reliable American ally into an apologist and virtual advocate for Pyongyang. China has greatly expanded bilateral economic ties with South Korea, thus lubricating the latter's increasing estrangement from the United States and Japan.

Chinese Proliferation

China's own proliferation activities continue unabated, particularly in the area of ballistic missiles. Despite rhetorical support for multilateral efforts to curb the spread of weapons of mass destruction and their delivery systems, China's export control regime remains porous—surely reflecting the Communist regime's desire to be seen to be exercising restraint without interfering with strategically useful WMDs technology transfers. In any event, chemical precursors, biological weapons infrastructure, and even some nuclear materials continue to make their way from the PRC to nations with long-standing ties to terror, including Iran, North Korea, and Pakistan.

China's "Far Abroad"

The PRC's bid for hegemony through proxies extends far beyond the East Asian littoral.

◆ China routinely uses military exercises, "advisory teams," and, not least, vast quantities of cash as it jockeys to secure a dominant position from the Western Pacific to Central Asia and beyond. The subtext of these efforts is a bid to shift allegiances or at least to neutralize U.S. allies.

◆ For example, since 1999, Chinese military advisory teams in Burma have overseen air-land-sea communications exercises carried out by the junta's forces. Such exercises have taken place along the coast of the Andaman Sea and the Bay of Bengal, some 300 nautical miles from democratic India, and within 450 miles of the strategic Straits of Malacca.

◆ The covert efforts of the PLA to foster regional instability are further demonstrated by its direct or indirect support for military aggression, terrorism, and narcotics trafficking across Southeast Asia. For example, the main national security threat to Thailand at present is the rapid expansion of methamphetamine narcotics trafficking by the twenty-five-thousand-strong Wa tribal army in Burma, with the backing of the PLA.

- ♦ China has engaged in a well-coordinated campaign to foster, finance, and militarize pro-Beijing regimes surrounding India, including in Burma, Bangladesh, Nepal, and Sri Lanka, as well as several other strategically situated Central Asian and Indian Ocean states.

Chinese Political Warfare

China is pursuing its strategy through diplomatic means as well. It has been the driving force behind the creation of new regional groups, such as the Shanghai Cooperation Organization and two organizations related to the Association of Southeast Asian Nations (ASEAN). These have been tailored in large part for the purpose of excluding the United States and marginalizing Japan. As discussed in the section of this step on Russia, Beijing teamed up with the Kremlin in one such forum. The purpose? To prevail on several former Soviet republics to suspend U.S. use of their bases—facilities relied upon to support military operations in neighboring Afghanistan.

Strategic Economic Developments

The PRC's long-term strategy also involves dominance over the world's key energy resources, materials and minerals, and technologies—all aimed at providing a civilian economy that will, consistent with Deng Xio Peng's famous "16 Character" dictum, serve China's military needs.[8]

- ♦ China is trading cash, arms, and political protection to Islamist and other energy-rich nations to secure access to oil, natural gas, coal, and other fuels. Such deals serve to prop up the worst of such regimes and to make them more dangerous enemies of freedom. Chinese control of such energy resources also has the potential to translate into significant strategic advantage in the future, at our expense.
- ♦ The PRC continues to pursue mercantilist trade policies, notwithstanding its repeated pledges to act as a responsible member of the international trading and financial communities. Specifically, the PRC continues to
  - breach a number of its World Trade Organization obligations.
  - manipulate its currency exchange rate.
  - make a mockery of intellectual property rights.

---

8   As noted in the report of the Cox Commission (see note 5), this mantra attributed to the Chinese leader in 1978 and adopted by the Chinese government in 1997 literally means: "Combine the military and civil; combine peace and war; give priority to military products; let the civil support the military."

♦ By fueling its export growth with subsidies, predatory pricing, and other instruments of systemic unfair trade, Beijing is accomplishing the withering of what is left of America's manufacturing capacity (including that of our defense-industrial base)—not to mention counterpart capabilities in Japan, Taiwan, certain ASEAN members, and many other nations around the globe.

♦ As discussed elsewhere in Step 9, China's commercial enterprises—many of which are directly tied into the PLA and the Communist Party—are making strategic inroads in Africa, Europe, the Middle East, and even in Latin America and the Caribbean. At the very least, such transactions represent important influence operations for Beijing, usually at the expense of the United States and the Free World's interests. At worst, they are covers for ominous intelligence, technology theft, military, and/or proliferation activities.

♦ The stock and bond offerings of some of China's most questionable state-owned enterprises continue to cascade into our capital markets. Among the most troubling proposed IPOs are those being issued by several so-called government banks. In fact, they are really just funding arms (or slush funds) for the regime's favored projects and businesses. None of them meet Western accounting standards; a number are effectively bankrupt.

The effect of such offerings is to draft unwitting American investors into contributing to the PRC's military buildup, proliferation activities, and oil-producing schemes in terrorist-sponsoring nations—like those generating cash for the genocidal Islamofascist regime in Sudan. Other unsavory Chinese behavior made possible, in part, by such investments include:

- rampant human rights abuses at home.
- authoritarian control of the Internet (see Section B in Step 10 on the United Nations).
- ruthless suppression of free speech and journalistic independence.

The additional danger is that many Americans, having invested their fortunes in such enterprises, may become part of a vastly expanded "China Lobby"—opposing the imposition of U.S. economic sanctions or other penalties on the PRC or its firms should that become necessary.

What Needs to Be Done

This sample menu of China's strategic activities illustrates the range of problems it poses for the Free World, problems that may rapidly metastasize into serious threats to our interests and well-being. The following are among the measures we need to adopt to mitigate this danger and, with luck, to help the Chinese people free themselves from the odious Communist regime in Beijing.

1. Encourage Change in China

As we have seen, political warfare is an instrument of statecraft that the United States must bring to bear to contend with the fiercely determined enemies of freedom. Communist China has always been hostile to freedom-loving peoples. But, until recently, it was principally occupied with oppressing its own population.

Successive U.S. administrations have therefore generally perceived China as unthreatening to American interests. Beijing was, accordingly, given a pass, as the United States sought to cultivate a strategic axis with China or to encourage commercial ventures with the Chinese.

Now, however, the Chinese Communists' ambitions have begun to pose a more palpable threat to those in Asia and elsewhere who aspire to live in freedom—starting with Taiwan. Worse yet, they are beginning to *act* on those ambitions, sometimes in their own right and sometimes in league with Islamofascist states that sponsor terror.

◆ **Use political warfare techniques to mitigate the danger posed by the government of China.** Fortunately, there may be an opportunity in China today for a successful political transformation strategy.

There is widespread unhappiness with the regime. The government-controlled Chinese press has acknowledged that there have been many thousands of demonstrations or other forms of public dissent against the regime (or its surrogates) in cities, towns, and villages all across China—and especially in rural areas. We can safely assume that there have actually been many more that have not been reported.

This domestic ferment raises the distinct possibility that the regime, in the time-worn tradition of totalitarian regimes, may try to secure popular support—or, at least, to justify intensified repression—by conjuring up a foreign threat. The technique, known as "social engineering," appeals to nationalism to help perpetuate the party's control. It can suddenly translate without warning or provocation into violent acts of aggression. This prospect is especially worrisome in light of the geo-strategic infrastructure and political arrangements China is assiduously putting into place around the world.

China's demographics add to the danger of military adventurism. The effect of China's long-standing one-child policy has been to create a generation in which there are a great many more young males than females (who are traditionally the less valued offspring). In general, young men represent the most favorable "market" for such nationalistic programs; moreover, their presence in large numbers can also encourage dictators to think of them as cannon fodder.

♦ **Support Taiwan.** The best model for the sort of change that would make a real difference for the Chinese people, and for the rest of us, is the Chinese democracy on Taiwan. All efforts must be made to help Taiwan survive.

♦ **Identify, encourage, and strengthen pro-freedom and democratic groups within China.** That may mean, as it did during the Cold War, publicly recognizing those who have had the courage to resist the regime and who have been punished for it—dissidents, political activists, journalists, scientists, and so forth. Their story needs to be told throughout the Free World, as a powerful reminder of what is at stake in this war. By telling it often and publicly in the West, we can help save their lives.

♦ **Engage in subtle but effective "strategic communications" with dissidents and their potential supporters.** That will require expanded U.S. government-supported radio and television broadcasts (see Step 8) and much more intensive use of the Internet to communicate with the Chinese people.

That priority is just one of the reasons why we must keep control of the Internet out of the hands of the Communist Chinese (pursued under the guise of "internationalizing" its operations; see Step 10). We must also develop ways of penalizing U.S. companies that help China to shut down this remarkable instrument for the free flow of information and ideas.

♦ **Along with Japan and South Korea, develop a strategy for the end of the Kim Jong-Il regime**, which could come about suddenly and far sooner than many "experts" predict. Plans should now be made for the stabilization of North Korea should that occur.

2. Deter China

In conjunction with its political warfare strategy, the United States is going to have to work hard—particularly with the other demands on its military forces at the moment—to establish a more formidable forward presence for the Free World in East Asia. Components of such a posture should include the following:

♦ **Station more military assets** (ships, fighter aircraft, bombers, logistical units, etc.) in or rotate them through Guam, Japan, Singapore, and other friendly nations.

♦ **Put China on notice** that the inevitable result of its continuing aggressive behavior and military buildup will be to drive other states in the region to acquire their own nuclear-deterrent capability. (This outcome will be all the more certain to occur—and sooner rather than later—if the United States does not take steps to restore confidence in its own nuclear deterrent; see Appendix II.)

♦ **Encourage Taiwan to provide more fully for its own defense**, notably by increasing its spending as a percentage of GNP and initiating immediately the long-overdue modernization of its armed forces (including the purchase of weapon systems offered by President Bush in 2001).

♦ **Increase bilateral military-to-military ties with Taiwan.**

♦ **Foster three-way defense relationships** and exercises with two of the Free World's most important outposts in the region—Japan and Taiwan.

♦ **Develop and exercise contingency plans** for implementing President Bush's commitment to defend Taiwan, including deploying sea-based missile defenses (see Appendix III).

♦ **Encourage other democratic regional powers**, notably, South Korea and India, to join us in our commitment to prevent a successful attack on Taiwan. Australia, which has said it would not come to Taiwan's aid, should be encouraged—as part of a larger effort on the part of the Free World—to revisit that decision.

3. Cultivate India

We must build on the efforts made to date by the Bush administration in developing our mutual interest in countering the growth of Chinese power in Asia. This has been a particular priority for President Bush from the day he took office.

Although some progress has been made, both the United States and India have acted at times in ways that raise questions about the strength of their commitment to this strategic relationship—the United States because of its dealings with Pakistan and China, and India its dealings with China and Iran. In addition, care needs to be exercised about compromising U.S. security interests, for example, through dismantling sensible U.S. proliferation safeguards or weakening American export control arrangements in pursuit of improved relations.

4. Use America's Economic Leverage

The United States has failed for too long to appreciate the *strategic purpose* behind China's economic and financial transactions. The congressionally mandated U.S.-China Economic and Security Review Commission is an invaluable resource and "second opinion" on China—for decision makers and the public alike. The commission has been usefully examining, documenting, and reporting on various ominous aspects of the PRC's military and economic agenda.

The commission should be asked to assess the *cumulative* effect of China's unfair trade practices, investments, technology thefts, and diversions, as well as its acquisitions of long-range, offensive military capabilities and dominant positions in strategic choke points around the world and in key industries. The commission should also be tasked with developing options for responding appropriately in those areas.

Components of such a strategy might include the following:

♦ Americans should approach their state pension systems and other fund managers to insist that their hard-earned retirement and other investment dollars *not* be used to purchase the stock of large Chinese state-owned enterprises, particularly the upcoming multibillion-dollar stock offerings by the Bank of China and the China Construction Bank. (The DivestTerror.org model described in Step 4 could be useful in this regard.)

♦ U.S. investors should divest immediately their equity holdings of any publicly traded Chinese companies doing business in genocide-ridden Sudan and terrorist-sponsoring Iran (see Step 4). This applies also to American holders of stocks of companies willing to partner with the brutal and dangerous North Korean regime.

♦ Businesses in the United States should be encouraged to diversify their international investments and overseas commercial partnerships with Indian and Southeast Asian entrepreneurs, rather than deal largely—still less, *exclusively*—with China.

- ◆ China's activities in Central and South America, the Middle East, and Africa must be more closely monitored and contested; U.S. policies must be crafted to publicize and challenge China's predatory trade practices, strategic/political partnerships (particularly with respect to oil and gas contracts with terrorist-sponsoring states), and weapons-proliferation practices in these regions.
- ◆ The U.S. Congress must become more activist in shaping U.S.-China policy, particularly in the areas of trade, acquisitions in our country, the defense of Taiwan, meaningful sanctions for proliferation abuses, and championing human liberties and the free flow of information.

The United States hardly needs a new enemy at this point. It is a mistake, however, to think that we can neutralize an emerging adversary by choosing to overlook it. We will not avoid a military conflict with Communist China simply by hoping that it will not occur—or, worse yet, by thinking that we can appease the PRC.

The best chance for avoiding the impending conflict with the PRC lies in using the sorts of strategies outlined above. In particular, we must help the Chinese people eliminate the danger their government poses both to them and to us by dispatching the regime that has brutalized and misruled China for nearly five decades and that threatens to harm the Free World badly in the years ahead.

D. Counteract the Reemergence of Totalitarianism in Latin America

With Contributions from Thor Halvorssen and Dr. J. Michael Waller

---

I f people in the United States think about Latin America at all, it is usually in a patronizing way—as "our backyard"—with little regard for the importance of this region to the U.S. economy, social fabric, and strategic interests. This is all the more remarkable because, in addition to being the locus of immense natural resources and vital American markets,[1] the Western Hemisphere south of the Rio Grande is increasingly in turmoil.

During the past two decades the region has deteriorated dramatically, and today it risks wholesale collapse. Rotten with corruption, overblown bureaucracy, ineptitude, and waste, many Latin American countries are imploding rather than developing. The region's most influential leaders are thugs. It is a magnet for Islamist terrorists and a breeding ground for hostile political movements, with most of the landmass now under the control of anti-U.S. politicians who are fueled—like Saddam Hussein, Muammar Gadhafi, and the Iranian mullahs before them—by seemingly endless streams of oil revenues. In this case, the key leader is Hugo Chavez, the billionaire dictator of Venezuela who has declared a Latino *jihad* against the United States.

Our focus is on the threat to U.S. national security interests—and to freedom more generally—emerging today in Latin America, and what we can do to mitigate it. In the background, however, there looms the distinct possibility

---

1 Latin America is home to some of the world's largest cities, most fertile plains, and greatest treasure houses of minerals, metal ores, precious gems, oil, and natural gas. Blessed with its endless stretches of grain and beef ranges (rivaled only by the American West), its tens of thousands of miles of coastal fishing grounds, and its vast farms of coffee, fruits, and vegetables, Latin America could feed itself and most of humanity.

that rising civil strife and violence may result in unheard-of numbers of immigrants and refugees flooding over the Mexican border into the United States (see Step 7).[2]

If Americans wish to secure and protect their own liberty, we must put effort into pressing the region to shed itself of the corrupt socialistic ideologies that have kept the region mired in injustice and senseless poverty for far too long. And Latin America will need to adopt its own War Footing against the purveyors of subversion and violence.

The bottom line is clear: There can be no assurance of American safety and liberty, let alone defense of the Free World, unless we help secure freedom elsewhere in the hemisphere.

Chavismo: A Regional Threat

Hugo Chavez is Fidel Castro's most successful and most dangerous pupil. He is an ex-paratrooper and mutineer who once led an unsuccessful coup against the democratically elected government of Venezuela. After he was released from prison, Chavez was subsequently elected to replace that government, campaigning on a populist platform of property confiscation and obsessive anti-Americanism.

Chavez now exercises increasingly despotic control over the nation that owns the largest petroleum reserves in the hemisphere—and that supplies the United States with much of its imported oil. Unlike Castro, or even the old Soviet Union, he has an almost endless supply of cash to finance political parties, revolutionary groups, violent underground movements, and terrorists. Chavez's money also allows him to buy the services of Washington power brokers (from both parties) who act as his agents of influence, downplaying concerns about this new threat to U.S. national security.

Until Chavez came to power, Venezuela had long enjoyed one of the hemisphere's strongest traditions of democracy. Widespread political and economic corruption, however, had produced a level of public discontent that Chavez was able to mobilize—playing to the expectations of millions of desperately poor people with his promises of ending official thievery and of redistributing the nation's wealth to the least fortunate. Once in office,

---

2   Latin America is the single largest source of illegal immigration into the United States. Rather than make their economies more open and efficient, most Latin American governments have relied on large-scale emigration of their poor and undereducated to the United States. This deliberate policy has two principal purposes: to reduce local unemployment without having to make badly needed reforms; and to create new sources of hard currency infusions from abroad, as illegal workers pump billions of dollars back into their local economies.

Chavez seized the opportunity systematically to dismantle Venezuela's democratic institutions. He did not, of course, end the corruption and abuse of power, but rather turned them toward his own ends.

The coup-plotter-turned-president has nevertheless cast himself as a latter-day Simón Bolívar, the founding father of Venezuela, who shepherded Latin America to independence from Spain. Chavez has named his movement (and even his country) "Bolívarian"—a grossly distorted caricature of Bolívar, a classical liberal who considered himself one of Thomas Jefferson's greatest fans.[3]

A more accurate name for Chavez's ideology is "Chavismo," a term that captures the egomaniacal form of tyranny with which the democratically elected Chavez has supplanted his nation's democracy. The following are among its manifestations:

- Since his election, Chavez has restructured Venezuela's institutions and policies to extend his rule. He has concentrated power, militarized the government, and essentially disabled the democratic opposition. Attentive to the need to keep up the appearance of legality, he has used a constituent assembly to establish a new constitution (approved by just 30 percent of the electorate) that gives him wide and effectively unchecked powers to tax and spend, seize private property, and limit freedom.[4] He used the same mechanism unconstitutionally to declare a national emergency, suspending and then sidelining the elected congress.

- As with other totalitarian takeovers, Chavez has stacked the courts with loyal judges and purged the military of anyone he thinks might oppose his orders. His administration has imposed gun control, ensuring that only its supporters are armed. It has also severely restricted freedom of speech, most recently by banning any public or private expression of opposition to the government. *It is now a crime in Venezuela to criticize the president.*

---

3   Simón Bolívar, who liberated most of South America from Spanish rule, was a great admirer of the American Revolution. During the early 19th century, Bolívar tried to establish republics in what are today Bolivia, Colombia, Ecuador, Panama, Peru, and Venezuela, based on the ideas that animated the American Revolution: limited government, separation of powers, rule of law, and respect for individual rights.

4   The Constituent Assembly was heavily stacked. Groups opposing the regime received 38 percent of the votes, marginally less than the 42 percent for the pro-regime slates. Nevertheless (in a move unremarked by the foreign press), *93 percent of the seats in the Constituent Assembly went to regime supporters.* This distorted representation is the basis of claims that Chavez enjoys overwhelming support.

◆ Meanwhile, political control is assured in part by the presence of the Cuban secret police, an institution created for Fidel Castro by the Soviet KGB, which operates in Venezuela as freely as it does at home. Colonel Chavez has become so fearful of his own generals—including those he has retained—that he surrounds himself with Cuban bodyguards.

◆ This dictator—taking a long view—has also secured full political control of the country's educational system, ensuring that Venezuela's youth will be indoctrinated along rigid ideological lines. The regime is one of the worst human rights violators in the hemisphere, using torture, arbitrary imprisonment, and confiscation of private property as tools of repression. Since winning a referendum in August 2004—in a vote that was certified as free and fair by former President Jimmy Carter, even though it was clearly marred by fraud and voter harassment—Chavez has revved up his revolutionary project. He now asserts that he wishes to rule until the year 2030.[5]

In short, Venezuela is now in a state of permanent centrally controlled revolution. Hugo Chavez is systematically pursuing a fascistic program aimed at maximizing and consolidating governmental power at the expense of individual freedom. Toward these ends, he has replaced every key institution in government and civil society. Every element of Venezuela's political infrastructure (including its government departments, currency boards, judicial framework, military establishment, police forces, banking structures, educational system, and independent labor unions) has been politicized and purged of those not deemed loyal to Chavez. Only the Roman Catholic Church, a steadfast opponent and target of the regime, remains outside the government's control—for now.

Chavez's Ominous International Agenda

Chavez is an enemy of freedom not only at home but abroad as well. To further the radical anti-American agenda long promoted by his mentor, Fidel Castro, the Venezuelan president is lavishly applying his nation's oil resources to counter U.S. interests and influence in Latin America and beyond.

◆ For this purpose, Chavez is establishing a loosely aligned federation of revolutionary republics as an anti-U.S. bloc in the Americas. He has made no secret of its strategic orientation as a counterweight to what he

---

5   "Venezuelan Opposition Must Join Forces To Defeat Chavez—Spokesman," *BBC Monitoring International Reports*, August 18, 2005.

calls "the most negative force in the world today. . . . the government of the United States."[6]

Under Chavez, Venezuela is funding militantly anti-U.S. political movements across the hemisphere.[7] His regime is also financing, sheltering, and providing military support to the FARC narco-guerrillas of Colombia.[8] In 2003, Chavez helped the producers of coca (raw material for cocaine) to overthrow Bolivia's elected, pro-American president, and then did the same to his successor in 2005. He is now financing political subversion in El Salvador as well as in Nicaragua, Ecuador, Peru, and Paraguay.[9]

♦ Chavez's government is also providing Venezuelan identity papers to hundreds, perhaps even thousands, of Islamist extremists, to allow them to enter the United States as Venezuelan nationals.

♦ Openly copying from al Jazeera (the Arabic satellite TV channel that serves to inflame world opinion against the United States), Chavez started a Spanish-language equivalent called Telesur.

---

6   Hugo Chavez, January 30, 2005 speech, World Social Forum, Porto Alegre, Brazil.
7   Today, Venezuelan government money is covertly funding the electoral ambitions of a half-dozen former terrorists in the region. For example:

  ♦ Chavez supplies funding to Shafik Handal, leader of El Salvador's FMLN, the leftist guerrilla-group-turned-opposition-party.
  ♦ In Bolivia, Chavez funds Evo Morales, the leader of the coca-growers' movement and head of the Movement Toward Socialism (MAS) party. With the backing of Chavez, Morales used mass protests to overthrow Bolivia's pro-U.S. President Sanchez de Losada in 2003 and President Carlos Mesa in 2005. An avowed enemy of the United States, Morales is now leading the polls in the run-up to the Bolivian presidential election scheduled for 2007.
  ♦ In Peru, Chavez funds the activities of the Ollanta and Antauro Humala, the brothers (and former army officers) who run the Peruvian Nationalist Movement (MNP). The Humalas once led a rebellion seeking to topple the government of Peru. Now, with Venezuelan oil money, they aim to seize power in the 2006 elections.
  ♦ In Nicaragua, Chavez is funding Daniel Ortega's Sandinista party. Recall that during the Cold War, Nicaragua was a satellite state of the Soviet Union and that its Sandinista dictatorship, led by Ortega, was the primary source of political violence and repression in the region. Ortega's chances of winning a democratic election are high; if he does win, he will establish a Chavismo-style dictatorship in Nicaragua.

8   In December 2004, high-ranking FARC terrorist Rodrigo Granda was arrested in Caracas. Granda had been living in baronial splendor under the protection—and at the expense—of the Chavez government. Bounty hunters kidnapped Granda and drove him to Colombia, where he is now imprisoned and awaiting trial. See: Thor Halvorssen, "Guerrilla Nation; The Arrest of FARC Terrorist Ricardo Palmera Sheds New Light on Hugo Chavez's Ongoing Support of Terrorism," *The Weekly Standard Online*, January 25, 2005.
9   The movement Chavez heads has awakened regional insurgencies that had been largely inactive for almost two decades. The guerilla groups and terrorists in the region, formerly dependent on illegal drug-trafficking, income from kidnapping, and organized crime, now have access to billions of dollars generated by sales of Venezuelan oil.

Total war with the United States. There is no doubt that Hugo Chavez is committed to picking a fight with the United States, proclaiming again and again that it "is not invincible."[10] With active Cuban participation, his revolutionary command has made public its plans for what Chavez has described as an "asymmetric war." This is a military term describing warfare in which the two sides are mismatched in their military capabilities. The model being used by the Venezuelan dictator is the Iraqi terrorist insurgency against U.S. forces there.

Although many in Washington consider the idea preposterous, Chavez is, in fact, preparing for *total war* against American security interests. Chavez's warlike intentions are underscored by an unprecedented arms buildup (starting with a reported intent to purchase high-performance military aircraft and hundreds of thousands of assault rifles from Russia) and by the exponential growth of the Venezuelan fighting force. A reserve army, with *twenty times* the number of soldiers currently in active units, is being established.[11]

A key element of Chavez's strategy is a *global network*—composed of rogue regimes, terrorist states, demagogic dictators, and narco-terrorists—extending well beyond this hemisphere, with a view to challenging the United States on every conceivable front. His allies make up a veritable *Who's Who* of global terror sponsorship.

Days after the September 11, 2001, terrorist attacks, Chavez declared that "the United States brought the attacks upon itself, for their arrogant imperialist foreign policy." Chavez also described the U.S. military response to Osama bin Laden as "terrorism," claiming to see no difference between the invasion of Afghanistan and the terrorist attacks on New York and Washington.[12]

Lubricating these relationships is Venezuelan oil money. Chavez has signed treaties for "technological cooperation" (a euphemism for weapons transfers) with the terrorist regimes of Libya, Iran, and Syria. For their part, Iran, Libya, and North Korea have invested hundreds of millions of dollars in Venezuela.

To put the magnitude of the potential problem in perspective, Venezuela has more energy resources than Iraq and supplies one-fifth of the oil sold in America. When Chavez took over Venezuela, oil prices were below $10 a

---

10 "Venezuela: Chavez Criticizes Colombia, USA; Insults Condoleezza Rice," *BBC Monitoring International Reports*, January 26, 2005.

11 "Venezuelan State Companies Reportedly Training Workers For Guerrilla Warfare," BBC Monitoring International Reports, May 19, 2005; "Many Venezuelans join guerrilla armies, plan to fight," *Miami Herald*, April 19, 2005; "Venezuela: Chavez Training Militia To Defend Against 'Aggression'," IPS-Inter Press Service, April 14, 2005.

12 Thor Halvorssen, "Comandante Chavez's Friends," *The Weekly Standard Online*, March 11, 2003.

barrel. Since then, prices have quintupled, making the Chavez government the richest in Venezuelan history and vastly multiplying the damage it can do.

Given his country's vast resources and his commitment to exporting revolution, Chavez's plans could result in a level of political instability never before experienced in this often turbulent region. More than 130 million Latin Americans could be affected—and with them, the United States, through its porous borders, among other means.

Fidel Castro: Back from the Crypt

Fidel Castro's regime was nearly dead when Hugo Chavez resurrected it. In exchange for Chavez breathing new life into the Cuban economy with endless oil subsidies and hard currency infusions, Castro has mentored his Venezuelan protégé.

Chavez represents what Castro always wanted to be: the leader of a revolution that extends well beyond his own territory. Castro has helped Chavez learn how to undermine and destabilize liberal democracies throughout the region by using Castro's own tested methods of political warfare. He has also supplied the personnel: literally tens of thousands of Cuban agents are now operating inside Venezuela. Hundreds of them serve openly in government offices and control every aspect of the state security apparatus. (As mentioned in Section B of this step, the Cuban dictator has also provided medical cadres to Venezuela in another time-tested technique to help establish political control.)

Castro has decades of experience; Chavez has money and power. Theirs is a partnership with Chavez in charge. The struggle for Cuban freedom—and, indeed, for freedom throughout Latin America—now depends heavily on whether or not freedom can be restored in Venezuela.

How Did We Get into This Fix?

Though few in the United States appreciate it, Chavez is emerging as the pre-eminent anti-American figure on the world stage, with stunningly little resistance. Although most Latin American and European governments understand the authoritarian nature of Chavismo, they remain neutral toward Venezuela—principally because Chavez has oil. He has also successfully cast his current political odyssey as the struggle against the "American imperialism" of the widely resented George W. Bush. But this neutrality also reflects the fact that—in violation of the principle of political warfare described in Step 8—Washington has done little to make it costly either for Chavez to oppose us or for others to support him.

Spain, France, and Germany remain mute about the real nature of Chavez's power, despite the significant damage he has done to the region and to Venezuelan democracy. Many Latin American governments also tolerate his activities, partly in response to the "carrot" of lucrative oil contracts, arms purchases, infrastructure projects, emergency relief, giveaways for the poor, and cash handouts. But there is a stick as well: Chavez threatens uncooperative leaders and nations with the same destabilizing forces that he currently exports throughout the region.

In contrast, the United States has failed to impose any political or economic costs on countries supporting him. In fact, the United States paid shockingly little attention as Chavez consolidated and expanded his power. During the Clinton administration and the first term of the George W. Bush administration, the U.S. policy on Venezuela was one of almost total disengagement, notwithstanding our historically close ties to that country.

Such American indifference has persisted despite efforts over many years by Venezuelan citizens, businessmen, political leaders, military officers, clergymen, and others who urged the Bush administration to acknowledge the Chavez threat and to help build international pressure in support of freedom in Venezuela.[13] These concerns have largely gone *unacknowledged*. Needless to say, they have not produced any constructive U.S. action in response.[14]

Indeed, aside from trade-related matters—which we tend to take very seriously—the U.S. strategy toward our own hemisphere has been reactive at best, with little consideration for the political and security stakes, and still less engagement in the "war of ideas." Today, the United States finds itself increasingly isolated in the American hemisphere. Whereas the governments of Communist China, Libya, and Iran are hailed as heroes and partners, America is routinely described as an "evil" nation with an imperialistic plan.

---

13 Notably, House International Relations Committee Chairman Hyde wrote to President Bush and Secretary of State Colin Powell in October 2002, advising them that "the leadership of all the pro-democracy elements of the society" in Venezuela met to demand the resignation of the dictator and the holding of free and fair elections. Hyde described the illegitimacy of the Chavista regime, itemizing its steady progress toward creeping dictatorship and arguing that the United States should "declare itself in sympathy with the pro-democratic civil-military coalition in Venezuela which seeks to restore democracy and should do so at once."

14 The Americans remained uninvolved during the brief period in April 2002 when Chavez was briefly removed from power by a coup. Worse yet, former president Jimmy Carter put a stamp of international approval on a 2004 referendum Chavez had gone to great lengths to rig, calling it "free and fair." In fact, Chavez did everything—including granting citizenship to a half-million illegal aliens in a crude vote-buying scheme, and "migrating" existing voters away from their local election offices—to fix the results. An independent statistical analysis by a joint team of Harvard University and MIT professors, in August 2004 concluded that fraudulent activity in the electronic voting process had skewed the results. This report was, like much of Chavez's other activities, widely ignored outside Venezuela.

The Breaking Point

The situation has now reached a critical juncture. It is a great mistake to discount Chavez as a madman who can easily be removed from power. Such an idea severely underestimates the character of the forces Chavez has unleashed and the extent to which he has entrenched his ideological agenda in Venezuela and in Latin America.

This is especially true because opposition to Chavismo's growing regional power is scattered, disorganized, and weak. To be sure, there remains some local resistance, in the form of a few citizen opposition groups still struggling on in Venezuela and in Bolivia. The government of President Alvaro Uribe of Colombia also opposes Chavismo's advance—alone among Latin American governments. Chavez has successfully portrayed those who oppose him as right-wing alarmists who are unduly obsessed with an insignificant provincial trend.[15]

Left unchecked, Chavez will pose a real and growing threat to stability, safety, and freedom in the Americas—including in the United States. As elsewhere, if we are to preserve the Free World, America must take the lead in its own "backyard," counteracting Chavismo in ways that are comprehensive, disciplined, methodical, and international.

What Needs to Be Done

American leadership must expose Chavez and his agenda as a threat to the Free World. We must assist those inside Venezuela and Cuba who are on the front lines in opposing the Chavez-Castro axis. And before it is too late, we must assist the resistance elements in countries threatened by Chavismo by implementing the following steps:

1. **Design and implement a political warfare strategy to empower the Venezuelan people and to undermine the Chavez government.** The Venezuelan people do not share Chavez's vitriolic hatred of the United States. Indeed, the majority of Venezuelans have great affection for America and its freedoms.[16] This is why the Venezuelan government is funding numerous "educational" programs to shift affinity away from the United States.

---

15 One Latin American expert at the American Enterprise Institute, Marc Falcoff, considers Chavez "merely a nuisance" and a "moderate inconvenience" that the U.S. should ignore. "The Chavez Challenge: Venezuela's leader is a regional nuisance," *National Review*, August 16, 2005.

16 Polling data suggest that, although much of the world—and nearly all of Latin America—resents and mistrusts the United States, the population of Venezuela ranks among the greatest global admirers of the United States and its people, far more so than Western Europe.

One cabinet minister declared that the government in Caracas must prepare for war and invest in "sowing hatred toward the United States. Evidently the ties that bind us with the United States, even political and historic, are too strong. But we must prepare to see, and start seeing, the 'gringos' as enemies and that is the first step for combat."[17]

Elements of the needed political warfare strategy include the following:

- ◆ Sustain and protect—through monitoring and material support—the democratic and human rights movement in Venezuela that provides a viable alternative to the dictator.
- ◆ Make a far more concerted effort to help dissidents who have had the courage to stand up to Chavez and Castro. President Bush's White House meeting in May 2005 with Venezuelan dissident Maria Corina Machado was a start, but much more needs to be done.
- ◆ Expose Chavez's efforts to silence his opposition by calling attention to such abuses as the false arrest of the movement's leaders.

2. **Strengthen the Organization of American States (OAS).** This organization has, in the past, served as a constructive mechanism for addressing hemispheric issues, including those posed by enemies of freedom. Such a resource is especially important because (as discussed in Step 10) the United Nations cannot be relied upon to play a constructive role in contending with the threat posed by dictatorships in Venezuela and Cuba. We should treat the OAS as the hemisphere's preeminent multilateral political and security body, supplanting the UN wherever possible.

- ◆ Invoke the OAS's Democratic Charter, violated by the Chavez regime on dozens of occasions, to demonstrate support for the cause of anti-Chavez Venezuelans, and to pressure other freedom-loving nations to address the illegitimacy of Chavez's rule.

3. **Engage in public diplomacy in the region.** We need to reconstitute the necessary communication tools for building relationships with the public in countries where the United States still has friends—and where it might someday need them.

- ◆ The urgency of such efforts will grow only as Chavez's Telesur network comes online to fill, for example, the vacuum created by the termination of U.S. broadcasts in Bolivia. As discussed above,

---

17 See http://www.quintodia.com.ve/archivos/437/edicion/index.php.

in that supposedly "marginal" country, America's withdrawal enabled cocaine producers, assisted by the Chavez regime, to mobilize the poor in a successful campaign to overthrow the country's democratically elected, pro-U.S. president.

4. **Help stop Islamist infiltration.** Arab immigration to Latin America posed no problems for more than a century. To the contrary, Arab immigrants often became important pillars of the region's politics and economies and assimilated into the local cultures. In recent years, however, the region has seen an influx of tens of thousands of Arab Muslim immigrants, including substantial numbers of Islamists who sympathize with or support terrorist groups.

   ♦ Islamist terrorists are now finding safe haven, logistical support (including, as noted above, false Venezuelan identity papers), and other assistance from the Chavez regime. In fact, Castro and Chavez have gone out of their way to build "strategic relations" with Islamic fundamentalist leaders, as well as nominally Muslim leaders hostile to Washington. Urban slums whose walls once bore Marxist revolutionary propaganda now feature spray-painted slogans supporting terrorist sheiks half a world away.

   ♦ We need to work with others in the region—especially non-Muslim Arabs and non-Islamist Muslims—to ferret out and neutralize this threat. In addition, we need to make it far more difficult for such Islamist operatives to sneak into the United States (see Step 7).

5. **Give the native peoples of Latin America an alternative to Chavismo.** The only real answer to the poverty exploited by ideologues like Hugo Chavez is the creation of wealth. The indigenous people of Alaska demonstrated that such a transformation can be done *in one generation*. The Alaskan Native Claims Settlement Act (ANCSA)—a historic piece of legislation little known outside of Alaska—provides a model for transforming the lives and conditions of millions of Andean peoples in the Western Hemisphere.[18]

---

18 The history of this initiative warrants close scrutiny as an alternative to the current practice, which amounts to leaving the indigenous Andean people to the tender mercies of Chavez's political warfare.

By 1971, the native peoples of Alaska (Aleuts, Eskimos, and Indians) were becoming increasingly insistent that land taken from them, first by the Russians and then by the Americans, be returned or that they be fully compensated. Unrest and violence were a definite possibility. In response, Congress passed the most successful piece of economic/social legislation since the Homesteading Act of 1862: the Alaskan Native Claims Settlement Act (ANCSA).

Continued on 203

The native Alaskans who proved this model should, ideally, be enlisted to assist with its adoption in such countries as Ecuador, Peru, and Bolivia, which are endowed with natural resources similar to Alaska's. This initiative is being advanced currently by the Indigenous Enterprise Institute (IEI) and its affiliate, Instituto Empresarial Indigena of Ecuador.

6. **Become part of the solution.** Individual Americans can play a direct role in winning the War for the Free World against Hugo Chavez and his allies through the following steps:

   ♦ **Make sure your elected officials do their job.** Call, write, or send e-mails to get the attention of your congressmen and senators. Ask them what they are doing to counter the threat to democracy in the Americas. What are they doing to assist the political prisoners of Venezuela and Cuba? How are they strengthening the democratic alternatives inside these countries? What they are doing to assist the resistance in other countries besieged by Chavez?

   ♦ **Don't fund terrorism.** The Venezuelan regime owns Citgo Petroleum Corporation. Every time an American fills his tank with Citgo gasoline, he hands cash to Chavez. Make a statement about your opposition to what Chavez is doing with our money by taking your business elsewhere—and, ideally, to drive a car designed to use alternative fuels produced here at home, or in Latin American and Caribbean nations not hostile to America (see Step 3).

   ♦ **Reach out to dissidents via the Internet.** Independent blog sites, such as www.vcrisis.com, are crucial to finding out what is happening and how best to help. These tools can be expanded creatively to develop still more ways to show support and generate awareness of the growing problems in Latin America.

Note 18 (*continued*)

According to the terms of ANCSA, 44,000,000 acres were returned to native control (much less than the natives were demanding). In addition, thirteen regional native corporations and almost two hundred village corporations were established and capitalized with almost $1 billion (half paid from the Treasury over an eleven-year period, and half from mineral royalties as they became due). Every man, woman, and child who could prove at least one-quarter native blood received 100 shares of a regional corporation and a village corporation. The shares could be inherited but not sold for 19 years (later the natives themselves voted to make the prohibition on sale of the shares permanent).

All of the regional corporations and most of the village corporations have been successful, some spectacularly so. They are in oil, gas, mining, fishing, forestry, tourism, and many other activities. Of the ten largest corporations in Alaska, five are native corporations. Thirty billion dollars of wealth has been created over the past three decades.

♦ **Support resistance to the regime.** To find out more about how you can help, contact the U.S.-based Atlas Foundation for Economic Research, which is devoted to assisting think-tanks throughout the world. (See their Web site, www.atlasusa.org, for a full directory of the freedom-based movement in Latin America.) An affiliated group in the United States is the Hispanic American Center for Economic Research (www.hacer.org). HACER provides up-to-date information about the struggle for liberty in Latin America.[19] (More resources are listed at this book's companion Web site, www.WarFooting.com.)

♦ **Pressure the media.** The media has, by and large, given Chavismo a free pass. Chavez's wealth and power have won him many friends. In Washington, he has obtained support from prominent Democrat and Republican power-brokers. And pro-Chavez propaganda outlets in the press and online regularly attack critics of the regime, who lack support networks of their own.

The enemies of freedom count on our ignorance to shield their misdeeds. In this case, they intone the mantra that Chavez was democratically elected—as if this fact excuses, or even *justifies*, his government's subsequent, blatantly antidemocratic actions. Americans need to be far better informed about what is happening outside our borders and should demand greater coverage of the Latin American region by mainstream media outlets.

Hugo Chavez's scandalous record is public and must be widely and relentlessly exposed. Misinformation needs to be challenged: everyone is entitled to his opinion, but no one is entitled to his own set of facts. As individuals, we can hold the press accountable with letters to the editor and calls to talk radio. Each time you take such steps, it helps impress editors and producers that what Chavez is doing in Venezuela is a matter of public concern. In turn, this can prompt more stories and attention on the subject.[20]

---

19 A handful of nonprofit groups is doing the important job of communicating the ideas that can defeat Chavismo in the hemisphere: Fundación Libertad (Argentina: www.libertad.org.ar); Instituto Cultural Ludwig Von Mises (Bolivia: www.fulided.org.bo); Instituto de Ciencia Política (Colombia: www.icp-colombia.org); Instituto Ecuatoriano de Economía Política (Ecuador: www.ieep.org.ec); Instituto Liberal (Brazil: www.institutoliberal.org.br); Instituto de Libre Empresa (Peru: www.ileperu.org); Centro de Divulgacion del Conocimiento Economico para la Libertad (Venezuela: www.cedice.org.ve).

20 The law firm of Patton Boggs in Washington, D.C., has received millions of dollars to lobby for Chavez. Hundreds of professors and activists routinely jump into action whenever anyone criticizes Chavismo. The Venezuelan government has underwritten a propaganda operation in the United States called the Venezuela Information Office, devoted to spreading misinformation to the U.S. media. In addition, the Chavez government reportedly funds online media sources such as vheadline.com and venezuelanalysis.com that profess to be "independent."

Latin America must be considered one of the most important fronts in the War for the Free World. What happens there can affect us directly and materially—whether by disrupting our markets or oil supplies, through socially disruptive, illegal migration flows, or through negative strategic developments. We cannot hope to win this war unless we help secure our neighbors against the combined ideological assaults of a homegrown Chavismo and imported Islamofascism.

E. Challenge Russia's Emerging Autocracy

With Contributions from David Satter

S ome weeks before the first anniversary of the Beslan schoolhouse massacre, the mothers who had lost children there were instructed to report to the cemetery where their loved ones had been buried. An ambulance pulled up and a coffin was removed. It contained body parts from some of the children who were murdered in the attack. Many of the women fainted. There was no official on hand to explain what was happening, or to offer words of comfort.

"We were outraged that no officials came," said Susanna Dudiyeva, one of the women. "These body parts were also our children."[1]

The incident in the Beslan cemetery was among the latest in a series of events that illustrate the utter callousness of the regime of President Vladimir Putin, who is moving Russia inexorably in the direction of authoritarian rule. The government can afford to be completely callous toward its own citizens, because the Putin regime actually has no further use for democracy.

Because the regime, for the moment, is unthreatened—buoyed by historically high prices for oil, and natural gas, Russia's principal exports—this emerging dictatorship is relatively "soft." The West has so far failed to perceive, let alone respond to, the systematic way in which Putin is establishing absolute control over the instruments of power. The Russian president is relentlessly tightening his grip and successfully crushing those who oppose him.

Unless effectively challenged, both from within the country and outside, Putin will soon finish erecting a system in which the Kremlin once again dominates all aspects of Russia's political and economic life. Although we can only speculate about the ends to which Putin will ultimately apply Russia's vast natural wealth and its still formidable nuclear and conventional

---

1 Henry Meyer, "Grieving Russian parents, feeling brushed off and lied to, turn their hopes to a court trial," Associated Press, August 24, 2005.

military-industrial complex, these objectives are unlikely to be consistent with the interests of the United States and the Free World.

"Managed Democracy"

"Managed democracy" is the term Putin coined to distinguish the political system he envisages for Russia from those of traditional Western democratic governments. As recently as December, he insisted that there was no reason for concern that by "managed" he meant Kremlin controlled. "I don't think we should move toward an authoritarian state, especially a Soviet-style authoritarian state," he said. "That wouldn't help create favorable conditions for economic development and would limit the society's ability to control the government. That would be excessive."[2]

It is important, however, to take stock of *the totality* of Putin's actions to understand properly their potentially grave implications.

Political Control

If any question remained about what Putin meant by "managed," it has been dispelled in recent months. Alternative power centers have been systematically eliminated. Among the worrisome steps Putin has taken are the following:

+ **Ministry appointments**. He has installed in key posts fellow veterans of the KGB and Russian security services. The deputy chiefs of the Kremlin administration, Igor Sechin and Viktor Ivanov, are former KGB men. Half of the members of the Security Council are former officers in the police, military, or FSB (the largely unchanged successor to the KGB). So are nearly 70 percent of all senior regional officials. In addition, dozens of veterans of the security services have been appointed deputies in ministries far outside their expertise.

  The ministries of Economic Development, Heavy Industry, and Communications in fact have FSB deputies who remain in the FSB's active reserves and thus still clearly owe loyalty to the security organs. These and other representatives of the "force ministries" are the core of Putin's support. They are also the elements that are the most resentful of the Soviet Union's loss of the Cold War, most intent on restoring Russia's lost power, and most hostile to the West.

  An example of the mentality common in these circles was provided by the statements of Leonid Shebarshin, a former head of the KGB, in

2   "Putin's Paranoid Christmas Attack," NewsMax Wires, Friday, December 24, 2004. Available at http://www.newsmax.com/archives/articles/2004/12/23/214201.shtml.

an interview in September 2005 in the newspaper *Arguments and Facts*. He claimed that the terrorist acts of September 11, 2001, were a provocation by the American secret services. (This statement undoubtedly offers an insight into the readiness of the Russian special services to stage their own provocations.)

Speaking of provocations, it is worth recalling that the second war in Chechnya began after the bombings in 1999 of apartment buildings in Moscow, Volgodonsk, and Buinaksk. There is convincing circumstantial evidence that these bombings were carried out, not by Chechen terrorists, but by the Kremlin's security apparatus, the FSB.[3] (Not least, FSB agents were caught in September 1999 putting a bomb in the basement of a building in Ryazan—which they then tried to explain away as a training exercise.) In any event, the bombings and the renewed conflict they triggered catapulted Putin to political prominence and power.

- ♦ **Appointment of regional and local officials.** Putin has put into effect a *putsch* against previously independent, elected regional governors. The change—a clear violation of the Russian constitution—was cynically justified by the attack in Beslan, but it had actually been decided on months earlier. It was simply presented in the wake of Beslan in order to conceal the fact that Russians were losing another piece of their tattered freedom—the right to elect their local officials. The appointed governors will now, in all likelihood, begin to appoint mayors and other local officials, thus putting the entire administrative apparatus of the country once again squarely in the hands of the regime.
- ♦ **Control of parliament**. Similarly, the once-oppositional parliament—the State Duma—has been replaced with one utterly in the control of Kremlin loyalists and apparatchiks. The transformation was the result of the second Chechen war, which, in its successful early months, caused a sea change in Russian politics and allowed Putin loyalists to sweep the December 1999 parliamentary elections.

The new parliament has remained overwhelmingly pro-Putin from that time forward. It voted not to investigate charges that the FSB was involved in the 1999 terrorist acts. Recently, Putin demonstrated the confidence he now has in his control of the Duma by asking it to approve legislation that would allow the FSB to suspend the constitution on the strength of a simple FSB assertion that there is a threat of a terrorist attack.

---

3   David Satter, *Darkness at Dawn: The Rise of the Russian Criminal State,* Yale University Press, 2003.

Control Over the Media

♦ **Demise of independent media**. President Putin has returned all national television and most important print organs to state control. He has proved to be both adept and unscrupulous in exploiting that control for political advantage.

In the past national election, the government-run media provided extensive—and invariably favorable—coverage to Putin while largely ignoring his rivals. As Radio Free Europe/Radio Liberty has observed, "The year 2004 saw considerable restraints put on the already dwindling independent press in Russia."[4]

♦ **Assassination of journalists**. According to the Glasnost Defense Foundation, 130 journalists have been murdered in Russia since 1991, making Russia one of the most dangerous countries for journalists in the world. In almost all cases, the victims died because they unearthed information that challenged the local or national structures of power. Usually, the authorities do not even pretend to try to find the killers.

This seems to be true even in the case of a murdered *American* journalist, Paul Klebnikov, the Russian editor of *Forbes* magazine. Under intense pressure from the American embassy, the Russian authorities announced that Klebnikov was killed by a fugitive Chechen criminal leader, Khozh-Akhmed Nukhayev, supposedly angered by Klebnikov's depiction of him in a book. It is not clear what basis exists for such a charge.

Control Over the Economy

Fascism marries an authoritarian political system with capitalism, which is then put at the service of the state. Just as Putin is assiduously consolidating his power over all of Russia's political institutions, he is also reestablishing the Kremlin's control over Russia's economy.

♦ **State capitalism**. The immediate focus of Putin's economic program has been to exert his authority over the so-called oligarchs. These are mostly former Communist Party apparatchiks and factory managers who skillfully parlayed their connections with the Yeltsin regime into ownership of huge industrial enterprises and natural resources—and immense personal wealth. Some of the oligarchs who ran afoul of Putin have been banished and fled the country.

---

4 "Russia: Putin Defends Reforms, Condemns 'Revolutions,'" Radio Free Europe/Radio Liberty, Prague, 23 December 2004.

The poster child of Putin's anti-oligarch campaign, Mikhail Khodorkovsky, did not flee, however. He is now serving hard time in prison, after being subjected to a show trial and the loss of his once-huge oil company, Yukos. The impetus for such draconian punishment was not, as stated, Yukos's alleged failure to pay taxes. Rather, it was that Khodorkovsky dared to provide financial support to democratic, pro-Western, and anti-Putin political initiatives and operatives. Worse yet, he helped to underwrite media outlets that were independent of government control.

♦ **Renationalization and intimidation.** For his sins, Khodorkovsky's empire has now been renationalized. This was accomplished via a calculated and cynical ploy. A previously unknown front company, Baikalfinansgroup, bought Yukos's lucrative Yuganskneftez division at a secretive mid-December auction for $9.35 billion. Baikalfinansgroup was, in turn, almost immediately bought by another oil company, Rosneft, which was about to merge with the state-owned gas giant, Gazprom. Of this dubious transaction, Putin said, "Today, the state—using absolutely legal market mechanisms—is ensuring its interests. I consider this perfectly normal."[5]

In much the same way, Putin is ensuring the state's interests by going after another industry. As Garry Kasparov, the former world chess champion and one of Putin's most visible critics still operating inside Russia, noted in a December 2004 *Wall Street Journal* op-ed piece: "The latest example of this trend is the harassment of Russian mobile-phone operator VimpelCom. They are being targeted much in the same way as Yukos. The company has been hit with tax bills totaling over $450 million. It comes as no surprise that the owners of Megafon, one of VimpelCom's main competitors, have close ties to Mr. Putin."[6]

The message has not been lost on the other oligarchs: You can remain rich, powerful, and *even corrupt*—so long as you do not cross Vladimir Putin. It has also not been lost on Russian businessmen generally. The years of bandit capitalism in post-Soviet Russia that were thoughtlessly lauded in the United States and the West have left a legacy of business people who are vulnerable to legal prosecution.

Truth be told, in the Yeltsin years, everyone was invited to break the law, and virtually everyone who engaged in business in Russia did so. With the advent of Putin and an FSB government, those people are now

---

5   Ibid.
6   Garry Kasparov, "Say It in Russian: 'Caveat Emptor,'" *The Wall Street Journal*, December 21, 2004.

being reminded—most powerfully through the Khodorkovsky case—that if they want to avoid trouble over their ill-gotten wealth, they should forget about any political opposition to the regime.

As Kasparov notes, "The message that Western banks and companies should be receiving is that doing business in Russia is a risky proposition. Everything depends on loyalty to Mr. Putin. This loyalty is dubious, morally, and it is also weak, strategically. When an agreement has been negotiated in a lawless environment, there is no guarantee as to the future safety of that investment."

Control Over the Military

Nowhere is Putin's behavior more ominous for U.S. interests than with respect to military technologies, policies, and actions. This is true even though he frequently pays lip service to his solidarity with America. For example, he has declared that the United States is "one of our priority partners. We are unconditional partners in resolving a range of serious problems right now. First of all is the joint fight against terrorism. I would describe our relations, without exaggeration, not simply as a partnership, but as an alliance."[7]

Still, activities in several areas are the cause of serious concern.

♦ Earlier this year, Putin was personally and enthusiastically involved in exercises that simulated strategic nuclear attacks on the United States. Last February, the Russian president presided over Bezopastnost-2004, reportedly the largest mock nuclear attack on this country since Leonid Brezhnev ruled the Kremlin in 1982.

♦ Russia is working to develop, deploy, and market new technologies that are designed to defeat U.S. weapon systems. For instance, the Kremlin is aggressively deploying and offering for sale advanced maneuvering and hypersonic ballistic-missile warheads. The Russians explicitly advertise them as being designed to overcome America's nascent anti-missile defenses.

♦ Russia's most modern bombers were included, along with other weapon systems and ten thousand troops, in joint Sino-Russian war games held in August 2005 on Chinese territory (see Section C of this step). This was the most extensive show of military cooperation since the two countries allied against U.S.-led forces during the Korean War. The exercise scenario suggested that the American military is once again the enemy these two nations envision fighting.

7   "Russia: Putin Defends Reforms, Condemns 'Revolutions,'" op. cit.

A Worrisome Foreign Policy

Massively Arming Communist China

As noted in Section C of this step, the PRC is the largest purchaser of Russian arms in the world. Beijing is reported to be in the process of spending at least $2 billion to update its arsenal with Russian weapons this year alone. Having purchased large quantities of ships, missiles, and fighter aircraft from the former Soviet military-industrial complex, China is now expressing interest in buying long-range Russian bombers like the Tu-22 MC "Backfire" and Tu-95 Cs used in this summer's joint Sino-Russian exercises. These warplanes can carry conventional or nuclear-tipped cruise missiles; they could be used to attack U.S. forces in the event they are called upon to help defend Taiwan or other American interests in Asia.

Arming Iran

Putin's Russia has shown itself willing to facilitate Iranian nuclear ambitions. It is pressing ahead—despite growing evidence that Tehran is interested in nuclear *weapons,* not just nuclear power—with the construction and fueling of a reactor at Bushehr that will likely help advance the Iranian arms program.

The Kremlin has similarly seemed unconcerned about revelations from Ukraine that, in 2000, Iran spent millions illegally to purchase Soviet-made X-55 strategic cruise missiles. If tipped with nuclear warheads, these missiles could be used to threaten Israel, other U.S. allies, and American troops in the Middle East.

Even though these weapons were supposed to have been sent back to Russia under the terms of the START I nuclear disarmament treaty, Moscow has made no effort to recover them. To the contrary, it has continued to transfer military and nuclear technologies to Iran.

If the Iranians secretly divert several of the massive fuel rods intended for the Bushehr reactor (which the Russians are expected to deliver this year), the partially enriched uranium in the rods could be enhanced to weapons grade using a relatively small and undetectable centrifuge obtainable (illegally) from Pakistan. We know that the Iranians have been covertly acquiring large numbers of such devices for years (see Section A of this step). As Russian defense analyst Pavel Felgenhauer notes, "All the Iranians need to do is bribe Russian officials to turn a blind eye and the final component that would give a terrorist state a long-range, operational nuclear arms capability would be in place."

Regional Hegemony

In addition to promoting military and strategic ties to nations actively or potentially hostile to the United States, Putin is trying to reassert Moscow's hegemony over its neighbors. Although he acquiesced to a U.S. military presence in some of the former Soviet republics needed to help prosecute the war in Afghanistan, this was really the least he could do, given his stated support for the so-called War on Terror.

Of late, however, President Putin has displayed a much more aggressive attitude toward what he calls Russia's "near-abroad." Notably, Putin has joined forces with China in recent months to press Central Asian members of the so-called Shanghai Group to withdraw the welcome mat for American forces.

There are other examples of regional intervention.

- Putin connived in and subsequently supported the falsification of the results of the presidential election in Ukraine.
- He has encouraged secessionist movements and other subversion of the government of Georgia, declaring, "We stand for the territorial integrity of Georgia, but only if the interests of *all* the peoples who live on this territory [namely, including Russian nationals] are observed."[8]
- Putin also intends Russia to dominate once again oil-rich Azerbaijan and the Central Asian republics.

Russia and Iraq

Putin exhibited for a time a pragmatic accommodation with Washington after he proved unable to protect Russia's longtime Iraqi client, Saddam Hussein. He agreed to write off 90 percent of the estimated $8 billion debt that had been incurred by the Iraqi despot, most of it in connection with the purchase of Soviet arms. He has also encouraged other lender nations in the Paris Club to do the same.

In this case, too, Putin may simply have been acceding to reality. There is no chance Iraq would be able to repay these debts. Moreover, Iraq's then-interim prime minister, Iyad Allawi, responded to the Kremlin's gesture by saying that Russia will be given a "leading role" in helping to restore Iraq's oil and other industries. Given Putin's proclivities, such a presence could prove risky for Free Iraq.

---

8 Ibid.

Where Is Russia Headed?

In short, Vladimir Putin is pursuing a course that threatens simultaneously to subject the Russian people (once again) to an unaccountable authoritarian government and to conflict (once again) with U.S. policies and vital interests.

The effect of rising oil revenues has been to bring relative stability to Russia. This has made Putin understandably popular with some segments of the Russian population. Corruption, however, is believed to be even worse than during the Yeltsin period. Bribes in Russia grew from an estimated $36 billion in 2001 to $319 billion in 2005, according to two well-respected monitoring services.[9] And little of the country's new-found oil wealth has reached the general population.

As a result, Putin—or his hand-picked successor—could be vulnerable in fair elections. That is one reason why truly free and fair elections are unlikely to take place in Russia in the foreseeable future. In their stead, Russians will probably be obliged once again to participate in balloting that has nothing to do with choosing who leads their country or with such leaders' accountability.

What Needs to Be Done

The behavior of the Putin regime is an international tragedy. History has demonstrated convincingly that functioning democratic and free-market systems will afford far greater political legitimacy and economic prosperity than can any thuggish fascist regime. What is more, Moscow and Washington today have greater grounds for common cause than at any time since World War II. Specifically, both have much to fear from Iranian and other forms of Islamofascism, as well as from the burgeoning ambitions of Communist China.

As long as Putin fails to recognize these realities, however, President Bush—who once famously declared that he has "looked into Putin's soul" and found him "trustworthy"—would be well advised to reconsider that judgment. Putin can be trusted only to do one thing: *to pursue relentlessly his quest for power.* U.S. policy must be designed accordingly.

The days when the West could threaten Russia with a cutoff of loans are gone, however. Russia's oil bonanza is making it possible for Putin's Kremlin to pursue its domestic and foreign agenda without the need for Western financial help.

Still, the United States retains important moral influence in Russia, and this influence can be applied to help reverse the steady drift toward authoritarianism

---

9   Nikolai Popov, "A Billion a Day, the Price of the Matter," *Novoye Vremya*, No. 33, August 2005.

there—a drift that, if left unchecked, will lead to policies and behavior that become progressively more hostile to the West.

Specifically, we should do the following:

1. **Support the rule of law.** Fear has returned to Russia in part because selective prosecution is being used to eliminate opponents of the regime. The best-known case is that of Khodorkovsky—which we failed to make an issue in Russo-American relations. The United States needs to insist that selective prosecution for political purposes is a violation of the rule of law.

2. **The United States needs to make clear its opposition to Putin's undermining of Russia's democratic institutions.** When a regime controls the executive branch (in which all real power in Russia is vested) as well as the Duma and the judiciary, it cannot also appoint governors or ban minority party coalitions (for contesting elections) without forfeiting any claim to be treated as a democracy (see Section B in Step 10).

3. **Russia's strategic drift—most especially, its arms developments and sales—must be recognized as unfriendly to the United States.** That will require us to reassess the bilateral relationship and to consider necessary steps—for example, the need to rapidly develop and deploy more advanced missile defenses (see Appendix III)—to counter these Russian sales and their military implications).

4. **The United States should exert real pressure for a political settlement of the Chechen war.** Ever since Putin precipitated the current conflict to advance his political career, the Russians have murdered and kidnapped many thousands of Chechens in security sweeps and laid waste their land. This terror against civilians has inspired retaliation against Russian civilians by Chechen terrorists. Allowing the conflict to continue will further drive Chechen and other Muslims into the arms of Islamofascists, providing Putin with additional pretexts for restricting democratic liberties in Russia.

The U.S. influence in Russia is greatest with respect to our commitment to basic values, such as political freedom. In a poll taken in January 2004, 75 percent of the Russian respondents said they wanted their country to be an ally or friend of the West. Fewer than 3 percent thought that the West was Russia's enemy. Now, as the Putin regime steadily departs from the shared values that must underpin such friendship, it is incumbent on the United States to help reinforce the democratic instincts of the 75 percent.

F. Salvage Europe

With Contributions from Alex Alexiev

T he two principal pillars of the Free World are the United States and Europe. Despite periodic strains in the relationship—particularly with some of the states Donald Rumsfeld famously dubbed "Old Europe"—Americans have long taken for granted that, when the chips were down, our European allies could be counted on to help share the burden of securing freedom.

We now confront a very different prospect. Thanks to the political "perfect storm" of socioeconomic, demographic, military, and Islamist challenges, the European Union is poised to become, in the coming decades, a strife-ridden, second-rate power, unwilling or unable to help defend the Free World. It is not impossible that, in the foreseeable future, the EU may itself cease to be part of the Free World.

An Unraveling Economy

For decades past, Europeans of all political persuasions have shared a belief in the virtues of the "social market economy"—a modified capitalist system, characterized by considerable state intervention and the fabled "social safety net." This was an arrangement intended to guarantee economic growth and prosperity, on the basis of harmonious labor relations, social cohesion, and economic solidarity between the classes.

The viability of this model became an article of faith shared across the political spectrum in Europe. It stood in stark contrast to the American model, which represented generally the "creative destruction" characteristic of more genuinely free markets. And, indeed, the European social market economy worked fairly well for some time.

After World War II—with the support of the Marshall Plan and America's security umbrella—Western European countries quickly rebuilt their devastated economies, and by the 1970s they enjoyed unprecedented prosperity. When the Cold War ended and the European Community decided to form a single market with a common currency, overtaking and surpassing the United States was (many assumed) only a matter of time.

Today, however, the European project is in shambles. Somewhere along the way, its social market model lost steam and became counterproductive to economic growth. Current statistics indicate that by the mid-1990s, Europe had already begun falling behind the United States, as measured both by GDP and productivity growth.[1]

If the recent past does not look encouraging, the future is even more troubling. Structural problems are likely to limit EU growth to a maximum of 1.5 percent by 2015 and even less than that thereafter. Nor is there much likelihood that a "knowledge-based" economy—critical to success in the 21st century—will emerge to pull Europe out of its economic morass. After all, the EU is not only failing to progress in the high-tech area; it is actually falling further behind competitors such as the United States.

All this points to a sobering conclusion that few in Europe are willing to admit: the vaunted social market has come to the end of the line in the age of information and globalization.

The European Economic Model Implodes

This failure lies primarily in the fact that, over time, the "social market" became progressively more *social* and less *market*. Its foremost purpose came to be redistribution rather than production or trade.

Europe's social market has undeniably become a hindrance to economic growth.

+ Government expenditures may amount to 50 percent of national income.
+ Business is over-regulated.
+ Labor unions inflate pay scales, rendering companies and industries uncompetitive and contributing to huge unemployment.
+ Excessive social-welfare benefits, sustained by exorbitant tax rates, reduce incentives for employment.

The social and political implications of this economic predicament are still more alarming. Continued stagnation will inevitably be accompanied by rapidly falling living standards—and growing social instability and political conflict.

---

1   A recent OECD study asserts that "economic catching up (with the United States) started to stall in the 1980s and degenerated into relative decline during the 1990s." See the OECD publication, "Economic Policy Reforms," edited by Jean-Phillippe Cotis, March 2005. Available at www.oecd.org.

What Would It Take to Fix Europe's Dysfunctional Economy?

If Europe's economic problems are caused by misguided socioeconomic policies, it stands to reason that a sharp correction of these policies could arrest
and possibly reverse the economic malaise. This realization appears to be
spreading even among erstwhile advocates of the social market; the first halt-
ing efforts to begin reforming the system are currently on the agenda in a
number of European countries.

Although this is certainly a positive sign, it is possible that these modest
efforts will fail to bear fruit. The fact is, the most certain remedy is nothing
short of a *complete revamping of the system in a market direction.* This bitter
pill is very unlikely to be swallowed, however, given the powerful political and
economic interests arrayed against such a course.[2] A look at the proposed EU
constitution suggests that Europe will probably see, even now, yet *more*
socialism—and less market.[3]

More importantly, Europe is just entering a demographic maelstrom that
will severely limit its chances for reform.

A Depopulation Meltdown

The demographic crisis now engulfing Europe is a phenomenon unprecedented in human history, resulting largely from a long-standing rate of population growth at less than zero. European birth rates collapsed to a rate of
approximately 1.5 children per woman in 1995, from nearly twice that rate in
1965.[4] (The standard population replacement rate is about 2.1 births per
woman.) To put it another way, over the past ten years Europe has experienced
an annual deficit of more than *2 million births* below replacement levels.

As these smaller post-Baby Boom cohorts reach childbearing age, the
population deficit will widen further. This is expected to produce a *contrac-
tion* of the native European population of between 100 and 150 million by
2050; that is, the population may decrease over the next half a century by as

---

2   For example, more than half of the voters in Germany's September 2005 elections voted for parties
    that blame the free enterprise system for the country's problems.
3   The EU constitution's enunciated objectives outlined in Title 1, Article 3 read more like the electoral
    platform of a socialist party than a constitution of a free and democratic polity. It is chock-full with
    leftist shibboleths, oxymorons, and sloganeering such as "sustainable development," "balanced eco-
    nomic growth," "highly competitive social market economy," "full employment and social progress,"
    and other politically correct nostrums that have never been and cannot be legally defined and are
    therefore meaningless in constitutional terms. As the British commentator, William Rees-Mogg, put
    it succinctly: "If the European Constitution were American, it would raise numerous Supreme Court
    cases in every paragraph." See William Rees-Mogg, "Are We Fools Led by Liars," *The Times of
    London,* February 28, 2005.
4   *Eurostat Yearbook 2004,* p. 48.

much as *one-third* of today's population.[5] This implosion will shrink Europe's share of the world population to barely 4 percent in 2050, compared with 12 percent in 1950.

A Near-Term Problem

Unfortunately, the dire implications of this trend will not wait until mid-century to manifest themselves; they will start wreaking havoc on Europe's socioeconomic prospects in the immediate future. Long before significant depopulation begins to take place, low fertility will have produced an elder-skewed demographic that will render unsustainable the current unfunded, pay-as-you-go welfare system.

Rapidly shrinking and aging populations, furthermore, will decrease demand for everything—*except* health care and government services. Aging societies place extraordinary burdens on the public purse. At the same time, however, diminished consumption in the marketplace negatively affects the cost of labor, productivity, international competitiveness, innovation, and foreign and domestic investment. Ultimately, one can anticipate a massive out-migration of capital, companies, and skilled individuals to more attractive locales.

Possible Course Corrections

There are a number of options for mitigating these negative trends in the period before the population implosion begins in earnest, around 2020. All, however, entail considerable dislocation that could doom governments politically.

To keep the projected support ratio in balance, there are two measures Europeans could take that, combined, might add 32 million people to the workforce:[6]

♦ Raise the retirement age from fifty-eight years to sixty-five or sixty-six years.

♦ Increase the employment level, as a percentage of the population, from the EU's current level of 62 percent to that prevailing in Denmark, for example (75 percent).

---

5 European losses are likely to be considerably higher if one were to include Russia, Ukraine, and Belarus, which are projected to lose 30 percent, 36 percent, and 25 percent of their populations, respectively, for a total of more than 60 million, according to the UN World Population Prospects-2002 Revision. The UN's 2004 Revision projects an overall European population decline of nearly 172 million between 2005 and 2050 if current fertility rates remain unchanged. See http://esa.un.org/unpp/p2k0data.esp.

6 See D.A. Coleman, "Facing the 21st Century: New Developments, Continuing Problems"; paper delivered to the European Population Forum, January 12–14, 2004, Geneva, pp. 36–37.

More drastic—and therefore less likely—measures would involve deep cuts in welfare and pension benefits, and privatization of pay-as-you-go pension plans. Few politicians would want to defend such an unpopular platform.

Apart from these palliatives, there are only two possible solutions that could theoretically prevent the projected demographic crisis from becoming a reality: (1) increasing the birth rate, or (2) increasing immigration. Because the first is virtually impossible in the short-to-medium term and unlikely in the longer term, immigration would appear to be the solution of choice.

Yet the official policy of virtually all EU governments is to *discourage immigration* from outside the EU, except for highly skilled professionals and a few special categories such as family reunification and political asylum. Despite these restrictions, significant legal and illegal immigration—estimated at more than 2 million yearly—does take place. This, indeed, is the main reason Europe's population has not yet started declining.

Unfortunately, the sort of immigration taking place now is actually making things worse. The problem with current immigration to the EU is simply that much of it places additional burdens on the social welfare system rather than contributing to its solvency. Most of the new arrivals enter Europe either as part of the "migration chain" (that is, for family reunification reasons) or as illegal aliens. The vast majority in both categories lack employment and linguistic skills, and they do not join the tax-paying labor force in significant numbers.

The Islamist Time Bomb

There is growing evidence that failed immigration and integration policies may present an even bigger political challenge in the extensive and ongoing radicalization of the burgeoning Muslim population throughout Europe. It is difficult to establish even the basic parameters of Europe's Muslim populations, as most European governments avoid collecting or publishing relevant data regarding ethnic or religious affiliation. Nonetheless, we have some credible approximations.[7]

It is beyond dispute that, in the past half-century, the Muslim population in Western Europe has exploded from less than 250,000 to between 15 and 20 million. Although this still represents only a small percentage of the EU's total inhabitants, the Muslim subset is not only rapidly growing but has also become progressively radicalized.

---

7 The discussion here will be limited to the Muslim "diaspora" populations in Western Europe and exclude the very different native Muslim populations in Eastern Europe. The latter number more than 30 million and are concentrated in several geographic areas such as the Balkans, the Caucasus, and the Volga region in the European part of Russia.

Until very recently, most EU governments have avoided openly debating this issue, apart from rhetorical flourishes about the need to integrate the Muslim minority. Even now, policy discussions have tended to focus on its implications for terrorism. Relatively little attention, however, has been paid to the likelihood that the growing radicalized and unassimilated Muslim communities could have a dramatic impact on *political stability* in Europe.

Available data, however incomplete, demonstrate convincingly that Muslims are dramatically younger as a group and that they have fertility rates possibly two or even three times as high as those of native Europeans, depending on country. Demographically, these trends spell trouble for the non-Muslim population.

Chain Migration

Matters are made worse by the phenomenon known as "chain migration," a by-product of legal immigration. As European economies recovered from the devastation of World War II and went into "economic miracle" overdrive, millions of "guest workers" were needed. These were recruited principally from Turkey, North Africa, and South Asia to provide cheap labor for the booming economies of Western Europe, leading to a large-scale Muslim influx.

This effect was further compounded by "chain migration," a practice first instituted as a humanitarian family reunification measure. Of late, however, chain migration has become the leading method of gaining legal entry into the EU.

The most commonly used approach is arranged or forced marriages, where European-born individuals are married off to partners back in the home country. Not only is the new bride or bridegroom allowed to join the spouse in Europe, but very often the entire family follows. Muslim chain migration throughout the EU may be as high as half a million individuals each year.

These sorts of arranged (or forced) marriages have yet another important effect: they serve as a major barrier to assimilation in European society. By controlling and limiting their children's marriage choices, Muslim parents in Europe effectively undermine their chances for integration and economic betterment—at a significant cost both to the individuals involved and to the larger society.

Political Asylum

Another quasi-legal immigration category that contributes significantly to the growth of the EU's Muslim populations is political asylum. This practice is a noble and time-honored tradition of civilized nations. European societies, however, have allowed the asylum right to be abused by millions, for whom it provides a convenient way of gaining entry where they could not otherwise do so. New applications for asylum were running at a steady rate of about 350,000 per year as of 2003,[8] and a majority of asylum seekers make the request only *after* they have been apprehended for illegal entry.

Illegal Immigration

Finally, the Muslim populations in Europe are continuously augmented by large-scale illegal immigration. EU authorities estimate, probably conservatively, that there are already 3 million illegal residents in the EU, with half a million new illegal arrivals each year. Muslims appear to comprise a majority of the yearly influx.

The combined effects of natural population increase, chain migration, asylum seekers, and illegal immigration produce an increase in the EU Muslim population of more than 1 million each year, with a projected increase of at least 50 percent every decade. This implies a doubling of its current level by the year 2020 and doubling again by 2035. By that year, or possibly earlier, the majority of young people in most large European cities will be Muslims.

Islamofascist Europe?

The rise of a new dominant culture, reflecting a new demographic balance, is not necessarily cause for concern. Nor is the infusion of growing religious diversity in itself a problem.

It is undeniable, however, that an intolerant and violent extremist creed has taken hold throughout Muslim communities in Europe. Moreover, the fast-spreading Islamofascist strain is already on its way to becoming the dominant face of Islam in the EU. This profoundly anti-Western ideology, supported either directly or indirectly by Saudi sources, is marked by a wholesale rejection of such fundamental Western values as democracy, secularism, separation of church and state, human rights, and modernity.

One alarming implication of this phenomenon is already visible: Europe is no longer just a transit point for terrorists but has become a breeding ground hospitable to all stripes of Islamic extremism.

Hundreds of documented, European-born and -raised extremists have already taken part in terrorist activities worldwide. This is a matter of serious concern for EU governments and must become the focus of dramatically

---

8 Eurostat 2004, Asylum Applications, available at http://epp.eurostat.cec.eu.int/portal/ page?opageid=1996,39140985.

expanded efforts by law-enforcement and counterterrorist agencies. But terrorism is merely a symptom of the deeper malignancy, a totalitarian Islamofascist ideology that is on the march.

If the kind of radical, uncompromising, and violence-prone worldview currently on display should become dominant in European Muslim communities as they gain an increasing population share, Western Europe will be seriously challenged to preserve its character as a modern, democratic, and secular polity. France in fall 2005 is a leading indicator.

Troubling Prospects for Europe

Europe is facing an uncertain future. If it fails to undertake the urgently needed radical reforms of its flawed socioeconomic model, it will soon enter a period of economic decline. With an aging and contracting population, it will evolve into a second-rate economic power of growing political instability and marginal political relevance.

The EU itself is unlikely to survive the coming crisis intact. Continental Western Europe as a whole is performing far worse economically than the United Kingdom and most of Eastern Europe. These more successful countries are likely, sooner or later, to opt out of the EU, to avoid being dragged down by an imploding "Old Europe."

At the same time, radical Islam and its totalitarian ideology have become the dominant force in the burgeoning Muslim ghettos throughout Western Europe. If measures are not taken soon to counter this cancerous ideology, in three decades or less the continent's major cities will see their streets dominated by violent Muslim youth who completely reject Europe's fundamental values.

Change or Die

Much might be done to defuse Europe's existential and economic crisis, but none of it is easy—and time is now short. In spite of the clear need for radical reform, the political will is lacking, with little prospect for its emergence in the foreseeable future. Apart from the needed economic reforms, Europe's political, social, and military policies also require serious attention.

On the demographic front, there are no known policies that offer much hope for reversing the EU's demographic implosion in the near future. Moreover, the different rates of economic development and population loss in various parts of Europe will further accelerate the forces fracturing the Union.

Regarding Islamist extremism, however, much more could—and should—be done. It is high time for European officials to understand that Islamism is about *sedition*, not religion, and that it needs to be treated as such. Extremists preaching violence and jihad against their fellow citizens should be thrown in jail, and radical organizations, subversive "charities," and hate-preaching mosques should be closed down. European nations must also act without delay to jettison policies that facilitate the expansion of indigenous Islamist groups, such as chain migration, dysfunctional asylum policies, amnesties of illegal immigrants, and forced and arranged marriages.

Recent developments in a number of European countries (and in Australia) provide some reason for optimism in this respect. Some are now considering tougher sedition laws making "inciting violence," for instance, a criminal offense or facilitating preventive detention in suspected terrorist situations. Others, such as The Netherlands, are planning to deport tens of thousands of illegal aliens, make chain migration more difficult, and introduce a ban on covering one's face in public. If this is an indication that Europe is finally waking up from its complacency, it is a very hopeful sign indeed.

Internationally, Europe must finally realize that most extremism is state sponsored; Europe must initiate or support appropriate measures against the countries responsible, such as Saudi Arabia, Iran, Pakistan, and Sudan. The time has also come to put an end to the EU's coddling of terrorist groups seeking the "liberation of Palestine" and the destruction of Israel. Along the same lines, the EU must cease to tolerate (let alone encourage) hundreds of European companies doing business with, and thus propping up, designated terrorist-sponsoring states (see Step 4).

The Atlantic military alliance is in need of urgent attention. With the notable exception of Great Britain, Europe's stagnation has led to miserly defense spending, see-no-evil pacifism, and an ever-more-shrill anti-Americanism. A dangerous decoupling of Western Europe from America is manifested in rapidly diverging levels of military capabilities and equally divergent threat perceptions.

In a telling initiative, the EU is pursuing a European Rapid Reaction Force, intended, apparently, as a mechanism for standardizing Europe's shrinking military capabilities around technologies that are incompatible with those of the United States (but, at the same time, both inferior and more expensive).[9] What is more, European defense industries increasingly engage in selling weapons to America's enemies, potentially undermining the Atlantic alliance.

---

9   See Dr. Richard North, "The Wrong Side of the Hill: The 'Secret' Realignment of UK Defense Policy," The European Group of Democracies and Diversities, September 2005; and "Taking the 'Special' Out of the U.S.-U.K. Relationship," Center for Security Policy *Decision Brief* No. 05-D48, September 22, 2005. Available at http://www.centerforsecuritypolicy.org/index.jsp?section=papers&code=05-D048.

The implications of a complete breakdown in military standards between the United States and Europe—or, more particularly, between the United States and the United Kingdom—would be a grievous setback for the Free World. Freedom-loving people the world over would likely suffer from the rupture of the military underpinning this most important security partnership known as the Anglo-American "special relationship. Its value has been manifested most recently by the close cooperation in the military campaigns that have recently liberated Afghanistan and Iraq.

Faced with such prospects, it is imperative that the United States forcefully and publicly address this unfolding situation. It is likely that—if made aware of the EU's witting or unwitting attempt to weaken the trans-Atlantic military relationship—the European public might demand of their elected representatives at the national level a course reversal. Unlike elitist European bureaucrats, many ordinary European citizens are aware of the critical role this special relationship played in preserving their security in the past and the importance of maintaining it in the future.

The forecast is ominous for Europe's ability to preserve Western values and freedoms, much less to emerge as the European superpower envisioned by the EU's champions. Europe's decisions—now and in the very near future—in dealing with its economy, demographics and immigration, radical Islam, and the military will determine its future role in the new century. It is not too late for Europe to reverse course, but precious little time remains.

What Needs to Be Done

Europe's inexorable decline is a troubling development for the United States. There is not much America can do to address the deeply systemic nature of the continent's problems, but we should stand ready to offer our assistance whenever possible. And we need to understand the causes of Europe's predicament, in order to avoid repeating Europe's mistakes.

1. The United States must contemplate a future in which Europe is no longer the reliable ally, philosophical soulmate, and fellow pillar of Western civilization that it has been for the past two centuries. In the worst case, some regions or countries of an Islamicized Europe could conceivably become an adversary in the longer term.
2. It is likely that the European Union will splinter economically and politically in the coming decades, abandoning even the pretension of being a monolithic power. The United States should continue to offer friendship

and assistance to those Europeans that share our vision of freedom, individual responsibility, and opportunity.

3. A closer, specialized relationship with the United Kingdom and the Eastern Europe countries (for example) would include political, economic, and military ties as well as policy coordination. Out of this initiative, *a new alliance* could someday emerge—and expand beyond the borders of Europe.

STEP 10

Wield Effective Diplomacy

S killed diplomacy might make incalculable contributions to forging and strengthening alliances with other freedom-loving nations, attacking the legitimacy of hostile actors and their policies, and even expanding the numbers of free nations in the current conflict. Unfortunately, key diplomatic institutions—the U.S. State Department and the United Nations, buttressed by American academia and regional studies programs—have largely been unhelpful in furthering these objectives and have in fact contributed to the problem at a number of levels.

The following pages assess what has largely caused America to be significantly disarmed with respect to its diplomatic arsenal. They provide an unvarnished assessment of the bureaucratic, organizational, and political forces at work in each of these institutions and outline the prospects and possible approaches for constructive change.

To the extent such change *can* be achieved, we suggest ways in which to bring it about. And, where it seems unlikely—even with thoughtful and determined American effort—we offer ways in which at least the harm done to U.S. interests and those of the Free World can be mitigated.

A. Enlist the State Department

With contributions from Fred Gedrich and Maj. Gen. Paul E. Vallely, USA (Ret.)

U S. Sen. Jesse Helms once diagnosed the problem with the State Department with a characteristically colorful, yet insightful, comment. He noted that the department had a "Country Desk" for just about every nation in the world. The job of such offices usually seems to be to represent *the interests of those nations* to the U.S. government, rather than the other way around.

Senator Helms suggested that the State Department was missing one Country Desk, however, among the roster of nations with which it deals—that is, *America's* Desk. With that quip, he captured the essence of the well-documented phenomenon known as "clientitis": State Department positions are often shaped less to serve the interests of the United States than to make other countries (the State Department's "clients") happy.

The policy distortions tend to be relatively minor, if the foreign government in question is one of our Free World allies. Even here, however, there may be significant policy differences, as, for example, on such issues as the liberation of Iraq, the urgency of addressing North Korean and Iranian nuclear weapons programs, and the degree of deference to be accorded to the United Nations.

In dealing with some other "client" countries, however—especially those in the Un-Free camp—there are often radical differences in values and interests between our governments. In such cases, Foggy Bottom's[1] aggressive representation of the other country's views in U.S. government policy deliberations can be more than counterproductive. It can actually be dangerous.

This is especially true when such advocacy is taken to the press or Congress, in the classic form of leaked memos and off-the-record comments

---

1 "Foggy Bottom" is the designation for the neighborhood in Washington, D.C., where the State Department has been housed since 1947.

designed to sabotage the president's policy initiatives. Even in peacetime, such behavior represents a potentially damaging circumventing of America's constitutional processes, in which a chief executive is elected by the people to run the government and set its direction.

There's a War On

In time of war, however, the effect is clearly harmful. By playing out in public a policy disagreement with their elected superiors, our appointed diplomats transform the deliberative process and raise the stakes exponentially. Along the way, the American public can become demoralized, our allies confused, and our enemies emboldened by the impression that the U.S. government is seriously divided.

Worse still, foreign governments may be privately encouraged—even coached—by State Department officials to resist a U.S. policy that our diplomats find objectionable. Predictably, this produces an intensified international opposition, which can then be pointed to in interagency deliberations as further support for the State Department position.

This practice has certainly plagued George W. Bush's presidency. The State Department has repeatedly attempted to undermine announced presidential policies regarding, for example,[2]

- promotion of freedom and democracy in the Middle East.
- the Israeli-Palestinian conflict.
- the International Criminal Court (ICC).
- the Anti-Ballistic Missile Treaty.
- the Kyoto Protocol.
- counterproliferation strategies regarding North Korea and Iran.

Political Gamesmanship

One of the State Department's most egregious instances of insubordination to civilian authority was its opposition to Mr. Bush's efforts to liberate Iraq. In the run-up to war in spring 2003, President Bush was trying to persuade American and foreign publics that Saddam Hussein's ouster would spur democratic reform. He argued, in effect, that this instrument of political warfare was our best bet for countering the poison of Islamofascism and the terror weapon it wields.[3]

---

2   Lawrence F. Kaplan, "State's Rights," *The New Republic*, December 7, 2004.
3   As we have seen, the president's intuitive appreciation of the value of democratic change from a political warfare standpoint has been hampered by two things: (1) a reluctance to be precise about the ideological nature of the enemy (President Bush first used the term "Islamofascism" in October 2005); and (2) the lack of governmental infrastructure and strategies for waging political warfare.

Operatives in the State Department's highly politicized Bureau for Intelligence and Research (or INR, see Step 2)—citing an array of anonymous Middle East experts as well as unnamed State Department and CIA sources—produced a "classified" report and promptly released its contents to the *Los Angeles Times*. Its conclusion: the president's theory and policy were not credible.[4]

Fortunately, despite this deliberate attempt at sabotage, the liberation went forward. The successful elections that followed in Afghanistan, the historic balloting held on January 30, 2005, in post-Saddam Iraq, and, most recently, the stunning turnout of voters there for the October 15, 2005, constitutional referendum—despite threats and acts of violence—*have* inspired demands for democratic change in much of the Mideast. By contrast, if Saddam Hussein were still a force for despotism in the region, it is unlikely we would have seen any progress toward ending Syrian colonization of Lebanon, to say nothing of contested elections in Lebanon, in the Palestinian Authority, and in Egypt.[5]

Clientitis

In 2003, Beth Jones, a senior Foreign Service officer (FSO) serving as assistant secretary of state for European and Eurasian Affairs, exhibited the classic symptom of clientitis: an irrepressible identification with the views of the diplomatic client—in this case, the French and German governments.

The issue at stake was the question of U.S. participation in the International Criminal Court (ICC). President Bush determined, early in his first term, that the ICC is incompatible with U.S. interests (see the section on the UN in this step). The U.S. National Security Strategy reflects Bush's strong emphasis on the need to protect American leaders and members of the armed forces from unjust arrest and prosecution by such a politicized, UN-created tribunal.[6] The president in fact had "unsigned" the Treaty of Rome that established the court and went on to promote the Servicemen's Protection Act, enacting penalties for countries that do not agree to exempt U.S. personnel on their soil from possible ICC prosecution.

Assistant Secretary Jones nonetheless secured the signatures of her counterparts in the State Department's other regional bureaus on a letter addressed to the U.S. secretary of state, demanding that the United States abandon its campaign to negotiate such bilateral agreements. The letter naturally became public, so—although the demand was rejected—its point was achieved: the

---

4   Greg Miller, "State Dept. Report: Democracy Domino Theory Not Credible," *Los Angeles Times*, March 14, 2003.

5   Elections, of course, are not the same thing as democracy. The desire for accountable, representative government evident in each of these cases was unmistakable, however.

6   President George W. Bush, Chapter IX, "Transforming America's National Security Institutions to Meet the Challenges and Opportunities of the Twenty-First Century," National Security Strategy of the United States of America, October 2002.

signal was clearly sent that President Bush's policies were not supported by his own subordinates.

Rewarding Insubordination

The Foreign Service—the civil service organization for American diplomats—in fact *prides itself* on such acts of deliberate subversion of presidential policy. The diplomats' professional guild, the American Foreign Service Association (AFSA), actually rewards such acts, construing them to be "constructive criticism." For example, AFSA conferred one of its top honors in 2004 on Keith Mines, an FSO who, while serving as an American representative in Hungary, publicly accused President Bush of "going it alone" in Iraq and advocated giving the UN control of Iraq's political transition.[7]

An Unhealthy Dynamic

The intended effect of this unauthorized form of public diplomacy is to thwart presidential policies that are opposed by the Foreign Service and other State Department officers.[8] Whether one agrees with the president's policies or not, in time of war, it should be clear that such conduct divides us in the face of the enemy. In so doing, it injures the cause of the Free World, diminishes the prospects for a timely victory, and puts the lives of Americans at ever greater risk.

Newt Gingrich's Critique

In spring 2003, former speaker of the U.S House of Representatives Newt Gingrich called attention to the State Department's vocal opposition to the War for the Free World. In a powerful speech to the American Enterprise Institute, Gingrich challenged the State Department for what he saw as its abdication of U.S. values and principles in favor of "process, politeness, and accommodation."[9] He cited three examples of "diplomatic failure" in the run-up to the Iraq war:

- ◆ failure to counter French diplomacy against the war
- ◆ failure to obtain military transit rights through Turkey
- ◆ failure to obtain a UN Security Council resolution endorsing the war effort.

Speaker Gingrich pointedly challenged State Department officials for obstructing the orders of the president, noting their hostility to President Bush's foreign policy, especially toward Iraq. Warning that such dysfunctional behavior endangers U.S. national security, he called for bold reforms. His critique was right on the mark: the president is constitutionally entitled to the support of his executive branch, including the Department of State.

---

7   Peter Slevin, "Diplomats Honored for Dissent," *Washington Post*, June 28, 2004.
8   Civil service appointees are even less accountable for their actions, thanks to various federal government labor rights protections.
9   Newt Gingrich, "Transforming the State Department: The Next Challenge for the Bush Administration," American Enterprise Institute, April 22, 2003.

Without deigning to address the substance of the critique, the State Department savagely attacked the messenger and distorted his message. In harsh public statements and even more vicious off-the-record comments, this thoughtful and experienced public servant was personally assailed by senior officials, including Secretary of State Powell and his deputy, Richard Armitage. Armitage went so far as to suggest to the press that the speaker was mentally ill: "off his meds and out of therapy" was his colorful phrase.[10] Their only substantive response was a rather brilliant (if outrageous) example of "spin"—misrepresenting the speaker's position as an attack on the *president* rather than the State Department!

The Powell Legacy

On the occasions when he was moved to do so, Secretary of State Colin Powell acquitted himself very effectively as a loyal soldier fighting for the president's agenda. The most memorable example was his speech to the UN Security Council in February 2003, presenting the case for war on the basis of U.S. and allied intelligence reporting about Iraq's WMDs programs.[11]

But support for the president's policies was something of an aberration in the State Department under Secretary Powell. From their first days in office, Powell and Armitage seemed determined to foist the policy views of the State Department and its clients onto the White House rather than to assure the implementation at "State" of the president's policy views and directions.

In fact, during Secretary Powell's tenure, the State Department leadership devolved into a sort of established opposition, indulging its own worst tendencies toward institutional privilege, self-regard, ideological bias, and an element of barely disguised partisan hostility. The full intensity of this hostility was demonstrated in October 2005 when Powell's chief of staff, Lawrence Wilkerson, unleashed a bitter public tirade against the Bush administration, accusing it of secretive decision making, which "one would associate more with a dictatorship than a democracy."[12]

Business as Usual

Although this pattern of insubordination during time of war is particularly reprehensible, the behavior that Speaker Gingrich denounced also fits a long-standing pattern of State Department misconduct.

---

10 Barbara Slavin, "Gingrich Takes Swipe at State Department," *USA Today*, April 22, 2003.

11 Colin Powell, "U.S. Secretary of State Colin Powell Addresses the U.N. Security Council," The White House, February 5, 2003. Available at www.whitehouse.gov/news/releases/2003/02/20030205-1.html.

12 Speech by Col. Lawrence Wilkerson USA (Ret.) to the New America Foundation, October 19, 2005, subsequently reprised in an op.ed. piece entitled "The White House Cabal" published in the Los Angeles Times on October 25, 2005.

♦ Twenty-five years ago, former Ambassador Laurence H. Silberman pointed out problems arising from the Foreign Service's rejection of "presidential control and the legitimacy of political direction."[13]

♦ A congressionally mandated commission, chaired by former U.S. Sen. Gary Hart and U.S. Sen. Warren Rudman, reached a similar finding in February 2001:

> The Department is a crippled institution . . . rarely speaking with one voice, thus reducing its influence and credibility in its interactions with the Congress and in its representations abroad. . . . [FSOs] needed remind[ing] that *their group does not serve the interest of foreign states, but is a pillar of U.S. national security.*[14]

♦ A report drafted by two organizations traditionally sympathetic to the State Department offered its own harsh assessment: "The Department simply falls short in mission, organization, and skills relative to what is needed to navigate our way sensibly through the new international universe."[15]

♦ A more diplomatic assessment of State's *modus operandi* was provided in 1979 by former national security adviser and secretary of state Henry Kissinger in his memoir, *White House Years*. Without a strong hand at the helm, he noted, "clannishness" tends to overcome discipline, and State officers will become advocates for the countries they deal with and not spokesmen of national policy. He observed wryly that, although Foreign Service officers will carry out clear-cut instructions with great loyalty, it may be difficult to convince a Foreign Service officer that an unpalatable instruction is really clear-cut.[16]

Major Problem Areas

America confronts today enormous diplomatic and national security challenges—challenges that would be difficult to contend with even if the U.S. government could field a disciplined and integrated team. Several serious

---

13 Ambassador Laurence H. Silberman, "Toward Presidential Control of the State Department," *Foreign Affairs*, Spring 1979.

14 The Phase III Report of the U.S. Commission on National Security/21st Century (Hart-Rudman Commission), February 15, 2001. [Emphasis added.]

15 The Council on Foreign Relations/Center for Strategic and International Studies (CFR/CSIS) Non-Partisan Task Force, Report on State Department Reform, February 2001.

16 Henry Kissinger, *White House Years*, Little, Brown. 1979, p. 27.

problems must be overcome in order to bring the State Department into the team as a key contributor to our War Footing.

The "Institutional Culture"

◆ **"We know best."** The downside of cultivating a highly skilled diplomatic elite is that, like most elites, its members tend to take a dim view of nonmembers, particularly those who may be unfamiliar with the world of foreign languages, cultures, and relations. Such attitudes can easily translate into contempt for people like average Americans—and the men and women they may choose as their elected representatives.

Not infrequently, this contempt for elected leadership is expressed in the conviction of many State Department careerists that they know best what to do about foreign policy. Worse yet, they actually believe their agency needs to *operate independently* of the elected administration in order to act in ways they deem best—irrespective of policies laid out by the president and the Congress.

This often dysfunctional bureaucracy hurts U.S. policy by conveying an unclear (and occasionally even incoherent) message to the world regarding America's foreign policy. And it poorly serves the president, who relies on State Department personnel not only to represent him abroad, but also to provide sound advice and accurate reporting on international developments.

◆ **Hostility to political appointees.** A related syndrome is the intense hostility often exhibited toward political appointees assigned to the State Department to foster effective cooperation with the rest of the administration and supportive management at Foggy Bottom. Unless they concur with the permanent bureaucracy's program, these officials are typically made unwelcome and are excluded from decision making as much as possible.

In some cases, admittedly, political appointees may truly be ill-qualified for their positions, appointed as a reward for past political service or contributions rather than on the basis of merit. (This is conspicuously the case with ambassadorships in certain European and other capitals.) A political appointee who is unqualified for the position is likely to harm U.S. interests and the president's policies.

But there is nothing wrong with appointing competent, highly skilled Americans *from outside the Foreign Service* to represent the United States, whether at Foggy Bottom or abroad, and there is a real benefit from such appointments of qualified individuals who also have a personal relationship with the sitting president.

♦ **"Civil serpents."** A different challenge is presented by some in the State Department's career civil service. More than ten thousand civil servants make up the department's permanent bureaucracy in Washington (most of them in administrative, technical, and maintenance positions), and many of them—unlike career diplomats—remain in their positions for decades. Some are political appointees (mostly of Democratic administrations) who "burrow in" at the end of the presidential term; if the successor administration is of a different philosophy, they will work to thwart it in jobs from which they cannot easily be removed.

♦ **The inside game.** Politically inclined State Department civil servants have a variety of obstructionist techniques at their disposal. "Lifers" in the civil service have the great advantage over newer political appointees of knowing how to "work the system" to their advantage, by

- preventing the timely approval of a decision memorandum.
- leaking damaging information to the press or to friendly members of Congress.
- sending "uncoordinated" guidance cables without the approval of all appropriate administration representatives.
- having the secretary of state preempt a foreign policy decision via an uncleared speech.

If they are unsuccessful in hindering or scuttling an unfavorable decision, skilled infighters know that there is always an opportunity to reopen decisions after they have been made. As former secretary of state George Shultz once declared in exasperation, "Nothing is ever decided in Washington!" And if all else fails, the permanent bureaucrats know that they will outlast the administration and its appointees, and they can seek to revisit these decisions later, under more favorable political circumstances.

♦ **"Professional courtesy."** Elite Foreign Service officers have a great affinity for their counterpart elites in other countries—perhaps more than with their countrymen. And in general, they typically have in common a shared contempt for politicians. This is especially true with respect to politicians like presidents Ronald Reagan and George W. Bush, who came to office with the reputation of not being as smart or well educated as the average FSO. (Naturally, the American voters who elect uninformed leaders may also be held in low esteem.)

These biases may be reinforced when FSOs assigned overseas are unable to have much contact with non-elites in their host countries. Particularly where such contacts would be most valuable—as in closed societies or countries in which terrorism is a daily concern— our embassy personnel are accustomed to shuttling between their offices and their other official functions; living in diplomatic compounds, they have little contact beyond the world of officials and fellow diplomats. (In a closed society, moreover, diplomats' interactions with the host country's citizens would actually endanger their local contacts.)

♦ **Attachment to multilateralism.** The special affinity of Colin Powell and Richard Armitage for the UN contributed significantly to the problems experienced there by the Bush administration during its first term. But the fact is, most State Department officers reflexively support the UN and other multilateral organizations; many see their Foreign Service careers as a stepping-stone to higher paid positions with the UN and its various agencies[17] (see Section B of this step).

This bias is particularly evident for State Department officers assigned to work with international organizations. For example, State employees attached to the International Atomic Energy Agency tend to revere the organization—not troubled in the least by the irresponsible and highly politicized conduct of its director general, Mohamed El Baradei.

A Tradition of Dedicated Service

This critique of State Department institutional culture should not detract from our appreciation of the great contributions made by many of its personnel at all ranks in service to this country—today, as in the past. Many perform difficult and dangerous duties on our behalf, often at considerable personal sacrifice. For example:

♦ In 1973, 1976, and 1979, assassins took the lives of the U.S. ambassadors to Sudan, Lebanon, and Afghanistan, respectively.

♦ Bombings of the U.S. embassy in Beirut in 1983 and 1984 claimed 60 lives and wounded 92 others.

♦ In 1979, Iranian "students" (also known as *terrorists*) seized 52 American hostages at the U.S. embassy in Tehran and held them captive for fourteen months.

---

17 UN salaries are approximately 15 percent higher than comparable salaries of U.S. government employees, and the United Nations and other international organizations adjust salaries to compensate for taxes owed by employees to their home governments.

◆ In 1998, terrorists bombed the American embassies in Kenya and Tanzania, killing 223 and wounding 4,700.[18]

Given the global nature of the Islamofascist menace, Americans serving overseas are perhaps in even greater danger today. Therefore, the State Department has a special stake in America's prevailing in this War for the Free World.

Where there are differences in policy views, Foreign Service officers and State Department civil servants are of course entitled to express their views, in the course of normal internal U.S. government policy deliberations. Even in the middle of a war, the development of national security policies benefits from give-and-take between officials and agencies with different portfolios, responsibilities, and perspectives.

In the event they disagree with the resulting decision, such individuals are certainly still entitled to express their opposition—*from outside the government, following their resignation.* Short of resigning, it is incumbent upon them to support the government's policies, not to persist in dissenting or obstructing them. And it is an abuse of professional ethics for a government official to seek, while continuing to hold office, to sabotage unsatisfactory decisions in the public arena.

What Needs to Be Done

Leadership Is Essential

President Bush's second-term decision to replace Secretary Powell with Condoleezza Rice—someone intimately familiar with and supportive of his approach to the War for the Free World—was clearly a necessary step. It opened up the possibility of engaging the U.S. State Department as an engine for the president's foreign-policy initiatives, pulling steadily and effectively in the same direction he intends to go.

Unfortunately, the personnel changes of Preident Bush's second term have not yet alleviated the institutional problems of the State Department. At risk are several of the president's foreign-policy priorities.

◆ The president was adamant in his first term that North Korea not be rewarded for renewed promises to forego nuclear weapons—promises it has repeatedly made (and been rewarded for) and has disregarded in the past. Yet, Ambassador Christopher Hill has now been authorized to arrange exactly this kind of unverifiable and ill-advised deal (see Step 9).

---

18 Fred Gedrich, "Foreign Terrorist Attacks against the United States," Freedom Alliance UN Update, November 2, 2001.

- Bush was also opposed to negotiating with the Iranian regime during most of his first term. Yet, the United States today is fully supportive of European efforts that have bought Iran time to realize its nuclear weapons ambitions (see Step 9).
- As noted above, the president not only rejected the International Criminal Court but took steps to ensure it enjoyed no jurisdiction over U.S. military or other personnel. Yet, in his second term, he has acquiesced in the ICC's first mandate, to prosecute Sudanese war crimes in Darfur.
- The president signed off on the World Summit Outcome Statement in September 2005 that endorsed language supporting (for example) the Kyoto Protocol, UN control of the Internet, and globotaxes—in contradiction to his standing policies (see Section B of this step).

The *Los Angeles Times* placed these trends in the context of an overall policy shift:

> R. Nicholas Burns, the Under Secretary of State for Political Affairs, said in an interview that Rice had emphasized from the beginning of her term that *she intended to stress diplomacy and international institutions to advance the president's agenda.* Burns cited the administration's approach in the North Korea and Iran talks, the International Criminal Court abstention, and the U.S. decision at last month's meeting of the UN General Assembly to soften ambitious demands for reforming the world body's management.[19]

But "diplomacy and international institutions" were consistently mobilized to *thwart,* rather than advance, the president's agenda in his first term. And, to judge from Burns's list of policy "successes," the new approach is simply to adapt the president's policies to the international "consensus" (as discussed in Section B of this step).

To succeed, as he must, the president needs to go beyond the leadership changes he has made to date in Foggy Bottom. He and Rice need to install, in the State Department and its foreign embassies, a cadre of high-ranking officials who are committed to supporting the president's agenda. These individuals, in turn, must seek out the department's talented and loyal career officers, promote them, and give them consequential national security assignments.

A "Goldwater-Nichols" Reform for State

Excessive power is concentrated in the State Department's regional bureaus, which have traditionally exercised undue influence over policy and personnel

---

19 "Under Rice, Powell's policies are reborn," *Los Angeles Times,* October 11, 2005, (Emphasis added.)

decision making within the department. They also tend to be the locus of the most intense outbreaks of clientitis: the Near East/South Asia Affairs Bureau is notoriously Arabist, the East Asia Bureau is pro-Beijing, and the Europe and Eurasia Bureau is reflexively attuned to the Franco-German line.

Under current Foreign Service and departmental procedures, the regional bureaus define a successful diplomatic career. Tours involving assignments in the "functional bureaus" (such as nonproliferation, counternarcotics, and counterterrorism), whose portfolios cut across regional lines, are viewed as setbacks, if not the kiss of death, for the future aspirations of ambitious young officers.

The Defense Department once faced a similar problem. Prior to the implementation two decades ago of legislation known as Goldwater-Nichols, professional success in the military meant serving entirely in one's own branch of the armed forces.

Because a leaner U.S. military, facing nontraditional enemies, would increasingly require multiservice (or "joint") operations, it was essential to overcome this single-service orientation. Goldwater-Nichols made officers' advancement contingent upon serving tours in interservice organizations such as the Joint Staff, in multiservice combatant commands, and in other government agencies.

A similar approach to the assignment of FSOs could help lessen the parochialism—and clientitis—associated with the predominance of the regional bureaus. Favorable "fitness reports" and career advancement should require experience in the State Department's functional organizations (which currently have a hard time getting FSOs to staff them). This would help the State Department make more efficient use of its resources—and foster an *American* perspective among its personnel.

This goal can also be advanced by bringing into the State Department more mid-level people from other agencies and, for that matter, outside the government itself. This approach would (1) diversify the experience base from which American diplomacy draws, and (2) train a far broader group of professionals to support the diplomatic program of the War for the Free World.[20]

No More "Business as Usual"

Such personnel initiatives will, of course, require changes in the way business is done today and will therefore be resisted by Foreign Service officers and AFSA (which serves as the sole bargaining agent for twenty-three thousand active and

---

20 Such individuals would have to serve outside of the Foreign Service; otherwise, its selection process would ensure only those who adhere to the party line will be allowed in, defeating the purpose of the exercise.

retired officers).[21] FSOs currently control the department's policies pertaining to hiring, evaluation, promotion, assignments, and discipline.

Yet the need for change is clear. U.S. missions in many areas around the world have inadequate numbers of trained linguists and other regional specialists, reflecting an assignment system that is employee driven; the department does not *require* FSOs to serve at hardship posts. As a result, places like China, Russia, and Saudi Arabia typically experience significant staffing shortfalls, unlike such desirable posts as Paris and Berlin. This is obviously unacceptable in time of war, when the hardship posts are where our best diplomats are most needed.

Furthermore, under the current personnel arrangements, the State Department rarely uses directed assignments to fill staffing shortfalls and critical language-designated positions. The GAO, Congress's watchdog, found that more than 50 percent of language-designated positions were not filled with qualified linguists, even though the department had an abundance of trained resources in the workforce.[22] Without proper staffing, overseas missions cannot perform such important tasks as collecting information for national security and foreign-policy purposes or properly screening visa applicants.

Finally, the State Department's promotion process works against FSOs and civil servants who do not share the political views prevailing in the agency. Apart from a handful of political appointees, a conservative president is likely to find very few like-minded individuals staffing this crucial government institution.

Throughout its history, the United States has been blessed with dedicated individuals who performed with diplomatic daring and vision. As America faces enormous challenges in a dangerous and unfriendly world, it would be a great tribute to their memory—to say nothing of a tremendous benefit to America's security—were the State Department to resume its place as an institution that plays its unique, constitutional, and much-needed role in defending American values and promoting U.S. interests.

---

21 See http://www.afsa.org.
22 Foreign Languages: Human Capital Approach Needed to Correct Staffing and Proficiency Shortfalls, U.S. General Accounting Office, GAO-02-375, January 2002.

B. Marginalize the UN

With Contributions from Claudia Rosett and Cliff Kincaid

In recent years, some of the problems with United Nations operations have become painfully public.

- The ongoing investigations of the UN's Oil for Food scandal demonstrate colossal incompetence or, worse, that systemic corruption and venality, have reached the highest levels of the organization and its bureaucracy. Saddam Hussein exploited these failings to embezzle perhaps as much as $17 billion dollars of funds intended to provide food and medicine for his suffering people.

- UN "peacekeepers" operated rape squads and engaged in sex-slave trafficking in Africa.

- The organization's shameful past inaction in the face of "ethnic cleansing," mass murder, and other human rights abuses in the Balkans and Rwanda is being repeated today in Sudan.

- Large-scale graft has been revealed not only in the now notorious Oil for Food program but also in the UN procurement department, which spends the bulk of the U.S. tax dollars contributed to the organization.

- The UN's International Atomic Energy Agency has been grossly negligent with respect to monitoring and preventing proliferating nuclear weapons programs in Iran and North Korea. (The Nobel Committee added insult to this considerable injury by awarding its 2005 Peace Prize to the IAEA and its highly politicized chief, Mohamed El Baradei.)

Such episodes have brought public confidence in the UN to a new low, prompting widespread calls for its reform. Even Secretary General Kofi Annan has been obliged to acknowledge the need for change in a wide variety of UN functions and offices—including his own secretariat.

Political Warfare at the UN

Unfortunately, even the most sweeping of these changes will not address what *really* is wrong with the United Nations. If the UN apparatus and its admirers succeed in focusing attention on such superficial "reforms," the most essential reforms will drop off the public agenda.

The UN and the Internet

A case in point is unfolding at this writing and involves a UN bid to take over from the United States "control" of the Internet. On October 6, 2005, the London *Guardian* published a report titled "Breaking America's Grip on the Net." The following is an excerpt:

> For the vast majority of people who use the Internet, the only real concern is getting on it. But with the Internet now essential to countries' basic infrastructure—Brazil relies on it for 90 percent of its tax collection—the question of who has control has become critical.
>
> And the unwelcome answer for many is that it is the US government. In the early days, an enlightened Department of Commerce (DoC) pushed and funded expansion of the Internet. And when it became global, it created a private company, the Internet Corporation for Assigned Names and Numbers (ICANN) to run it.
>
> But the DoC retained overall control, and in June stated what many had always feared: that it would retain indefinite control of the Internet's foundation—its "root servers," which act as the basic directory for the whole Internet.
>
> A number of countries represented in Geneva, including Brazil, China, Cuba, Iran, and several African states, insisted the US give up control, but it refused. The meeting was "going nowhere" . . . [until] the European Union took a bold step and proposed two stark changes: a new forum that would decide [Internet] public policy and a "cooperation model" comprising governments that would be in overall charge.
>
> Much to the distress of the US, the idea proved popular. Its representative hit back, stating that it "can't in any way allow any changes" that went against "the historic role" of the US in controlling the top level of the Internet.
>
> But the refusal to budge only strengthened opposition, and now the world's governments are expected to agree on a deal to award themselves ultimate control. It will be officially raised at a UN summit of world leaders next month and, *faced with international consensus, there is little the US government can do but acquiesce.* [Emphasis added.]

Consider what is going on here. The United States is being told by "an international consensus" that it must surrender "control" over an asset invented, developed, and made freely available to the world, *exclusively with American taxpayer funds.* (The Internet was a creation of the Pentagon's Advanced Research Projects Agency.)

International "Consensus"

Although the usual meaning of "consensus" is unanimous agreement, the UN's General Assembly, and its various politicized tribunals and organizations, routinely cast votes with which the United States does not agree. (In this case, the decision-making body is the ad hoc UN Working Group on Internet Governance, or WGIG.)

Here is how the negotiating process normally unfolds at the UN and its franchises.

1. Member nations and international bureaucrats hostile to the American point of view—often with the active encouragement or even participation of like-minded nongovernmental organizations (NGOs)—draft conventions or treaties reflecting the majority view.
2. To avoid being isolated or relegated to a small minority, our diplomats press Washington to make tactical concessions (see Section A of this step for a discussion of State Department operations). In most cases, such arguments eventually prevail.

   In this instance, it is expected that the November 2005 "World Summit on the Information Society" will direct the WGIG to prepare a document establishing not one, but *two*, international organizations to be put in charge, respectively, of the Internet's "public policies" and "coordination" (read, management).
3. The draft document gathers momentum. In this case, well over a hundred other countries will probably sign on. The United States will be subjected to intense pressure internationally, as well as lobbying at home, to join (or at least submit to) the "consensus." To avoid the accusation of acting "unilaterally," even a principled American administration may opt to go along.

The Stakes of the Game

In the case of the Internet controversy, as the *Guardian* report makes clear, the Bush administration has expressed its strong opposition. There is indeed much at stake.

♦ The Internet has become the most important engine for freedom—in particular, for the free flow of information and ideas—in the history of the world. It has also become an indispensable element in the growth of international capitalism.

♦ The Internet, on the whole, works flawlessly, as currently managed—*not* "controlled"—by a U.S. corporation. It is a perfect metaphor for Pax Americana in the best sense of the word: an example of the largely benign, generous, and constructive use of U.S. power to benefit the entire planet.

♦ The very nature of the Internet requires the current form of entrepreneurial, unstructured, user driven, and rapidly adaptive management arrangement. The surest way to destroy the Internet is to surrender it to international bureaucrats and their multilateral masters.

Those who are leading the campaign for control of the Internet have made no secret of their hostility to it; Chinese, Russian, Iranian, and Saudi officials detest it precisely because it is an engine for freedom. The PRC, for example, reportedly employs forty-thousand computer programmers to monitor Internet usage in China, to block access to Web sites and other information flows, and to crack down on those who are making use of the net for other than approved purposes.[1] Moreover, Beijing has obliged Western companies like Yahoo!, Cisco, and Google to help it accomplish these repressive tasks.[2] This task would be far simpler with "proper" international control mechanisms.

Even if those put in charge refrained from sabotaging the Internet and its future growth, another by-product is predictable. Granting control to China and other nations with sophisticated cyber-warfare capabilities would create serious vulnerabilities for the United States and the rest of the Free World. At the very least, the security of business information and credit card data risks being compromised.

One motivation for the international community's designs on the Internet is the expectation that taxes can be levied on transactions, possibly creating new sources of hard currency for corrupt regimes. Such taxes could also aid the UN's efforts to create its own independent revenue streams—allowing the institution to become even less accountable for its conduct in the future.

The attempt to commandeer the Internet exemplifies what is wrong with the United Nations. Its initiatives are not necessarily designed to serve the best interests of mankind and may indeed be harmful to the common good. They are almost invariably injurious to the economic and geopolitical interests of the United States, its largest contributor. And—despite the putative moral authority of the UN—the U.S. position is not *wrong* just because most other countries are lining up on the other side.

---

1 Melinda Liu, "Big Brother Is Talking," *Newsweek*, October 17, 2005.
2 Dan Gillmor, "Censorship Has Found All Too Willing Helpers," *The Financial Times*, October 5, 2005.

Malign Intent

The UN's grab for the Internet is but one example—though a particularly clear one—of the larger purpose to which freedom's enemies often put the institution: its use as an instrument for political warfare against nations like this one that stand in their way. Other examples include the following.

The Iraq Oil for Food Program

Oil for Food was poorly designed from the start: It amounted to a protection racket for Saddam Hussein, who was accorded the right to negotiate his own contracts to sell Iraqi oil and to choose his own foreign customers. He was also allowed to draw up the shopping lists of "humanitarian" supplies and to choose his foreign suppliers. The UN also granted Saddam a say in the choice of the bank that would be primarily responsible for handling the funds and issuing the letters of credit to suppliers.

Saddam was thus invited by the UN to sell oil at below-market prices to his hand-picked customers—principally, the French and Russians—who could then resell it at a fat profit. Part of this profit was kicked back to Saddam as a "surcharge," paid directly into bank accounts outside the UN program in clear violation of existing UN sanctions. It is estimated that Saddam embezzled as much as $17 billion in illicit income through this comfortable arrangement. Equally important, however, was the influence he thus acquired over those countries' leaders and policies.

Worse yet, in the course of the Oil for Food program, Secretary General Annan approved an expanded shopping list requested by Saddam, adding ten new sectors to be funded by the program, including labor and social affairs, "information," and "justice." None of these, of course, fit under the rubric of *relief*; they were, however, essential underpinnings of Saddam's totalitarian state. Labor, information, and justice translated (respectively) into Baathist party patronage; propaganda and censorship; and Saddam's secret police, rape rooms, and mass graves. The UN thus was actively, and perhaps knowingly, sustaining a particularly hideous tyranny.[3]

Hindering the Liberation of Iraq

Russia, China, France, and Germany used the machinery and bureaucracy of the United Nations to delay for six months the removal of the Iraqi dictator's regime—precious time that was used to lay the groundwork for today's

---

3   Claudia Rosett, "The Oil-for-Food Scam: What did Kofi Annan Know, and When Did He Know It?" *Commentary*, April 16, 2004.

bloody insurgency, at great cost of American, Allied, and Iraqi lives (see Step 2). Even after Saddam's overthrow, Kofi Annan gratuitiously encouraged the enemies of freedom in Iraq by declaring the invasion to have been "illegal" because it had not been formally approved by the UN.

Human Rights?

For years, the UN's Commission on Human Rights has worked against the interests of global freedom and security. By routinely seating nations like China, Cuba, Libya, Sierra Leone, Togo, and Sudan on this panel, it has rendered the commission an international laughingstock. The larger political warfare purpose was further served, however, by the *eviction of the United States* from this commission.

Unfortunately, the greatest losers are the world's oppressed peoples. In 2004 alone, of the eighty-six separate votes of the commission, the United States was on the losing side 85 percent of the time, as it stood up for those whose rights are being abused.[4]

Free Pass for Proliferators

Today, the UN is running interference for the world's two most dangerous nuclear proliferators—North Korea and Iran—again, with the acquiescence or connivance of several U.S. allies. In both cases, the UN's IAEA has helped create a public impression that the "international community" is (as the diplomats are fond of saying) "seized" with the problem of Pyongyang and Tehran "going nuclear."

It is clear, however, that the endless deliberations inside the IAEA, as well as the parallel multilateral negotiations outside of it—the so-called six-party talks involving North Korea and the EU-3's discussions with the Iranians—have merely served to stymie action and to allow the despots to run out the clock.

The greatest hope for UN action would be that, at some point, these proliferators will be referred to the Security Council. This hope is sure to be proved unfounded: the veto-wielding Russians and Chinese (joined, in the case of Iran, by Germany and India)[5] have made it clear that they will *not agree* to any authorization of punitive measures—even economic sanctions, to say nothing of military action. The losers, once again, are the United States and the rest of the Free World, which are threatened by the possession and proliferation of nuclear weapons by such hostile regimes.

---

4   Anne Bayefsky, "W's UN Mandate," *National Review Online*, November 9, 2004.
5   Interestingly, these two nations are pressing hard to be made permanent members of the Security Council.

These many-faceted initiatives and programs demonstrate the UN's enormous value to antidemocratic countries as an instrument of political warfare against nations that stand in their way. As this instance suggests, the lowest common denominator—that is to say the prevailing side in most UN votes—is not motivated by the ambition to make the world "safe for democracy" (as Woodrow Wilson once put it). The driving force at the UN typically is a group of dictatorships and their allies, clients, and proxies.[6] They are interested only in preserving their own power and that of fellow despots.

Their purpose is advanced by building up the UN and its numerous franchises, many of which are controlled by the Un-Free World through the diplomatic equivalent of mob rule—assisted by the connivance of sympathetic international bureaucrats and the accommodation of Western nations that put commercial interests before principle or even prudence.

Globotaxes and Other Mischief

The September "World Summit 2005" was a high-level plenary meeting of the UN General Assembly. The stated intention was to use the event to "review progress" on the Millennium Development Goals. The unstated purpose was to maximize pressure on developed nations—and, most of all, on the United States—to honor commitments made at a UN conference in Monterey, Mexico, in 2002.

At a time when no one in Washington was paying sufficient attention, the United States went along with the "consensus" at the Monterey meeting—presumably, as usual, so we would not be isolated. On that occasion, we agreed that rich countries like ours should promise to give 0.7 percent of our gross national income to developing countries in foreign aid (also known as Official Development Assistance, or ODA).[7]

The growing consensus, however, is that ODA has been conclusively shown to be the least efficient way to help poor people around the world. It is frequently squandered by corrupt regimes that use it not to help the needy but to prop themselves up and enrich their cronies. (This is almost certainly

---

6   One hundred three of the 191 nations that are members of the UN are not full-fledged democracies—and most of them are influential in the 115 member "non-aligned" movement. This group of nations accounts for less than 1 percent of the UN's total budget (compared with 22 percent for the United States). Yet these are the nations that, thanks to the majority they represent in the General Assembly and their representatives throughout the Secretariat, control the funds, programs, and overall agenda of the United Nations. (See Anne Bayefsky, "The Right Reform," *National Review Online*, July 18, 2005; and Brett D. Schaeffer, "The United Nations Reform Act of 2005: A Powerful Lever to Advance UN Reform," Heritage Foundation Webmemo 759, June 10, 2005.)

7   The United States is by far the leader in another, likely more effective form of international assistance—that provided by privately funded nonprofits and corporations.

equally true of spending by many UN agencies as well. They tend to conduct themselves with such an astonishing lack of transparency, however, that it is impossible to know whether their funds are better or worse deployed than this low standard.)

Nevertheless, if the UN wants more official development assistance, the question becomes, how might that be arranged?

According to Kofi Annan's special adviser, Dr. Jeffrey Sachs of Harvard University, under the Monterey formula the United States "owes" the international community, for this year alone, foreign aid funding amounting to *an extra $65 billion*, above what the United States is currently expected to spend. Extrapolating this commitment over the fifteen years of the Millennium Declaration, we would be obliged to come up with a whopping *$845 billion* more than anybody thinks likely.

Rather than try to get this kind of money out of the Congress, Dr. Sachs and others at the UN have seized on an idea that has been kicking around the "world body" for a long time: giving the UN taxing authority on various international transactions, through what might be called "Globotaxes." The rationale is that both the UN and its wealthier member nations could, thereby, be spared the nasty business of coming up directly with money for foreign aid—let alone the vastly inflated sums pursuant to the Monterey deal.

The Law of the Sea Treaty

The UN Convention on the Law of the Sea Treaty (LOST) was the first and (so far) only instance in which the UN, through one of its agencies, obtained taxing authority. LOST was originally drafted in the heyday of the New International Economic Order in the late 1970s and early 1980s—a brainchild of one-world government proponents at the World Federalist Association (WFA), supported by the former Soviet Union and the so-called nonaligned movement (the caucus of developing states, generally very much aligned with Moscow).

The treaty created an international authority to govern the exploitation of seabed minerals a well as subterranean oil and gas underneath international waters. As WFA documents concerning LOST have made clear, the framers of the treaty intended it also as a model for managing—and taxing—international energy flows, airline travel, currency transactions, and commerce, outer space, and now the Internet.[8]

---

8   See also Ralph B. Levering and Miriam L. Levering, *Citizen Action for Global Change: The Neptune Group and the Law of the Sea,* Syracuse University Press, 1999.

An organization is already in the process of being developed to control the exploitation of ocean resources, and similar agencies could be created to govern Antarctica and the moon. . . . By means of these voluntarily funded functional agencies, *national sovereignty would be gradually eroded until it is no longer an issue.* . . . Eventually, a world federation can be formally adopted with little resistance.[9]

In fact, LOST set up a mini-world government for the seabeds, complete with a multinational executive, permanent bureaucracy, legislature, and judiciary. The last of these would have mandatory dispute-resolution authority, working through either binding arbitration or a classic, politicized UN international court (with dozens of jurists from member states serving on a rotating basis).[10] It also was given the ability to levy what amounted to taxes on resources taken from the international seabeds.

To his credit, President Ronald Reagan decided he did not want to encourage such a sovereignty-sapping arrangement, either in its own right or as a prototype for future UN endeavors. He refused to sign LOST, although he agreed that the United States would conform to its generally laudable arrangements governing transit of territorial and international waters and straits.

During fall 2003, following the diplomatic maelstrom over the liberation of Iraq, the UN's standard operating procedure kicked into gear. The Bush administration sought to demonstrate that the United States was not, after all, a unilateralist "cowboy" by going along with the "consensus" on LOST. President Reagan's concerns were said to have all been addressed in subsequent negotiations and agreements, fashioned during an earlier effort, by the Clinton administration, to get with the UN's program. (This claim is highly debatable even with respect to some of the treaty particulars, and it is certainly not true with regard to President Reagan's strongly held philosophical objection to creating world-governing supranational organizations.)

---

9   *The Genius of World Federation: Why World Federation is the Answer to Global Problems,* World Federalist Association, undated report. (Emphasis added.)

10 Another example of such courts is the International Criminal Court. As noted above, the Bush administration adamantly opposed this court and refused to participate in it, and Congress enacted the Servicemembers' Protection Act to prevent the court from being used capriciously to prosecute U.S. military personnel and others for "war crimes." Recently, however, in the interest of "consensus," the United States agreed to allow the ICC to be used to prosecute crimes in Sudan's Darfur region.

Even more troubling is the growing tendency among American jurists to allow rulings of international courts (and, for that matter, other organizations such as UN conferences, conventions, etc.) to influence the application of U.S. law. U.S. Supreme Court Justice Anthony Kennedy recently even suggested that international law should inform the interpretation of the U.S. Constitution (see *Roper v. Simmons,* US Supreme Court, No. 03-633, March 1, 2005, p. 21).

As a result, the Bush administration has asked the U.S. Senate to ratify LOST "as soon as possible." The timing is a bit awkward, however, coming just as the UN effort to gain international taxing authority is getting under way, based in part on the LOST precedent.

The "World Summit 2005" and Its Outcome Statement

Push came to shove in September 2005. The UN planned to use an "Outcome Statement" of the World Summit to advance a broad agenda, including globo-taxes. With only a month before the statement's release, President Bush named John Bolton, in a recess appointment, as U.S. ambassador to the United Nations. For the first time, the United States had a representative in these negotiations who would be unafraid to break with "consensus" on matters of principle and importance to the sovereignty and security of the United States. Ambassador Bolton promptly sought hundreds of changes to the statement as previously drafted (largely behind closed doors).

One of the changes sought by Ambassador Bolton was to drop all references to the Millennium Development Goals and international taxes. By the end of the draft's negotiation, however, the United States—in the interest of achieving "consensus"—had agreed to accept nuanced revisions of the language it opposed. Washington claimed its positions were preserved on this and other fronts, but the emerging picture suggests otherwise.

A reference to the Millennium Development Goals did in fact remain in the final document. Still more discouraging, in his address before the General Assembly, President Bush actually announced that "We are committed to the Millennium Development goals."

The State Department spin is that the president is not talking about *the same* Millennium Development Goals that the UN uses that phrase to describe. Rather, he meant the "development goals of the Millennium Declaration"—not the detailed and mandatory "Millennium Development Goals" subsequently whipped up by the UN bureaucracy; hence, the use of the crucial lowercase "g" in Bush's speech. (Of course, those listening to the speech might not have discerned that the president used the *lowercase* letter rather than the *uppercase* one.) In any event, it is certain that this compromise will undermine future U.S. efforts to resist "consensus" on implementation of the Millennium Development Goals (uppercase), through the adoption of international taxes.

In fact, the Outcome Statement language actually reflects further progress down that proverbial "slippery slope." The document recognizes the initiative by "some countries" (notably, France, Germany, and Brazil) to impose a "solidarity contribution on airline tickets" (UN-speak for an international tax on plane travel). The idea is to raise money for development assistance from tourists, other travelers, and businessmen. The statement also notes that—at least for the moment—these "contributions" will be garnered by the countries "utilizing their national authorities," not through the UN or some other global facility.

Here again, the nuanced formulation allowed the United States to say that it did not endorse globotaxes in signing onto the Outcome Statement. We should be clear, however: the UN *modus operandi* is in full gear. The United States has agreed to yet another step toward institutionalizing self-financing arrangements for the UN.

Washington also accepted the document's reference to "innovative sources of financing," a formulation that will surely come back to haunt us. The United States glosses that phrase to mean "public, private, domestic or external basis" for raising funds. That, however, is surely not what is intended by one-worlders, UN bureaucrats, nongovernmental organizations, and political warfare-minded member nations who champion globotaxes.

There are a number of other troubling elements in the agreed Outcome Statement.

- Some references to "strengthening the UN" specify the objective of "the prevention of armed conflict"—further reinforcing the idea that all armed conflict is a matter for UN approval or veto.
- Reaffirmation that the Security Council has "primary responsibility for the maintenance of international peace and security" further underlines this point.
- The endorsement of the creation of "an initial operating capability for a standing police capacity" ushers in the precursor for a UN army.
- Nongovernmental organizations are encouraged to referee UN affairs. Such groups, almost uniformly hostile to the United States, are prime movers behind much in the organization's agenda that is contrary to U.S. sovereignty and interests.

Finally, the United States signed onto one other ominous item in the Outcome Statement—urging the implementation of the recommendations of the World Summit on the Information Society. As we have seen, if matters run true to form, those recommendations will require the United States to turn over the Internet to the United Nations.

What Needs to Be Done

The UN as currently constituted is now—and *will remain*—an instrument of political warfare wielded by enemies of the Free World. The UN is not merely resistant to the sort of systemic change that might bring it into closer alignment with its founding principles of protecting and promoting freedom.[11] Such changes are, as a practical matter, *impossible*.

Consequently, the United States, joined by other freedom-defending nations, should recognize that an alternative approach must be employed.

1. **Marginalize the United Nations.** We must stop legitimating the organization and deferring to its assertion of higher moral authority. Particularly in time of war, the Free World cannot afford to allow an organization *dominated by the Un-Free* to be the arbiter of our security, let alone the determinant of what we do to safeguard it. The World War II analogy would have been a League of Nations whose initiatives were orchestrated by the Axis powers. The UN has no standing whatsoever to dictate to or otherwise interfere with the exercise of sovereignty by freedom-loving peoples and their elected representatives.

   ♦ There are activities the UN performs (notably, in the humanitarian relief area) whose continued U.S. funding might be justified. *American contributions to the UN* should be earmarked for these limited purposes, however, and not made available to support the bloated, inefficient, and generally hostile bureaucracy of the secretariat.

   ♦ We need to stop turning a blind eye to *Secretary General Kofi Annan's* undisguised anti-Americanism and his unhelpfulness in the War for the Free World.[12] We must no longer lend our support to enable Kofi Annan to retain a position to which he has brought disgrace and dishonor through his incompetence or possibly his corruption.

   ♦ Under no circumstances should the U.S. government or its citizens agree to or be obligated to pay *international taxes* of any kind. "No taxation without representation" was the founding principle of this country, and we cannot acquiesce in its abrogation

---

11 This deviation from the UN's charter and intended mission is powerfully documented in *Broken Promises: The United Nations at 60*, a film released in October 2005 by Ron Silver and Citizens United.

12 Examples of Kofi Annan's public maneuvering include documented efforts to sabotage President Bush's September 11, 2002, speech laying the groundwork for war with Iraq; his subsequent declaration that that war was "illegal," as it had not be authorized by the UN; and his declaration that it was "shameful" that the United States was "among the least generous" nations in the world.

by unelected international bureaucrats and unaccountable multilateral institutions. This is particularly true given the UN's now-well-documented corruption and malfeasance in managing the funds administered through the Oil for Food program.

2. **Create a new organization: the "Free Nations."** U.S. leadership, prestige, and resources should, instead, be directed toward establishing a new entity for the defense of the Free World. Only bona fide democracies would be invited to join—in contrast to the UN's parody of a Democracy Caucus, whose 125 member nations include 25—*one-fifth*—that are *not* democracies.[13]

Presumably, those 25 countries are the ones Kofi Annan had in mind when he announced that the UN Democracy Fund (which was launched, naturally, in the World Summit 2005 Outcome Statement) "will not support any *single* model of democracy." But the UN should not be supporting so-called democracies that are not rooted in the institutions of representative, accountable, and fairly elected governments (the only model of democracy that can reliably deliver more than one-man, one-vote, *one-time* elections). These crypto-dictatorships would not, certainly, be eligible for membership in the Free Nations.

Such an organization would have *real* moral standing, would represent the best aspirations of mankind, would give force and effect to the sentiments embedded in the UN Charter and UN Declaration on Human Rights, and would provide a ready basis for forming coalitions for the defense of the Free World.

The Free Nations would, of course, have a place for democratic Taiwan—a nation of nearly 23 million people, blocked from representation in the UN at the insistence of un-free Communist China. In this organization, Israel would be a welcome member, allowed to participate fully in its deliberations (something it is not permitted to do in the UN). The Free Nations would forego the endless stream of resolutions condemning the Jewish State and funding its enemies (which, in fact, make up a large share of the UN's work program and "relief" activities).

3. **Stop thinking of the world's oceans, international commerce, outer space, and the Internet as so-called *global commons* to be turned over to UN organizations.** The idea of a socialist bureaucracy administering an invaluable and delicately structured resource—such as the Internet— is an obvious nonstarter. No less unwelcome are similar initiatives in

---

13 Anne Bayefsky, "The Right Reform," *National Review Online*, July 18, 2005.

other areas vital to American national security, economic interests, and sovereignty.[14]

The United States and other freedom-defending nations can no longer afford to ignore the insidious role played by the UN in support of our enemies. It is time to say aloud that the emperor's cloak of moral authority is in tatters, and that the international organization—far from being the best hope for world peace and human dignity—has degenerated to the point that it makes a travesty of its original charter.

As long as the UN remains a going concern, U.S. policy should be directed toward marginalizing it. That will be far easier to do if we refuse to go along with further rounds of U.S. concessions or "consensus" decisions that are calculated to be inimical to the interests of America and the Free World.

---

14 For example, if the United States were a party to the Law of the Sea Treaty, it is entirely possible that it would have been enjoined from pumping the toxic liquids that had flooded in New Orleans into Lake Pontchartrain and the Mississippi River. Note that (1) such a measure would surely violate the parties' obligations not to pollute the international waters downstream; and (2) the Law of the Sea Tribunal has already established the precedent that its jurisdiction extends onto the sovereign soil of member states.

C. Recruit Academia

With Contributions from Sarah N. Stern and Dr. Michael Rubin

I n the last great struggle against a hostile ideology with global ambitions—the Cold War—this nation recognized the need for its young people to be equipped with skills in foreign languages, cultures, and regions. Early Soviet space and military programs created a sense of American vulnerability and the widely shared conviction that corrective action was needed.

Accordingly, in 1958, the United States adopted the National Defense Education Act (NDEA). Its goal was to supply knowledgeable specialists to government, business, industry, and education. Today, under Title VI of the Higher Education Act (successor to the NDEA), the government allocates some $120 million to support regional studies centers on campuses around the country that specialize in such areas as Africa, the Middle East, and Asia.

As a result of the cumulative efforts of this federal investment over nearly five decades, the United States has developed a formidable regional studies industry. Unfortunately, that industry has, with few exceptions, scarcely supported the advancement of the original legislative objective—namely, "to ensure that the national security interests of our nation are being met." In time of war, it is simply unacceptable that the country's national security-related educational needs remain largely *unmet*, due to serious deficiencies in much of the curricula, values, and faculty of our federally subsidized regional studies centers.[1]

---

1 Another egregious example of academia's hindrance of the war effort is its attempt to deny military recruiters access to college campuses. (Such recruitment is critical to our ability to avoid conscription by maintaining an all-volunteer force; see Step 2.) Incredibly, it took an act of Congress to guarantee the military's admission, through the Solomon Amendment (1996), which bars institutions of higher education from receiving federal funding if they do not permit entrance to recruiters.

A coalition of academic and other antimilitary groups has nonetheless pursued a lawsuit—currently before the U.S. Supreme Court—seeking to declare the Solomon Amendment unconstitutional. The justification (namely, that the military's "Don't Ask, Don't Tell" policy on homosexuals in the armed forces violates the schools' nondiscrimination policies) is specious. (See Brief of Amici Curiae Admiral Charles S. Abbot, et al., Rumsfeld v. Forum for Academic and Institutional Rights, et al., 125 S. Ct. 1977 (2005) (No. 04-1152)). This case reflects, rather, the academy's determined hostility toward the military and American national security more generally.

Unmet Needs

As the need for those with Middle East language and regional skills reaches a historic high, universities—and particularly the Title VI–supported international studies centers—are failing spectacularly to meet that need.

- The FBI has such a serious shortfall in the number of available Arabic translators that it has *120,000 hours* of pre-September 11 "chatter" still undeciphered.[2]
- The dearth of Americans trained in relevant regional languages is so acute that law-enforcement and intelligence communities have been forced to "outsource" the work to foreign nationals, some of which are of uncertain reliability. One FBI whistleblower raised an alarm about the translation of critical wiretaps of organizations with suspected ties to Islamist terrorists: foreign nationals, relied on for these translations, were failing to translate accurately and expeditiously.[3]

In an effort to remedy this dangerous lack of American expertise, Congress allocated additional funding of $20 million to the Title VI centers after September 11, 2001—a 26 percent increase. The legislators wrote this substantial check in good faith, with the understanding that these centers would promote language study, particularly in regard to "Islamic and/or Muslim culture, politics, religion and economy."[4]

The increased spending, however, has not increased the output of the academic pipeline as intended. Dr. Martin Kramer, a recognized authority on regional studies centers, cited this representative example: "[Berkeley] has been continuously subsidized under Title VI for the last forty years. So you have to shake your head at reports that Berkeley has actually been *cutting* its introductory Arabic offerings for four years running, regularly leaving more than a hundred undergrads stuck on a waiting list."[5]

The problems of international studies centers and American academia run deeper than funding allocations. The most serious of such problems arise, instead, from the radical politicization of universities that has been precipitated

---

2   Eric Lichtblau, "FBI Said to Lag on Translators of Terror Tapes," *The New York Times*, September 28, 2004.
3   On March 2, 2005, the whistleblower, Sibel Edmunds, testified before the House Committee on Government Reform, on the topic of "Problems with the FBI's translation unit involving criminal conduct against our national interests, potential espionage, serious security breaches threatening our intelligence, intentional mistranslation, and blocking of intelligence."
4   As quoted by Dr. Stanley Kurtz in a special briefing before the Washington Institute for Near East Studies, November 20, 2003. (For complete transcript, see http://www.washingtoninstitute.org/distribution/pos813.doc.)
5   See http://sandbox.blog-city.com/arabicoscandaloatoberkely.htm.

by academics and characterized by the routine abuse of their roles as educators and the quiet but consistent suppression of professorial dissent.

Deep-Rooted Troubles in the American Academy: Professors and Their Curricula

Although the radicalism of the 1960s may have been a passing phase in American society, it has left a lasting imprint on the academy in this country. Indeed, the professoriat is overwhelmingly populated with professors whose ideological rigidity has had the effect of largely driving dissent from the classroom. One utterly unfashionable—and thus unacceptable—concept on the contemporary campus is the traditional American belief in the universality of freedom and democracy.

The professoriat's contempt for this country, and particularly for American exceptionalism, has naturally been passed along to impressionable students. On many campuses, indeed, students' academic careers will suffer if they fail to reflect their professors' anti-American sentiments.[6] They are often actively discouraged from supporting the war effort, thus depriving the country of the contributions of an enormous pool of able young people.

Taxpayers, of course, are underwriting the academic industry that actively discourages American students from properly understanding, let alone contributing to, the War for the Free World. Indeed, many of the professors who benefit most from Title VI funding have made no secret of their hostility toward this country's government and its policies and, in some flagrant cases, their sympathies for our foes. And these professors routinely use their bully pulpit to preach politics.

Arguably the most egregious example of this phenomenon was the late Columbia University professor of English and comparative literature Edward Said. His 1978 book, *Orientalism*, opened a Pandora's box of politicization. *Orientalism* quickly became the dominant intellectual prism through which many leading academics and their students came to view the world.

The Said paradigm—subsequently enhanced by the now-dominant intellectual fashion known as "post-colonial theory"—argued that the United States had become the successor to the European colonial powers. It was victimizing in particular the people of the Middle East through its oppressive exercise of power, both directly and indirectly through its proxy, Israel. This thesis encouraged many Americans studying in U.S. regional centers to

---

6   The pattern holds true also in reverse: junior faculty may suffer in the institutionalized student-feedback process, particularly at elite institutions, if they do not project the proper degree of leftist political concern.

believe that their country was responsible for inflicting immense psychological, economic, physical, and political damage on those it was "colonizing."

Said gained still greater currency and influence in the academy by denouncing professors who supported American foreign policy, comparing them with 19th-century European intellectuals who propped up racist colonial empires. The core premise of post-colonial theory is that it is *immoral* for a scholar to put his knowledge of foreign languages and cultures at the service of American power. He secured such a following that, before his death, it was said of him that he "is one of only two academics today (the other is Noam Chomsky) who draws an overflow crowd on any campus he visits and who always gets a standing ovation."[7]

Two other examples of tenured radicals abusing their position of trust to indoctrinate and place politics before scholarship are worth noting:

♦ At his podium, University of Michigan professor Juan Cole unabashedly preaches a virulent form of anti-Semitism. Cole teaches that the Iraq war was orchestrated by Jews on behalf of the Israeli government who wanted "someone else's boys to do the dying."[8] To Cole, everything from the Sudan civil war to the Iranian nuclear crisis to the Iraq war is actually a plot conceived either in Israel or by American Jews in Washington.[9]

♦ Professor Lisa Hajjar of the University of California at Santa Barbara, a recipient of Title VI funding, served on the self-appointed "world tribunal" that found Saddam Hussein *innocent* of war crimes and human rights abuses—and the United States *guilty* of both "war crimes" and "abuses of human rights" of suspected al-Qaeda terrorists held in Guantanamo Bay.[10] Dr. Hajjar defines her instructional goal as "debunking the false belief that Western history constitutes a progressive move from more to less torture."[11]

The Effects of Politicized Universities

Not surprisingly, the infiltration of such anti-American indoctrination in regional studies centers has produced the opposite effect of what was intended

---

7   Martin Kramer, "Congress Probes Middle East Centers," personal blog, June 23, 2003. Available at http://www.geocities.com/martinkramerorg/2003o06o23.htm.

8   Juan Cole, "Pentagon/Israel Spying Case Expands: Fomenting a War on Iran," *Informed Comment*, August 29, 2004.

9   Alex Joffe, "Juan Cole and the Decline of Middle Eastern Studies," *Middle East Quarterly*, Winter 2006.

10 Steven Plaut, "The Jihadnik Prof of UC-Santa Barbara," FrontPageMag.com, June 7, 2005. Available at http://www.frontpagemag.com/Articles/ReadArticle.asp?ID=18236 .

11 Ibid.

by our national leaders. Instead of equipping and encouraging young people to pursue careers in support of the nation's security and intelligence needs, students are often actively *discouraged* from pursuing work in such fields.

Consider an official advertisement soliciting employment postings to run in the journal of the Middle Eastern Studies Association of North America (MESA, a recipient of Title VI funding). It warns prospective advertisers that "MESA reserves the right to refuse ads it deems inappropriate or in conflict with MESA's objectives. *MESA publications will not accept advertising from defense and intelligence related agencies from any government.*" (Emphasis added.)[12] The clear implication is that MESA—a federally funded entity, created with a primary objective to train and support the government's needs for Middle East expertise—believes that America's defense and intelligence agencies are at odds with MESA's objectives.

Due to the indoctrination provided by professors such as Edward Said, Juan Cole, and Lisa Hajjar and the environment cultivated by such radical thinkers, taxpayer-funded Middle East studies have continually produced students unable or unwilling to provide the skills the nation needs so desperately at the moment. Dr. Anthony Cordesman, of the Center for Strategic and International Studies, summed up the situation in congressional testimony:

> Many U.S. Middle East experts . . . provide a chorus of almost ritual criticism of any U.S. military role in the region, and any use of force. [They] generally do a far better job of speaking for the country, or countries, they study than for the U.S."[13]

MESA has also engaged in an official boycott of another initiative aimed at meeting America's wartime needs: the National Security Education Program (NSEP). NSEP is a Pentagon-funded effort intended to develop a cadre of professionals to help the U.S. government "make sound decisions" on national security issues. The stated reason for the boycott is professors' concerns that students could be harmed abroad if they are suspected of being spies.

In fact, students do not have to disclose where the funding for their academic work comes from, nor are they required to perform any government-related service until after graduation. The MESA boycott is merely another instance of the ideological academic barricade, keeping students from cooperating with the American government.[14]

---

12 See http://fp.arizona.edu/mesassoc/advertising.htm.
13 As cited in Martin Kramer, *Ivory Towers on Sand—The Failure of Middle Eastern Studies in America*, Washington Institute for Near East Policy, 2001, p. 97.
14 Stanley Kurtz, "Ivory Scam" *National Review Online*, May 20, 2002.

As Dr. Kramer has observed, the opposition to NSEP by academics has more to do with the political biases of the professors than the welfare of the students. In his landmark study *Ivory Towers on Sand: The Failure of Middle Eastern Studies in America*, he noted:

> Not surprisingly the [NSEP] immediately became a rallying point for academic radicals of every stripe. They . . . conjured up the image of intelligence agencies sending tentacles into the academy and the mainstream area studies programs from the Department of Defense.[15]

Compounding the effects of this pervasive ideological hostility, elite colleges also hinder the serious study of sensitive regions by forbidding students to study in areas that university administrators consider dangerous. For example, in the aftermath of September 11, many schools began to force students to avoid trouble spots and countries with State Department travel advisories. Such a prohibition handicaps a student's ability to gain full knowledge of a region, conflict, or language—thus, further hampering our expertise in these tumultuous regions.

The regional studies centers proselytize to other educators as well. For example, well-intentioned legislators stipulated that in order to receive Title VI funding, university professors must conduct "outreach seminars" to the community, in the form of workshops for teachers of kindergarten through 12th grade.

Often, these teachers are not well informed about the subjects addressed by regional studies programs. They tend to defer to the academic elite, namely, those teaching at the university level who are specialists in the field. The virus of anti-American ideology is thus methodically introduced into the American educational bloodstream at every level.

What Needs to Be Done

For American diplomacy, military, and intelligence services to function effectively during this War for the Free World, steps must to be taken to change the attitudes—and perhaps the personnel—associated with the politicized university system. For too long, we have failed to reap the vitally needed return on our investment in the regional studies centers. We simply can no longer afford to muddle through.

The following are the sorts of steps a War Footing will require us to adopt to ensure that this country develops the necessary knowledge and skills to understand, confront, and defeat America's enemies.

---

15 Martin Kramer, *Ivory Towers on Sand*, op. cit., p. 94.

◆ **Revise the tenure system.** U.S. universities will not return to their core educational mission until the practice of tenure as we have known it is abolished. Although there must be protection for the free speech so necessary for the exploration of ideas, consideration needs to be given urgently to replacing tenure, at least in publicly funded centers, with long-term contracts as a practical compromise—for example, by establishing an escalating review and renewal process, evaluating scholarship and productivity at five-year intervals.

◆ **Revise the hiring process.** In order to prevent academia from becoming a wasteland of "group think," government-funded universities must break the monopoly of the hiring process. At present, candidates are evaluated solely by those academics within their particular field and mainly from a single department.

Such a process contributes to professors becoming echo chambers of each other's theories. Scholars in the humanities and social sciences can spend their entire careers communicating with only a handful of their peers, without having to subject themselves and their work to rigorous challenge from others who might give a more objective evaluation. In support of the war effort, it should be mandatory that academic evaluations involve professors from outside the professor's own discipline, with a view to inducing scholars to remain better grounded and well connected to a more realistic macro-picture.

◆ **Cultivate foreign language experts.** A priority must be placed on the rigorous study and mastery of relevant foreign languages. Area studies programs should not receive federal funding if their students are unable upon graduation to demonstrate proficiency in one or more of the foreign languages of interest to our current and prospective national security needs.

Many academics claim fluency—but practicality matters. If they cannot explain how to fix a clogged drain or change a flat tire in Arabic, Persian, or some other foreign language, then they are not fluent.

◆ **Foster students' field research.** Federally funded curricula should ensure that regional studies address the world *as it is*, not just politicized imaginings about foreign peoples, cultures, and religions. They should be encouraged, not discouraged, from undertaking educational travel to critical regions. As Margaret Thatcher once wrote, "We make a great mistake when we transpose our beliefs onto the rest of the world."

◆ **Refuse foreign funding.** Too many universities hesitate to offer programs sponsored by U.S. government agencies but happily accept money from foreign states whose interests are inimical to U.S. standards of democracy, liberalism, and human rights. For example, Georgetown University has accepted more than $1.2 million from the United Arab Emirates.[16] Columbia University accepted money from Palestinian Authority and Saudi interests.[17] Arab governments, in particular, and their registered agents spend money not for the sake of education but to buy influence. The absence of foreign funding for regional centers and other foreign-studies programs should become the hallmark of unbiased, neutral scholarship.

◆ **Ground students in the American tradition.** Our regional studies programs must root American students in an accurate appreciation of America. It is unacceptable to spend federal tax dollars to support curricula that amount to little more than indoctrination in a skewed and vehemently anti-American view of this country and the world. A core curriculum of the great American writers and thinkers should be included as contributing to the diverse strains and intellectual antecedents that have gone into making American foreign policy.

As long as our students are imbued, instead, with an education grounded in radical anti-Americanism, future generations will make foreign-policy decisions operating under the weight of misplaced guilt and moral ambiguity. We confront powerful forces that suffer no corresponding uncertainty about the rightness of their own cause and who are adept at exploiting the sometimes disabling divisions of a democracy.

For the duration of this War for the Free World, we need to restore among our youth a sense of America's outstanding moral, ethical, humanitarian, scientific, and intellectual contributions to the community of nations. We will need a wealth of such properly equipped students to fulfill diplomatic and other functions that rely on personnel with robust regional awareness, language skills, and well-developed common sense.

We should expect nothing less from our enormous investment in academic support for our diplomatic arsenal.

---

16 See http://chronicle.com/prm/daily/2004/07/2004072903n.htm.
17 See http://daily.nysun.com/Repository/getFiles.asp?Style=OliveXLib:ArticleToMail&Type=text/html&Path=NYS/2003/07/23&ID=Ar00103.

Conclusion

This book begins with former CIA Director R. James Woolsey ruminating about what to call the bloody conflict in which we are engaged. He observes—and the intervening pages have confirmed—that America is not, in fact, fighting a "global war on terror."

To be sure, it *is* a global war. But what we have established is that, given its complexities and stakes, this conflict should be called what it plainly is—the War for the Free World.

The preceding pages document those complexities and stakes. Reduced to their essence, these factors mean that those who live in and love freedom are once again locked in a struggle to the death with totalitarian enemies, foes with a fanatical attachment to ideologies that require our destruction.

We have faced such enemies before. And, as when the Nazis, Fascists, Imperial Japanese, and Soviet Communists sought to destroy and enslave the Free World, we must do now what we did then: Wage war creatively and effectively, using nonmilitary as well as military means, on a global scale. Now as then, we must understand the necessity of fully mobilizing the energy, courage, and imagination of freedom-loving people—starting with putting the country on a War Footing—as if our lives, and way of life, depend on it. For indeed, they do.

In this book, we have seen that the threat posed to today's Free World by the totalitarian ideology known as Islamofascism masquerades as a religion. That simply makes it more dangerous to freedom-loving societies that pride themselves on their religious tolerance.

We have also learned that the danger posed by these Islamists is not confined to non-Muslims in the West. Islamofascism poses an even more immediate menace to the majority of Muslims, both in the Free World and elsewhere, who do not subscribe to the Islamist agenda.

If we fail to make common cause with the non-Islamist Muslims, they will inexorably be forced to embrace that agenda or at least to go along with it, under threat of violence or other coercive techniques. We would then lose natural allies in our own struggle and face precisely the sort of apocalyptic "clash of civilizations" sought by the likes of Osama bin Laden and his sponsors.

If, on the other hand, we demonstrate our resolve to resist the Islamofascists and to help non-Islamist Muslims do so as well, we can enlarge the Free World and secure the allies we will need to prevail.

There can no longer be the least doubt that this war is simply about Iraq or Afghanistan. Indeed, it had begun long before our engagement in either of those countries. Seductive as the idea sounds, withdrawing from such far-flung battlefields is no solution. Because the fight is about nothing less than whether there will continue to *be* a Free World, one in which we are able to speak, publish, assemble, vote, and practice our religions as we wish, ceding more ground to our enemies will only bring closer the day when we can no longer do any of these things.

By recognizing this conflict as the War for the Free World, we are able to restore the moral clarity that Americans—and other democracies—need to sustain war's expensive costs (in both human and financial terms). Doing so also helps in one other, critical way. It serves to strip away the *false moral equivalence* some assert between our Islamofascist enemies on the one hand and, on the other hand, those who are fighting and dying to protect freedom here at home and to promote it elsewhere as a bulwark for our own security.

Shortly after September 11, 2001, President Bush rightly said to the nations of the world, "You are either with us or against us." That has never been more true than it is today. By putting America on a War Footing, as called for in this book, we will make it clear that people around the world who want to be on the side of the Free World can safely do so. And those who are on the side of freedom's enemies will be on the wrong side of history, as surely as were totalitarians of the past.

Finally, we hope to have helped the American people take ownership of this war—an indispensable precondition for its successful outcome. By understanding and mastering the instruments at our disposal, we can and will take the steps necessary, both at home and abroad, to secure the victory in this War for the Free World that we literally cannot live without.

AFTERWORD

We Have to Win

By Bruce Herschensohn[1]

I f there is anything that jolts us into a realistic sense of values, it's witnessing tragedy as we all did four years ago. . . . During the fourth year of the war, the year that has just passed, questions have been raised about fighting this war; more questions than were raised in the three preceding years. They are, in my view, invalid questions. The only question of validity is: Are we going to win this war or are we going to lose?

Wars generally conclude with a winner and a loser. If we win, the next generation can just read about it as victories in times that are done. If we lose, the United States will be done, and all democracies will be done, and civilization as we know it will be done.

There is a third course between victory and defeat. We can be the first generation to live in an age of terrorism in which your children, grandchildren, and generations after them will live in fear at best, and repeated 9/11s at worst.

There is no fourth course. And only one of the three courses available is acceptable. We have to win.

The Need for Perspective

I want to briefly go into some of the areas of dissent in the year that just passed.

- Much of it was dominated with accusations regarding humiliated prisoners at Abu Ghraib in Iraq and interrogations of prisoners at

---

1 This contribution was adapted from remarks made by Mr. Herschensohn at the Nixon Library in Yorba Linda, California, on (September 11, 2005) the fourth anniversary of the attacks.

Guantanamo Bay. Our continued public expression of remorse makes us laughingstocks among those who have known lifetimes of fear. When terrorists hear repeated apologies, they conclude that we are weak. They perform their acts of terrorism with greater ease knowing that if they are captured by the Americans, the consequences will be minimal: our public opinion will demand it.

It is said by so many that if we don't give such apologies they will retaliate by treating American prisoners with cruelty. In what war were American prisoners of war treated *without* cruelty? Make the terrorists afraid. Fear, valid or invalid, is the most potent weapon in the world.

◆ Another charge: In the past months there have been those who oppose the securing of our borders from the entrance of illegal immigrants. Not *legal*. *Illegal*. They say we shouldn't build another Berlin Wall. Among other things, that statement is an offense against history. Since communities on the earth began, walls have been built to keep invaders out. What made the *Berlin* Wall unique was that it was not built to keep invaders out but to keep their own citizens in. We are not seeking to keep our citizens in. We need to keep invaders out.

◆ And there is the argument heard so often since the presidential campaign that started year number four: Some say to leave more up to the UN and less up to the United States. That is a guarantee for defeat. The UN won't do anything in the interest of liberty. Naturally not. More than half its members are non-democracies. They don't want all the people of the world to be free. If all the people of the world would live in liberty, those governments would fall. The UN has a history of preference given to non-democracies.

Since the UN's Oil for Food scandal was exposed, and especially . . . with new revelations, there has been pressure for Kofi Annan to leave his post. Although his departure would be welcome and totally justified, he is just one of a string of terrible secretaries general. . . . Like the League of Nations, the major fault of the UN has been more than an individual; it is a foundation that admits non-democracies that do not represent their people. There is *no forum* for the *people* of the world.

◆ In the recent demonstrations in Crawford, Texas (led by Cindy Sheehan, the mother of a soldier killed in action in Iraq), there has been another charge: that this war is all about our lust for oil. That charge ignores U.S. contemporary military engagements. There was no oil in Vietnam or Cambodia or Laos. The protests were just as loud. There was no oil in Grenada or Panama or Haiti or Bosnia or Kosovo. Why did we fight in those places?

Should we say that we will always fight when people are endangered, except, *except,* if the people that need our help *have oil?* Then we won't? There was, however, oil in Kuwait. We liberated it, and Kuwait is now the master of its own house and the master of its oil.

It has become unfortunately obvious that for some, maybe not many, but for some—September 11 wasn't enough. What will it take to realize that we have to win on a world scale? And preemption is the only way, unless we want to wait for more attacks.

Defeat Is Possible

Can we lose? I am admittedly obsessed with that question and I'll tell you why.

During many of the years of the Southeast Asian War, I was with our government in positions that called for travel, much of it to Vietnam, Laos, and Cambodia. There wasn't one trip I took—not one—that I even considered the possibility that the war's conclusion would be the enemy's conquest of Cambodia, Laos, and South Vietnam.

Such a consideration was impossible. On those trips the plane would first land at Tan Son Nhut airport in Saigon, and as we taxied to the exterior of the terminal, there were the horizonless formations of U.S. aircraft: fighters, bombers, helicopters, all painted in camouflage colors, with the uncamouflaged symbol of the United States Air Force. No. There was not a thought that we could lose. There was not even a moment that I imagined that in the years just ahead, Saigon would be called Ho Chi Minh City.

But it happened. Not because of our military. It was superb. Not because of South Vietnam's military. It was superb. Surrender had nothing to do with the capabilities and the determination of our military or their military. It had to do with our home front, and members of the 94th Congress, and members of the major media. It had to do with streets of demonstrators. And there rest the Vietnam parallels with today. The ones who accuse us of now being involved in another Vietnam are themselves the creators of the scenario of which they warn.

What Losing Costs the Free World

It seems lost in history and intentionally lost in the memory of many Americans who held banners reading "Peace Now" in their rallies, that the peace they achieved brought more death, by far, than occurred during the war. That should be known by those who demonstrate *now* with the shouted word "peace" just as it was shouted thirty years ago.

Peace brought to South Vietnam about 1 million deaths or imprisonment in reeducation camps, while another million boat people escaped South Vietnam on anything that could float, with an estimated half of them drowned beneath the South China Sea. And in neighboring Cambodia there was a minimum of 2 million who lost their lives in the genocide there. Minimum. Somewhere between one-quarter and one-third of the population. That was the peace that was achieved. To the satisfaction of some who still say, with pride, they helped bring about peace, they are right. They did.

Look back at our history to see how easy it would have been to always have chosen such peace. Our Founders could have had peace easily. All they had to do was not be Founders. No War of Independence. No United States of America. And there would have been peace. President Lincoln could have chosen peace if he wanted to settle for two nations, one free, one slave, and he could have saved more than half a million American lives. They would have lived. And there would have been peace.

On the Monday morning after December 7, 1941, President Roosevelt could have asked the Congress for a declaration of accommodation with what was the Japanese Empire rather than a declaration of war. And there would have been peace. Peace without liberty is surrender. Always.

"Unity": The Need for a War Footing

One disadvantage that we have in the current war is that most Americans living today do not remember a war for our own survival. World War II is now a long time ago. Memories of most people today are limited to wars fought for the survival of distant friends—a fate that's bad enough—but they weren't wars for our *own* survival.

How did we do it in World War II? I remember how. I was a little kid but I remember how: unity.

- Our victory in World War II was not achieved by dominating the newsreels with pictures of those things a few American troops did to captured enemies.
- We didn't give false accusations against our own government for being in the war.

- We did not call for an end of domestic profiling.
- We did not demonstrate against our military involvement.
- We did not demand a date for an exit.
- Not one film was made against our involvement. Not one entertainment personality advocated such a course.

Instead of all that, we bombed our enemies into submission from Dresden to Berlin to Osaka to Tokyo. After our costly invasion of Europe with immense U.S. casualties, the atomic bomb was ready and to prevent another invasion, we used it twice on Japan.

During those years of war there was one issue: winning the war by demanding absolute and unconditional surrender of our enemies. There was not a simultaneous cry for saving the environment, and a demand for creating more jobs, and an insistence on government-provided health care, and lower costs for prescription drugs. All subjects other than victory were nothing more than luxury reserved for a later time. If we are not prepared to do that now, we are not prepared to win.

It *is* four years since September 11. Four years after Pearl Harbor we had already won the war. In fact, on the first day of September 1945, while General MacArthur was accepting the surrender on the battleship *Missouri*, President Truman said in a broadcast to the world from Washington, D.C.:

> Four years ago, the thoughts and fears of the whole civilized world were centered on another piece of American soil— Pearl Harbor. The mighty threat to civilization which began there is now laid to rest. It was a long road to Tokyo—and a bloody one. . . .This is a victory of more than arms alone. This is a victory over tyranny. . . . Back of it all were the will and spirit and determination of a free people who know what freedom is, and who know that it is worth whatever price they had to pay to preserve it.

Victory: "The Permanence of Our Nation"

We are going to win. No more praise for those who dissent. When they ask, "Wouldn't you fight for my right to dissent?" I have to answer, "Not right now. Later. *After* we *win* this war." Such dissent *is* a luxury for later times when we can look back at September 11 knowing the war has been won and knowing that those lives lost that day and lost in the war since that day have *eternal purpose.* It will come. And when it does we will do just what we did after World War II.

We are already doing it in Afghanistan and Iraq while fighting still goes on. We are building schools and hospitals and infrastructure and, most of all, building democracies. Not bad. I would hope that here on the homefront we would reinstate a Civil Defense Program second to none with marked shelters as we started during the late 1950s, early '60s, the Cuban Missile Crisis, and beyond: shelters loaded with food, water, and supplies that would be there for any disaster.

The real victory to be achieved is the permanence of our nation. Most things in life are temporary. We know that. Lives, themselves, are temporary. But this country, this nation, the United States of America *has* to be permanent: permanent from New York City, to Somerset County, Pennsylvania, to the Pentagon Building in Virginia. . . . And beyond those places that have endured such recent tragedies, the permanence of *every* place within our borders from Norwich, Connecticut, to Yorba Linda, California. And that permanence of our nation *has* to be the cause of our times.

APPENDIX I

"Set America Free"

A Blueprint for U.S. Energy Security

Introduction

Historically, the United States has pursued a three-pronged strategy for minimizing the vulnerabilities associated with its dependency on oil from unstable and/or hostile nations: diversifying sources of oil, managing inventory in a strategic petroleum reserve, and increasing the efficiency of the transportation sector's energy consumption. In recent years, the focus has been principally on finding new and larger sources of petroleum globally.

Rapidly growing worldwide demand for oil, however, has had the effect of largely neutralizing this initiative, depleting existing reserves faster than new, economically exploitable deposits are being brought on line. Under these circumstances, diversification among such sources is but a stop-gap solution that can, at best, have a temporary effect on oil supply and, hence, on national security. Conservation can help, but with oil consumption expected to grow by 60 percent over the next twenty-five years, conservation alone will not be a sufficient solution.

The "Set America Free" Project

Long-term security and economic prosperity requires the creation of a fourth pillar—technological transformation of the transportation sector through what might be called "fuel choice." By leading a multinational effort rooted in the following principles, the United States can *immediately* begin to introduce a global economy based on next-generation fuels and vehicles that can utilize them.

- **Fuel diversification:** Today, consumers can choose among various octanes of gasoline, which accounts for 45 percent of U.S. oil consumption, or diesel, which accounts for almost another fifth. To these choices can and should promptly be added other fuels that are domestically produced, where possible, from waste products and that are clean and affordable.
- **Real-world solutions:** We have no time to wait for commercialization of immature technologies. The United States should implement technologies **that exist today and are ready for widespread use.**
- **Using existing infrastructure:** The focus should be on utilizing competitive technologies that do not require prohibitive or, if possible, even significant investment in changing our transportation sector's infrastructure. Instead, "fuel choice" should permit the maximum possible use of the existing refueling and automotive infrastructure.
- **Domestic resource utilization:** The United States is no longer rich in oil or natural gas. It has, however, a wealth of other energy sources from which transportation fuel can be safely, affordably, and cleanly generated. Among them: hundreds of years' worth of coal reserves, 25 percent of the world's total (especially promising with Integrated Gasification and Combined Cycle technologies); billions of tons a year of biomass, and further billions of tons of agricultural and municipal waste. Vehicles that meet consumer needs (e.g., "plug-in" hybrids) can also tap America's electrical grid to supply energy for transportation, making more efficient use of such clean sources of electricity as solar, wind, geothermal, hydroelectric, and nuclear power.
- **Environmentally sensible choices:** The technologies adopted should improve public safety and respond to the public's environmental and health concerns.

Key Elements of the "Set America Free" Project

Vehicles

- **Hybrid electric vehicles:** There are already thousands of vehicles on America's roads that combine hybrid engines powered in an integrated fashion by liquid fuel–powered motors and battery-powered ones. Such vehicles increase gas-consumption efficiency by 30–40 percent.

- **Ultralight materials:** At least two-thirds of fuel use by a typical consumer vehicle is caused by its weight. Thanks to advances in both metals and plastics, ultralight vehicles can be affordably manufactured with today's technologies and can roughly halve fuel consumption without compromising safety, performance, or cost-effectiveness.
- **"Plug-in" hybrid electric vehicles:** Plug-in hybrid electric vehicles are also powered by a combination of electricity and liquid fuel. Unlike standard hybrids, however, plug-ins draw charge not only from the engine and captured braking energy, but also directly from the electrical grid by being plugged into standard electric outlets when not in use. Plug-in hybrids have liquid fuel tanks and internal combustion engines, so they do not face the range limitation posed by electric-only cars. Since 50 percent of cars on the road in the United States are driven twenty miles a day or less, a plug-in with a twenty-mile range battery would reduce fuel consumption by, on average, 85 percent. *Plug-in hybrid electric vehicles can reach fuel economy levels of one hundred miles per gallon of gasoline consumed.*
- **Flexible fuel vehicles (FFVs):** FFVs are designed to burn on alcohol, gasoline, or any mixture of the two. About 4 million FFV's have been manufactured since 1996. The only difference between a conventional car and a flexible fuel vehicle is that the latter is equipped with a different control chip and some different fittings in the fuel line to accommodate the characteristics of alcohol. The marginal additional cost associated with such FFV-associated changes is currently under $100 per vehicle. That cost would be reduced further as volume of FFVs increases, particularly if flexible fuel designs were to become the industry standard.
- **Flexible fuel/plug-in hybrid electric vehicles:** If the two technologies are combined, such vehicles can be powered by blends of alcohol fuels, gasoline, and electricity. If a plug-in vehicle is also a FFV fueled with 80 percent alcohol and 20 percent gasoline, fuel economy could reach *five million miles per gallon* of gasoline.

If, by 2025, all cars on the road are hybrids and half are plug-in hybrid vehicles, U.S. oil imports would drop by 8 million barrels per day (mbd). Today, the United States imports 11 mbd and it is projected to import almost 20 mbd by 2025. If all of these cars were also flexible fuel vehicles, U.S. oil imports would drop by as much as 12 mbd.

Fuels

- **Fuel additives:** Fuel additives can enhance combustion efficiency by up to 25 percent. They can be blended into gasoline, diesel, and bunker fuel.

♦ **Electricity as a fuel:** Less than 2 percent of U.S. electricity is generated from oil, so using electricity as a transportation fuel would greatly reduce dependence on imported petroleum. Plug-in hybrid vehicles would be charged at night in home garages—a time interval during which electric utilities have significant excess capacity. *The Electric Power Research Institute estimates that up to 30 percent of market penetration for plug-in hybrid electric vehicles with 20-mile electric range can be achieved without a need to install additional electricity-generating capacity.*

Alcohol Fuels—Ethanol, Methanol, and Other Blends

♦ **Ethanol:** Also known as grain alcohol. Ethanol is currently produced in the United States from corn. The industry currently has a capacity of 3.3 billion gallons a year and has increased on the average of 25 percent per year over the past three years. Upping production would be achieved by continuing to advance the corn-based ethanol industry and by commercializing the production of ethanol from biomass waste and dedicated energy crops. *P-Series* fuel (approved by the Department of Energy in 1999) is a more energy-efficient blend of ethanol, natural gas liquids, and ether made from biomass waste.

♦ **Methanol:** Also known as wood alcohol. Methanol is produced for the most part today from natural gas. Expanding domestic production can be achieved by producing methanol from coal, a resource with which the United States is abundantly endowed. The commercial feasibility of coal-to-methanol technology was demonstrated as part of the DOE's "clean coal" technology effort. Currently, methanol is being cleanly produced from coal for under 50 cents a gallon.

It only costs about $60,000 to add a fuel pump that serves one of the above fuels to an existing refueling station.

♦ **Non-oil based diesel:** Biodiesel is commercially produced from soybean and other vegetable oils. Diesel can also be made from waste products such as tires and animal by products, and is currently commercially produced from turkey offal. Diesel is also commercially produced from coal.

Policy Recommendations

♦ Provide incentives to auto manufacturers to produce and consumers to purchase, hybrid vehicles, plug-in hybrid electric vehicles, and FFVs across all vehicle models.

- Provide incentives for auto manufacturers to increase fuel efficiency of existing, non-FFV auto models.
- Conduct extensive testing of next-generation fuels across the vehicle spectrum to meet auto warranty and EPA emission standards.
- Mandate substantial incorporation of plug-ins and FFVs into federal, state, municipal, and covered fleets.
- Provide investment tax incentives for corporate fleets and taxi fleets to switch to plug-ins, hybrids, and FFVs.
- Encourage gasoline distributors to blend combustion enhancers into the fuel.
- Provide incentives for existing fueling stations to install pumps that serve all liquid fuels that can be used in the existing transportation infrastructure, and mandate that all new gas stations be so equipped.
- Provide incentives to enable new players, such as utilities, to enter the transportation fuel market, and for the development of environmentally sound exploitation of nontraditional petroleum deposits from stable areas (such as Canadian tar sands).
- Provide incentives for the construction of plants that generate liquid transportation fuels from domestic energy resources, particularly from waste, that can be used in the existing infrastructure.
- Allocate funds for commercial scale demonstration plants that produce next-generation transportation fuels, particularly from waste products.
- Implement federal, state, and local policies to encourage mass transit and to reduce vehiclemiles traveled.
- Work with other oil-consuming countries toward distribution of the above-mentioned technologies and overall reduction of reliance on petroleum, particularly from hostile and potentially unstable regions of the world.

A New National Project

In 1942, President Roosevelt launched the Manhattan Project to build an atomic weapon to be ready by 1945 because of threats to America and to explore the future of nuclear fission. The cost in today's prices was $20 billion. The outcome was an end to the war with Japan, and the beginning of a wide new array of nuclear-based technologies in energy, medical treatment, and other fields.

In 1962, President Kennedy launched the Man to the Moon Project to be achieved by 1969 because of mounting threats to U.S. and international security posed by Soviet space dominance and to explore outer space. The cost of the Apollo program in today's prices would be well over $100 billion. The outcome was an extraordinary strategic and technological success for the United States. It engendered a wide array of spin-offs that improved virtually every aspect of modern life, including but not limited to transportation, communications, health care, medical treatment and food production.

The security of the United States, and the world, is no less threatened by oil supply disruptions, price instabilities, and shortages. It is imperative that America provide needed leadership by immediately beginning to dramatically reduce its dependence on imported oil. This can be done by embracing the concepts outlined above with a focus on fuel choice, combined with concerted efforts at improving energy efficiency and the increased availability of energy from renewable sources.

The estimated cost of the "Set America Free" plan over the next four years is $12 billion. This would be applied in the following way: $2 billion for automotive manufacturers to cover one-half the costs of building FFV-capability into their new production cars (i.e., roughly 40 million cars at $50 per unit); $1 billion to pay for at least one out of every four existing gas stations to add at least one pump to supply alcohol fuels (an estimated incentive of $20,000 per pump, new pumps costing approximately $60,000 per unit); $2 billion in consumer tax incentives to procure hybrid cars; $2 billion for automotive manufacturers to commercialize plug-in hybrid electric vehicles; $3 billion to construct commercial-scale demonstration plants to produce nonpetroleum-based liquid fuels (utilizing public-private cost-sharing partnerships to build roughly twenty-five plants in order to demonstrate the feasibility of various approaches to perform efficiently at full-scale production); and $2 billion to continue work on commercializing fuel cell technology.

Since no major, new scientific advances are necessary to launch this program, such funds can be applied toward increasing the efficiencies of the involved processes. The resulting return-on-investment—in terms of enhanced energy and national security, economic growth, quality of life, and environmental protection—should more than pay for the seed money required.

Members of the "Set America Free" Coalition

Gary L. Bauer
President, American Values

Milton Copulos
National Defense Council
Foundation

Congressman Eliot Engel

Frank Gaffney
Center for Security Policy

Bracken Hendricks
Apollo Alliance

Jack D. Hidary
Coalition Advocating for Smart
Transportation

Col. Bill Holmberg (Ret.)
American Council on
Renewable Energy

Anne Korin
Institute for the Analysis of Global
Security

Deron Lovaas
Natural Resources Defense Council

Gal Luft
Institute for the Analysis of
Global Security

Cliff May
Foundation for the Defense
of Democracies

Hon. Robert C. McFarlane
Former National Security Adviser

Thomas Neumann
The Jewish Institute for National
Security Affairs (JINSA)

Daniel Pipes
Middle East Forum

Chelsea Sexton
Plug in America

William K. Shireman
Future 500

Professor Richard E. Smalley
1996 Nobel Laureate in Chemistry

Hon. James Strock
Former California Secretary for
Environmental Protection

Adm. James D. Watkins (Ret.)
Former U.S. Secretary of Energy

Hon. R. James Woolsey
Former Director of the CIA;
Co-Chairman, Committee on the
Present Danger

Meyrav Wurmser
Hudson Institute

NOTE: For more information about the coalition—its blueprint and its activities—see http://www.SetAmericaFree.org.

APPENDIX II

Regain Nuclear Deterrence

With Contributions from Vice Adm. Robert R. Monroe, USN (Ret.)

I n the previous pages, we addressed a terrifying reality: our Islamofascist enemies are determined to destroy this country and our way of life. They are trying to acquire the means to do so—and in some cases they already have.

In Step 6 we examined one scenario by which such destruction might be inflicted upon virtually all of us: high-altitude electromagnetic pulse attack. Other uses of weapons of mass destruction (WMDs) against American population centers, strategic targets, or both can also have devastating effects.

These dangers make *War Footing*'s ten steps not simply desirable but *absolutely necessary*. The threat to this country from WMDs demands the planning, preparation, and training called for in Step 5. Preventing such attacks, in some scenarios, could depend on our implementation of the recommendations in Step 7 concerning securing our borders and interior.

As we have seen, such measures must be complemented and enhanced by offensive strategies. These involve, as appropriate, using military force (Step 2), economic and financial means (Steps 3 and 4), political warfare (Step 8), and diplomatic techniques (Step 10). If combined with the sorts of regional strategies laid out in Step 9, we will have done *nearly* everything possible to protect ourselves and help the Free World prevail in this war.

There is, however, one thing more that must be done: We must be able to confront our enemies with the credible threat of nuclear destruction. During the Cold War, this capability effectively deterred the Soviet Union from launching thermonuclear weapons against us and from launching a conventional war against America's allies. This deterrent was so effective that, during this period, not a single nuclear weapon was ever used in anger, despite the hundreds of crises that occurred.

Although today's and tomorrow's adversaries are quite different from our Cold War foes, nuclear deterrence will be effective against many of them. Given the stakes involved, the prudent approach for America is to take such steps as have proved effective in the past.

At its core, deterrence involves having a decisive impact on the enemy's thinking. It requires convincing our foe that the consequences of an attack on us will be intolerable to him. We will surely destroy all he holds dear; we will do so in a rapid and devastating manner; and the loss to him will be far greater than any gain he might have achieved by his planned action.

By its nature, deterrence is not a constant, all-purpose capability. It must be fine-tuned for each adversary, for each situation, and for the specific action we wish to deter the adversary from taking. Again, some foes may simply be undeterrable. For them, we must hope that the ten steps will suffice to disable and defeat their ability to cause us harm. But, for those that *can* be deterred, we need to apply the lessons of the Cold War to make sure deterrence helps us succeed in the current conflict.

For example, during what Winston Churchill called the "long, twilight struggle" with the Soviet Union, we learned that deterrence required a nuclear arsenal that was seen by the leaders of the Kremlin to be *credible*. It needed to be modern, safe, reliable, and capable of destroying, on a moment's notice, the assets our adversary valued most.

A deterrent with these attributes required underground nuclear testing—proof positive of both the effectiveness of our weapons and our determination to keep them ready. It also required us to continually adjust our targeting to match the values of changing Soviet leaders. Our military forces exercised constantly in the realistic employment of these weapons. And our nation's leaders, in frequent statements, declared our absolute determination to respond to any attack with overwhelming nuclear force.

Unfortunately, far from applying these lessons in deterrence since the Cold War's end, we have largely ignored them.

- We stopped conducting underground nuclear tests thirteen years ago.
- For fifteen years our nuclear weapons laboratories have not conducted any advanced research on new nuclear weapons concepts.
- We have not designed or produced any new nuclear weapons.

♦ We have disabled much of the nuclear weapons infrastructure necessary to produce and maintain modern thermonuclear weapons and their components. In fact, we alone among the world's nuclear powers lack the capability to produce such weapons in quantity.

♦ Nearly all of the nation's scientists, engineers, designers, technicians, and operators with *actual experience* in the design, explosive testing, and production of new nuclear weapons have retired from government service. Their successors, who lack such experience, are at a huge, and possibly critical, disadvantage.

♦ As regards our nuclear weapons themselves, we have been frozen in time, attempting to preserve an aging Cold War stockpile of weapons designed for a different adversary and vastly different strategic conditions. Even if we could be absolutely certain these hugely destructive weapons will work as they are supposed to—*and we cannot be*—they are not seen as credible by *today's* adversaries.

For example, North Korea and Iran are continuing, undeterred, in their drive to acquire nuclear weapons, quite confident that we would never use our high-yield Cold War nuclear weapons to stop them, because doing so would surely require us to kill or injure many thousands of innocent civilians and spread radiation widely.

What Needs to Be Done

What must be done to regain a viable nuclear deterrent against today's WMDs threats, which are arguably just as dangerous as those of the Cold War, but more complex, more distributed, and more difficult to target?

1. We need to restore America's capability to fine-tune our deterrent for each key adversary. This will require identifying the action (or actions) we wish to deter, and then determining—to the extent possible—the assets this adversary values most (for example, regime survival, national leadership, military forces, WMDs production or storage sites, etc.).

2. We must, as a matter of great urgency, reenergize and rebuild our nuclear weapons enterprise so as to transform our nuclear weapons stockpile from that of the Cold War to the one needed today. Credibility of use is the key.

   Specifically, we will need newly designed, highly accurate, very-low-yield, penetrating nuclear weapons. These should be designed to reduce their residual radiation and to maximize their ability to defeat WMDs types of targets. These weapons are for deterrence, but to achieve this effect, the adversary must be absolutely convinced we will use them with decisive effect if we must. Immediate action is needed, because it will take us years to transform our nuclear weapons stockpile, while the threats are apparent today.

3. Our design, testing, and production of new-design nuclear weapons must be apparent to our adversary, as must our armed forces' training and exercising in their employment.

4. Nuclear deterrence requires something more than mere possession of credible and appropriate nuclear weapons. It requires clear, firm declarations by the president that we will use as much force as required to prevent the adversary's intended action. This must be backed up by other national leaders, civilian and military.

Such a forthright declaratory policy is important in two respects.

- ◆ First, in order to have the desired effect on the enemy.
- ◆ Second, to secure the necessary, strong, and bipartisan support of the American people and their elected representatives for the investments and other steps needed assure the credibility of our deterrent.

The latter purpose is particularly important given the lack of rigor in strategic thinking about deterrence for the past fifteen years. In its absence, some woolly-headed notions have become conventional wisdom. For example, some believe that U.S. efforts to ensure the viability of its deterrent must be resisted, lest they encourage proliferation on the part of rogue states.

In fact, regaining our nuclear deterrent in the above manner is the *only hope* for discouraging proliferation on the part of our enemies and, possibly, on the part of friends too. After all, the latter have had reason increasingly to be unsure of our nuclear guarantees, given the growing irrelevance of our deterrent. In the face of the sorts of threats described in the preceding pages, freedom-loving nations may soon move to seek their own nuclear arms.

Although we have no more desire to use nuclear weapons today than we did during the Cold War, a true War Footing requires that we do everything possible to protect ourselves against existing and emerging threats. Regaining America's nuclear deterrent must be part of our approach to waging the War for the Free World.

APPENDIX III

Deploy Sea-Based Missile Defenses

More than a decade ago, a group of distinguished national security experts was assembled under the auspices of the Heritage Foundation to provide a second opinion on the need for—and the options to achieve—effective, near-term ballistic missile defenses. Dubbed "Team B" (to distinguish it from the Clinton administration, "Team A"), this group reached a noteworthy conclusion: The fastest, most efficient, and most cost-effective way to provide the first stage of a global missile defense would be by adapting the U.S. Navy's vast investment in the AEGIS fleet air-defense system in order to give it a ballistic missile defense capability.[1]

At the time, the Clinton team, its friends on Capitol Hill, and arms control advocates scoffed at the findings. Earlier this year, however, the U.S. Navy confirmed that Team B's vision can be realized in a near-term and highly cost-effective way.

A successful test in February 2005—the fifth success out of six attempts to date—proved that U.S. Navy ships can track, intercept, and destroy a ballistic missile in flight. Best of all, they can do so using their *existing* AEGIS fleet air-defense systems and a new Standard Missile, known as the SM-3.

This test was particularly noteworthy for the confidence it provided in three areas. For the first time, the hardware and software used for the experiment were *the same* as will be installed in all other AEGIS missile defense ships. No less important is the fact that the SM-3 used to shoot down the target was one of the first of the *production rounds* to come off the manufacturing line. And,

---

1 See "Defending America: A Near- and Long-term Plan to Deploy Missile Defenses," The Heritage Foundation, 1995; and "Defending America: Ending America's Vulnerability to Ballistic Missiles," The Heritage Foundation, 1996.

the personnel who performed the test were the *regular crew* of an operational navy ship, the USS *Lake Erie*.

The February test featured another signal development. A second AEGIS ship, the USS *Russell*, brought to bear for the first time a powerful upgrade to the vessel's radar, known as the AEGIS Ballistic Missile Signal Processor (BMSP). This S-band radar provided real-time information that helped precisely identify and track the target, information that considerably enhances the likelihood of its successful interception. The AEGIS BMSP holds promise for greatly expanding missile defense radar coverage at a fraction of the cost of other approaches.

In other words, this was the "real deal." We can now begin with confidence to do what we should have done long ago: start deploying as quickly as possible sea-based missile defenses aboard AEGIS vessels to complement the land-based antimissile systems now being placed in silos in Alaska and California.

These achievements are all the more significant for one other reason: The sea-based missile defense program has, for most of the past thirteen years, suffered from minimal support from the navy's leadership—and outright hostility from the Pentagon's missile-defense bureaucracy. The former have tended to see this mission as a diversion of scarce resources from the other priority air- and sea-control duties for which the AEGIS ships were designed.

For the latter, sea-based antimissile systems have generally been anathema, for varying reasons. During the Clinton years, the 1972 Anti-Ballistic Missile Treaty—which banned almost all missile defense—was considered holy writ. Even seagoing missile defenses that were clearly not covered by the treaty (namely, those incapable of stopping *long-range* ballistic missiles) were considered to be problematic. Consequently, the navy's programs were often starved of funds.

Amazingly, things have not been much better under a George W. Bush administration. That has been true even though Bush, to his credit, came to office with the stated purpose of withdrawing from the ABM Treaty—which he subsequently *did*—and of deploying effective global missile defenses at the earliest possible time. The Pentagon's Missile Defense Agency has, nonetheless, been allowed largely to give short shrift to the development and deployment of navy antimissile systems, in favor of ground-based interceptors and longer-term research and development efforts.

Unfortunately, the ground-based missile defense has experienced a series of experimental setbacks. The threat of missile attack demands that that program be brought to completion—and that such further testing and developmental work be conducted as is necessary to get there. The achievements of the sea-based missile defense program to date demand that a much more assertive effort also be undertaken to realize its potential.

What Needs to Be Done

1. Accelerate procurement of SM-3 missiles. Present plans call for the deployment of just thirty such missiles by 2007, of which only a few would be the Block I interceptor successfully tested in February. The rest would be upgraded Block IA missiles that have yet to be proved, let alone put into full-scale production. An expedited purchase of a larger number of Block IAs could enable more ships to be made missile defense capable faster, thereby affording protection to larger areas of the globe and reducing the unit costs of the interceptors.
2. Retain AEGIS cruisers being decommissioned at roughly the halfway point in their planned service life. These vessels can be reconfigured to be effective antimissile ships at a fraction of the cost of new construction.
3. Resuscitate a program terminated several years ago to afford the U.S. Navy's fleets protection against short-range ballistic missile attack. Scuds and similar missiles available to North Korea, Iran, and China, among other potentially hostile states, demand the deployment at the earliest possible time of a capability like that of the SM-2 Block IVa program.
4. Maximize the interoperability of U.S. sea-based missile defenses with ship of allied fleets—including AEGIS-equipped vessels in the navies of those of Japan, Australia, Spain, Norway, and South Korea. Doing so can complement America's efforts to provide truly global protection against ballistic missile attack to our own forces, people, and interests, while helping to defray the costs of such protection.

Missile defenses are required now more than ever. The time has come to assign the Navy the mission and the resources necessary to provide comprehensive defenses from the sea—especially in light of the fact that such defenses may be the only kind available when we need them to prevent a high-altitude electromagnetic pulse attack of the kind described in Step 6.

APPENDIX IV

"Secure America" — A Pledge for Elected Officials and Candidates[1]

1. The purpose of U.S. immigration policy is to benefit the citizens of the United States.

2. Since immigration policy can profoundly shape a country, it should be set by deliberate actions, not by accident or acquiescence, with careful consideration to ensure that it does not adversely affect the quality of life of American citizens and their communities.

3. Immigration policy should be based on and adhere to the rule of law. Immigration laws must be enforced consistently and uniformly throughout the United States.

4. Non-citizens enter the United States as guests and must obey the rules governing their entry. The U.S. government must track the entry, stay, and departure of all visa holders to ensure that they comply fully with the terms of their visas or to remove them if they fail to comply.

5. The borders of the United States must be physically secured at the earliest possible time. An effective barrier to the illegal entry of both aliens and contraband is vital to U.S. security.

6. Those responsible for facilitating illegal immigration shall be sought, arrested, and prosecuted to the full extent of the law and shall forfeit any profits from such activity. This applies to smugglers and traffickers of

---

1 For more information about the "Secure America" Pledge, and to learn how you can help make it the basis for government policy, see http://www.WarFooting.com.

people, as well as to those involved in the production, procurement, distribution, or use of fraudulent or counterfeit documents.

7. U.S. employers shall be given a simple and streamlined process to determine whether employees are legally eligible to work. Employers who obey the law shall be protected both from liability and from unfair competition by those who violate immigration law. The violators shall be subject to fines and taxes in excess of what they would have paid to employ U.S. citizens and legal residents for the same work.

8. Those who enter or remain in the United States in violation of the law shall be detained and removed expeditiously. Illegal aliens shall not accrue any benefit, including U.S. citizenship, as a result of their illegal entry or presence in the United States.

9. No federal, state, or local entity shall reward individuals for violating immigration laws by granting public benefits or services, or by issuing or accepting any form of identification, or by providing any other assistance that facilitates unlawful presence or employment in this country. All federal and all law-enforcement agencies shall cooperate fully with federal immigration authorities and shall report to such authorities any information they receive indicating that an individual may have violated immigration laws.

10. Illegal aliens currently in the United States may be afforded a one-time opportunity to leave the United States without penalty and seek permission to reenter legally if they qualify under existing law. Those who do not take advantage of this opportunity will be removed and permanently barred from returning.

I promise to work for the implementation of these principles.

(Signed) _____

Sponsors of the "Secure America" Pledge

Frank Gaffney
President and CEO/**Center for Security Policy**

Roy Beck
Executive Director/**NumbersUSA**

Phyllis Schlafly
Founder and President/**Eagle Forum**

Paul M. Weyrich
National Chairman/**Coalitions for America**

Peggy Birchfield
Executive Director/**Religious Freedom Coalition**

Theresa Harmon
Co-founder/**Tennesseans for Responsible Immigration Policies**

Teela Roche
Co-director/**South Carolinians for Immigration Moderation**

Edward and Cynthia Kolb
Founders/**Desertvisions.us**

Rob Sanchez
Founder/**ZaZona.com**

Ron Woodard
Director/**NC LISTEN**

Mike Sizer
Chair/**Utahans for Immigration Reform and Enforcement (UFIRE)**

Glenn R. Jackson
Founder and Director/**American Reformation Project**

Scott A. Lauf
Executive Director/**CitizensLobby.com**

Stuart H. Hurlbert
President/**Rainbow Coalition for Commonalities and Cablinasians**

Maggie Whitlock Art
Founder/**Slow California Growth**

Joan Hueter
President/**American Council for Immigration Reform**

Billy E. Reed
President/**American Engineering Association**

Mary Martin
Chairman of the Board/**The Seniors Coalition**

Joyce Tarnow
President/**Floridians for a Sustainable Population**

Sadie Fields
State Chairman/**Christian Coalition of Georgia**

Peter Gadiel
Founder/**9/11 Families for a Secure America**

Charles L. Heatherly
President/**National Center for Citizenship and Immigration**

Arnold Harris
President/Owner/**Harris Environmental Safety Consultants, Inc.**

Tim Donnelly
Director/**Minuteman Party**

D.A. King
Founder/**The American Resistance Foundation**

Carolyn Galloway
President/**Citizens for Immigration Reform**

Robert Casimiro
Executive Director/**Massachusetts Coalition for Immigration Reform**

Paul Streitz
Executive Director/**CT Citizens for Immigration Control**

Phyllis Sears
Chair/**Citizens Council on Immigration**

Diana Hull, Ph.D.
President/**Californians for Population Stabilization (CAPS)**

Edward Nelson
Chairman/**United States Border Control**

Yeh Ling-Ling
Executive Director/**Diversity Alliance for a Sustainable America**

List of Contributors

Alex Alexiev is vice president for research at the Center for Security Policy. During his nearly twenty years as a senior analyst with the National Security Division of the Rand Corporation, he directed numerous research projects for the U.S. Department of Defense and other agencies. He is the author of several books and myriad monographs and articles on national security issues. His current research focuses on issues related to Islamic extremism and terrorism. Mr. Alexiev received his undergraduate degree in English from Sofia State University, Bulgaria, and his M.A. in political science from the University of California at Los Angeles (UCLA).

Congressman Roscoe Bartlett represents the Sixth Congressional District of Maryland and is serving his seventh term. Prior to his election, Bartlett pursued careers as a professor, research scientist, inventor, small-business owner, and farmer. In Congress, Bartlett is senior member of the Science Committee and is chairman of the Projection Forces Subcommittee of the Armed Services Committee. A recipient of the American Institute of Aeronautics and Astronautics Jeffries Award, Congressman Bartlett earned a degree in theology and biology from Columbia Union College and a Ph.D. in physiology from the University of Maryland, College Park.

Amanda Bowman is the New York director of the Center for Security Policy and president of the Coalition for a Secure Driver's License. In addition to heading her own consulting firm, Ms. Bowman's positions have included conference programmer at *The Economist*; vice president of marketing and public relations, Christie's; vice president, Hill & Knowlton; senior vice president for public affairs, United Way of New York City; senior vice president, Ogilvy Public Relations; and managing director of Fine Light Public Relations. Ms. Bowman is a graduate of the University of Cambridge.

Christopher Brown has been a Transitions to Democracy Program Member at the Hudson Institute since 2003. His duties include preparing research, providing testimony, and conducting briefings for officials at the U.S. Departments of Defense and State, the Central Intelligence Agency, National Security Council, the White House, and members of Congress and their staff. His articles have appeared in major publications, and he assisted the late Dr. Constantine Menges on the recently published book *China: The Gathering Threat*. Mr. Brown is a graduate of Utah State University with a dual major in political science and philosophy. He is fluent in both Afrikaans and Xhosa and is currently studying Arabic.

Mark Chussil is a founder and senior director of Crisis Simulations International (CSI), where he designed CSI's DXMAT crisis simulator. Mr. Chussil is also founder and CEO of Advanced Competitive Strategies, Inc., and designer of ACS's award-winning ValueWar business simulator. He has published extensively, and has thirty years of experience in consulting, simulation, teaching, and business war-gaming on six continents. Mr. Chussil earned his M.B.A. in general management from Harvard and his B.A. in political science from Yale.

Timothy Connors is director of the Manhattan Institute's Center for Policing Terrorism (CPT), helping police departments combat terrorism using a global network of counterterrorism experts to generate practical products, advice, and services. Mr. Connors is a decorated veteran who recently completed a combat tour in Konar Province, Afghanistan, where he led a Civil Affairs Team in support of 20th Special Forces Group. He is a graduate of West Point and was commissioned as a Second Lieutenant of Infantry. He received an M.B.A. and J.D. at the University of Notre Dame.

Lt. Col. Gordon Cucullu, USA (Ret.), a former Green Beret, is an editorialist and author. Born into a military family, he lived and served for more than thirteen years in East Asia, including eight years in

Korea. For his Special Forces service in Vietnam, he was awarded a Bronze Star, Vietnamese Cross of Gallantry, and the Presidential Unit Commendation. After separation from the Army, he worked on Korean and East Asian affairs at the Pentagon and Department of State and later as an executive for General Electric in Korea. His first major nonfiction work, *Separated at Birth: How North Korea became the Evil Twin*, is based in large part on his extensive experience in Korea and East Asia as a governmental insider and businessman.

Frank J. Gaffney Jr. is the founder and president of the Center for Security Policy, established in Washington, D.C., in 1988. Mr. Gaffney acted as the assistant secretary of defense for international security policy under President Reagan. In that capacity, he served as chairman of the High Level Group of NATO. He also served as a professional staff member of the U.S. Senate Armed Services Committee under its then-chairman, John Tower, and as an aide to Senator Henry "Scoop" Jackson. Mr. Gaffney is a weekly contributor to the *Washington Times* and numerous online publications. Mr. Gaffney holds a B.S. in foreign service from Georgetown University School of Foreign Service and an M.A. in international studies from the Johns Hopkins University School of Advanced International Studies.

Fred Gedrich is executive vice president for MobilVox Inc., a software development and wireless technology contractor developing anti-improvised explosive device technology. He formerly served as a U.S. Department of Defense and U.S. Department of State official. His State Department assignments included Beijing, Beirut, Haiti, several African countries, and several republics of the former Soviet Union. His articles have been widely published. He received his bachelor's degree from Wilkes College in 1973 and his master's degree from Central Michigan University in 1983.

Colleen Gilbert is a research associate at the Center for Security Policy responsible for issues pertaining to immigration and homeland security. Ms. Gilbert is also executive director of the Coalition for a Secure Driver's License, overseeing the coalition's legislative agenda at both the federal and state levels. She is also responsible for representing the coalition in various media forums, and her writings have appeared in publications such as the *Wall Street Journal*, *Newsday*, and *Human Events*. Miss Gilbert holds a B.F.A. from New York University and an M.A. from George Washington University.

Caroline B. Glick is the senior Middle East fellow at the Center for Security Policy in Washington, D.C. Ms. Glick, who lives in Jerusalem, Israel, also serves as the deputy managing editor and chief columnist for *The Jerusalem Post*. She is the senior editorialist and commentator for *Makor Rishon*, a Hebrew newspaper in Israel, a senior researcher at the Israel Defense Force's Operational Theory Research Institute, and an adjunct lecturer in tactical warfare at the Israeli Defense Force's Command and Staff College. Ms. Glick received her bachelor's degree in political science from Columbia University and her master's degree in public policy from Harvard University's Kennedy School of Government.

Dr. Daniel Goure is vice president of the Lexington Institute. Dr. Goure was a U.S. Defense Department official during the George H.W. Bush Administration. Dr. Goure teaches at both Georgetown University and the National Defense University and is an NBC military analyst. He received a B.A from Pomona College and an M.A. and Ph.D. in international relations from Johns Hopkins University.

Thor Halvorssen is president of the New York-based Human Rights Foundation and is the First Amendment Scholar at the Commonwealth Foundation. He currently serves on the Board of Directors of the Armando Valladares Foundation, the Advisory Council of the Atlantic Legal Foundation, and the Society of Fellows of the American Council of Trustees and Alumni. Mr. Halvorssen is a contributing author of *Bringing Justice to the People: The Story of the Freedom-Based Public Law Movement* (Heritage Books). Mr. Halvorssen received undergraduate and graduate degrees in political science and history from the University of Pennsylvania.

Victor Davis Hanson is the Martin and Illie Anderson Senior Fellow at the Hoover Institution. He was a full-time farmer before joining California State University, Fresno, in 1984 to initiate a classics program. His academic achievements have included the National Endowment for the Humanities fellow at the Center for Advanced Studies in the Behavioral Sciences (Stanford), the Eric Breindel Award for opinion journalism, and the Shifrin Chair of Military History at the U.S. Naval Academy. Dr. Hansen is the author of over 170 articles, book reviews, and editorials and is a biweekly contributor to National Review Online. He was educated at the University of California, Santa Cruz, the American School of Classical Studies, and received his Ph.D. in classics from Stanford University.

Bruce Herschensohn, author and television and radio political commentator for two decades, currently teaches at Pepperdine University, is an Associate Fellow at the Nixon Center for Peace and Freedom, and serves on the Board of Directors of the Center for Individual Freedom. After service in the U.S. Air Force, Mr. Herschensohn started his own motion picture company and was appointed director of motion pictures and television for the United States Information Agency. He served as the deputy special assistant to President Nixon, as a member of Ronald Reagan's transition team, and as a fellow at the John F. Kennedy Institute of Politics at Harvard and at the Claremont Institute.

Christopher Holton is vice president for administration, marketing & development at the Center for Security Policy. Mr. Holton came to the center after serving as president and marketing director of Blanchard & Co. and editor-in-chief of the Blanchard Economic Research Unit from 1990 to 2003. As chief of the Blanchard Economic Research Unit in 2000, he conceived and commissioned the Center for Security Policy special report, *Clinton's Legacy: The Dangerous Decade*. Holton is a member of the Board of Advisers of WorldTribune.com.

Rosemary Jenks is director of government relations for NumbersUSA, a nonprofit, nonpartisan, grass-roots organization. She has worked on immigration issues since 1990, first with the Center for Immigration Studies, a Washington, D.C.-based immigration think-tank, and then as a consultant. Her articles have appeared widely and she is the co-author of *Shaping Illinois: The Effects of Immigration 1970–2020 and Doctors and Nurses: A Demographic Profile*. Ms. Jenks earned a J.D. with honors from Harvard Law School and a B.A. in political science from Colorado College, and she is a member of the Virginia State Bar.

Cliff Kincaid is president of America's Survival, Inc. (ASI) and the editor of the Accuracy in Media (AIM) Report. A veteran journalist and media and policy analyst, he has been an advocate on behalf of the families of victims of terrorism. ASI was the first national organization to warn of global taxes and the proposed International Criminal Court, holding news conferences at the National Press Club and on Capitol Hill. Mr. Kincaid is the author of eight books and has published frequently in major media outlets. He received his degree in journalism and communications from the University of Toledo.

Anne Korin is co-director of the Institute for the Analysis of Global Security (IAGS) and editor of *Energy Security*. She is also co-chair of the Set America Free Coalition. Ms. Korin focuses on energy supply vulnerabilities, OPEC, maritime terrorism, energy security, energy strategies, and technological innovation. She has written articles for various foreign-affairs journals. Her education includes an engineering degree in computer science from Johns Hopkins University and study toward a doctorate at Stanford University.

Dr. Gal Luft is executive director of the Institute for the Analysis of Global Security (IAGS) and co-chair of the Set America Free Coalition. He specializes in strategy, geopolitics, terrorism, and energy security. He has published numerous studies and articles on security and energy issues and consults with various think tanks and news organizations worldwide. Dr. Luft holds degrees in international relations, international economics, Middle East studies, and strategic studies and a doctorate in strategic studies from the Paul H. Nitze School of Advanced International Studies (SAIS,) Johns Hopkins University.

Andrew McCarthy is a senior fellow at the Foundation for the Defense of Democracies, and a contributor at *National Review Online*. For 18 years, he was an assistant U.S. attorney in the Southern District of New York and in 1995 led the terrorism prosecution against Sheik Omar Abdel Rahman and eleven others in connection with the 1993 World Trade Center bombing. He became the chief assistant U.S. attorney for the Southern District's satellite office and supervised the office's Command Post near Ground Zero in New York City after the attacks of September 11, 2001. Mr. McCarthy also served as a special assistant to then-deputy secretary of defense Paul Wolfowitz.

David McCormack is research associate at the Center for Security Policy where he directs the African Security Project. His articles have appeared in publications such as the *Washington Times*, the *Jerusalem Post*, and the *Wall Street Journal Europe*, and he is the author of the CSP Occasional Paper "An African Vortex: Islamism in Sub-Saharan Africa." Mr. McCormack holds a B.A. in history and international affairs from the George Washington University.

Lt. Gen. Thomas McInerney, USAF (Ret.), served thirty-five years in the U.S. Air Force as a fighter pilot and commander at every unit level. He had four combat tours in Vietnam as well as commanding a major air strike against terrorists in the mid-1980s. His last assignment in the Air Force was assistant vice chief of staff as well as director of the Vice President's Defense Performance Review (Reinventing

Government) for all of the U.S. Department of Defense. Upon retirement as a lieutenant general, he served as a vice president for command, control, and intelligence for UNISYS and Loral Corporations until becoming president and CEO of Business Executives for National Security for four years. In 2000, he created his own consulting company, focusing on government reform and terrorism. General McInerney is a Fox News military analyst and co-authored the book *End Game: The Blueprint for Victory in the War on Terror.*

Vice Adm. Robert R. Monroe, USN (Ret.), served thirty-eight years in the U.S. Navy. During his career, he had combat tours in World War II and the Korean and Vietnam Wars. He was a systems analyst for the U.S. secretary of defense, and, as vice admiral, headed the Defense Nuclear Agency and then directed Navy Research and Development. Upon retirement, Admiral Monroe joined Bechtel, and, over the next twenty-one years served successively as business line manager, vice president, senior vice president, and partner. He is now a private consultant, also serving on several U.S. government advisory boards. Admiral Monroe graduated from the U.S. Naval Academy and holds a master's degree in international relations from Stanford University.

Claudia Rosett is journalist-in-residence at the Foundation for the Defense of Democracies, writing on tyranny and human rights, especially as these relate to the War for the Free World. Over the past twenty-four years, Ms. Rosett has reported from Asia, Latin America, the Middle East, and the former Soviet Union. She is an adjunct fellow at the Hudson Institute and a former member of the editorial board of the *Wall Street Journal.* Ms. Rosett received an Overseas Press Club Citation for Excellence for her on-site coverage of China's 1989 Tiananmen Square uprising. In 2005, she won the Eric Breindel Award for her coverage of the United Nations.

Dr. Michael Rubin is a resident scholar at the American Enterprise Institute and editor of the *Middle East Quarterly.* Rubin received a Ph.D. in history in 1999. His dissertation on the formation of modern Iran won Yale's top prize. He has spent twenty months in Iraq and more than seven in Iran. His most recent book (with Patrick Clawson) is *Eternal Iran: Continuity and Chaos.*

Al Santoli is president and founder of the nonprofit Asia America Initiative and the editor of the weekly e-publications China in Focus and Asia in Focus. He is the former senior vice-president of the American Foreign Policy Council and director of the Asia-Pacific Initiative and has worked as a foreign policy and national security advisor in the U.S. House of Representatives. Mr. Santoli has been a contributing editor at *PARADE* magazine, and his writings have appeared in a variety of publications He is the author of numerous books and monographs, including *Everything We Had: An Oral History of the Vietnam War.*

David Satter is an associate of the Hoover Institution, the Hudson Institute, and Johns Hopkins University and the author of two books on Russia: *Age of Delirium: The Decline and Fall of the Soviet Union* and *Darkness at Dawn: The Rise of the Russian Criminal State.* He writes frequently for the editorial page of the *Wall Street Journal* on the former Soviet Union and is currently working on a new book about the Russian attitude toward the communist past. Mr. Satter received a B.A. from the University of Chicago and a B.Litt. degree in political philosophy from Oxford University.

James M. Staudenraus has been involved with border security and immigration issues for more than ten years. He has developed a wide range of trusted contacts within state and federal law enforcement and has witnessed first-hand how these agencies continue to remain hindered in their counterterrorism efforts by a lack of a common database, ongoing turf wars, and mixed signals from elected officials at all levels of government. A graduate of Syracuse University, terrorism hit home for Mr. Staudenraus in December 1988, when thirty-five of his university schoolmates were killed aboard Pan Am Flight 103.

Sarah N. Stern is the director of the Washington Office of the American Jewish Congress. She has long been an advocate for robust U.S. and Israeli foreign policies in the War for the Free World. Ms. Stern is also the author of a recently released novel, *Cherished Illusions.* She was educated at Boston University and received her master's degree from Columbia University. Prior to her work in public policy, Ms. Stern worked with Montgomery County, Maryland, public schools as a child psychologist.

Kenneth R. Timmerman is executive director of the Foundation for Democracy in Iran, which he founded in 1995, and a journalist with more than two decades of experience tracking and exposing terrorist networks. His 1998 expose of Osama bin Laden appeared in *Reader's Digest* just weeks before the embassy bombings in Africa. In recent years, Mr. Timmerman has revealed how U.S. policies have helped create new threats from Russia, China, and Iran. Mr. Timmerman is the author of numerous books and articles. His latest book is *Countdown to Crisis: The Coming Nuclear Showdown with Iran.*

Maj. Gen. Paul E. Vallely, USA (Ret.), served in the U.S. Army for thirty-two years. He served in many overseas theaters including Europe, Pacific Rim countries, and two combat tours in Vietnam. General Vallely is a military analyst for Fox News Channel and chairman of the Military Committee of the Center for Security Policy. He co-authored the book *Endgame-Blueprint for Victory for Winning the War on Terror.* He and his wife, Marian, are the co-trustees of the Scott Vallely Soldiers Memorial Fund. General Vallely graduated from the U.S. Military Academy at West Point, Infantry School, Ranger and Airborne Schools, Jumpmaster School, the Command and General Staff School, the Industrial College of the Armed Forces, and the Army War College.

Dr. J. Michael Waller holds the Walter and Leonore Annenberg Chair in International Communication at the Institute of World Politics and directs its graduate programs on public diplomacy and political warfare. He is also vice president for information operations of the Center for Security Policy in Washington, D.C. A former staff member of the U.S. Senate, consultant to the U.S. Department of State, and journalist and author, Dr. Waller is an expert on terrorism, intelligence, the former Soviet Union, and the Americas. He has been a contributor to *Insight* magazine, *Reader's Digest*, the *Washington Times*, and the *Wall Street Journal*. Dr. Waller holds a B.A. from George Washington University and an M.A. and Ph.D. from Boston University.

Congressman Curt Weldon represents the Seventh Congressional District of Pennsylvania and is serving his tenth term. Congressman Weldon is a senior member of the House Armed Services Committee and the Homeland Security Committee. He is recognized as one of the Congress' leading authorities on military weapons and other systems and techonologies. Long before September 11, Congressman Weldon was an advocate of bolstering U.S. defenses, assisting first responders, and improving intelligence gathering. Congressman Weldon received his B.A. in Russian from West Chester University.

R. James Woolsey is vice president for global strategic security at Booz Allen Hamilton. Ambassador Woolsey was director of the Central Intelligence Agency from 1993 to 1995, was appointed by President Reagan as delegate-at-large to the U.S.-Soviet Strategic Arms Reduction Talks (START) and Nuclear and Space Arms Talks (NST), and was an advisor on the U.S. Delegation to the Strategic Arms Limitation Talks (SALT I). He received his B.A. from Stanford University, an M.A. from Oxford University, where he was a Rhodes Scholar, and an LL.B from Yale Law School.

Members of the Center for Security Policy Staff who rendered invaluable help:

Olivia Albrecht, John Tower National Security Fellow at the Center for Security Policy, is the project manager for the center's Islamist Project and lead research for homeland security and international relations topics. She has worked at the Pentagon in Non-Proliferation Policy and at the Heritage Foundation. Ms. Albrecht is a graduate of Princeton University with a degree in philosophy.

Patrick Devenny is the Henry M. Jackson National Security Fellow at the Center for Security Policy. Mr. Devenny researches various national security topics and has been published in American Spectator Online, *Middle East Quarterly*, the *Washington Times*, and FrontPageMagazine.com. He is a graduate of Rutgers University with a degree in history and is currently pursuing a master's degree in U.S. foreign policy at American University's School of International Service.

Lisa Firestone is the executive assistant to the president of the Center for Security Policy. She has worked in the fields of asset management, campaign administration, and public policy. Ms. Firestone received a B.A. in English, economics, and French from Duke University and is a graduate of the New York Institute of Finance.

Ryan Peterson is a research associate and project manager for the Center for Security Policy's Energy Security Initiative. His research focuses on issues of global security, U.S. energy policies, and law and sovereignty issues. His work on these topics has been published by FrontPageMagazine.com. Mr. Peterson holds a B.A. in international relations from Wheaton College.

Michael T. Reilly is vice president for operations at the Center for Security Policy. In that capacity, Mr. Reilly is responsible for the day-to-day operations of the center as well as the management of the center's employees. Additionally, and working in close coordination with the president of the center, he also manages the center's outside relationships and strategic development. Mr. Reilly is a former military legislative assistant to Congressman Jerry Lewis and a Marine Corps veteran of Operation Iraqi Freedom. He is a graduate of the Catholic University of America with a degree in civil engineering.

Index

293